The Social Scientist as Public Intellectual

The Social Scientist as Public Intellectual

Critical Reflections in a Changing World

Charles F. Gattone

ROWMAN & LITTLEFIELD PUBLISHERS, INC.
Lanham • Boulder • New York • Toronto • Oxford

ROWMAN & LITTLEFIELD PUBLISHERS, INC.

Published in the United States of America
by Rowman & Littlefield Publishers, Inc.
A wholly owned subsidiary of The Rowman & Littlefield Publishing Group, Inc.
4501 Forbes Boulevard, Suite 200, Lanham, Maryland 20706
www.rowmanlittlefield.com

PO Box 317
Oxford
OX2 9RU, UK

British Library Cataloguing in Publication Information Available

Library of Congress Cataloging-in-Publication Data

Gattone, Charles F., 1960–
  The social scientist as public intellectual : critical reflections in a changing world
    p. cm.
  Includes bibliographical references and index.
  ISBN-13: 978-0-7425-3792-7 (cloth : alk. paper)
  ISBN-10: 0-7425-3792-7 (cloth : alk. paper)
  ISBN-13: 978-0-7425-3793-4 (pbk. : alk. paper)
  ISBN-10: 0-7425-3793-5 (pbk. : alk. paper)
  1. Policy sciences. 2. Social sciences and state. 3. Social scientists. 4. Policy
scientists. I. Title.
H97.G38 2006
300—dc22   2005027300

Printed in the United States of America

∞™ The paper used in this publication meets the minimum requirements of
American National Standard for Information Sciences—Permanence of Paper
for Printed Library Materials, ANSI/NISO Z39.48-1992.

For Lizzie, Max, and Angela Rose
and for Arthur

Contents

Introduction   ix

1   Knowledge and Politics in Early Modern Social Thought:
Auguste Comte and Henri deRouvroy Saint-Simon   1

2   Max Weber: Social Science and Politics in the
Transition to State Capitalism   21

3   Thorstein Veblen: The Social Scientist as Innovative Thinker   35

4   Karl Mannheim and Joseph Schumpeter: Social Science,
Intellectuals, and Politics in an Age of Declining Liberalism   49

5   C. Wright Mills and John Kenneth Galbraith:
Institutions, Social Science, and the Role of
Intellectuals in the New Industrial State   77

6   Pierre Bourdieu: Intellectuals, Symbolic Power, and
Social Change   101

7   The Social Scientist as Public Intellectual   125

Bibliography   151

Index   163

About the Author   169

Introduction

Changes in today's society are so pervasive and are unfolding so quickly that it is difficult to understand them in a comprehensive manner. These transformations are global in nature, but have local consequences and go a long way toward shaping lives at the interpersonal level. As the forces of Western capitalism continue to spread to the far reaches of the planet, newer modes of communication and transportation are connecting disparate cultures more extensively than ever before. The political boundaries of the past have faded and are steadily being replaced by larger and more elaborate governing networks. Industrial nations are linked together in the form of intercontinental federations, and national businesses have grown exponentially to become transnational corporations with bases around the world. These developments increasingly clash with regional and indigenous traditions and have fostered new varieties of ethnic and religious conflict in the domestic realm.

A key outcome of all this is that the arena of politics has become much more complex than it was in the past. Political leaders today are unable to approach their responsibilities in an informal or cavalier fashion or act solely on the basis of their own experiences, but must consider a broad array of institutional factors underlying each of their decisions, and consult their advisors at every turn. They may present an image of self-confidence and independence in their public appearances, but behind the scenes they are required to tread carefully when weaving their way through the multifarious mazes of public administration.

These difficulties in understanding extend to members of the larger population as well, leaving many at a loss in their efforts to make sense of contemporary developments on the basis of informed judgments. The mix of messages in the mainstream media may provide some insight into current events, but this cacophony rarely offers the kind of analyses needed to form a broader worldview.

The attempt to comprehend today's society at both the institutional and individual levels has facilitated a renewed interest in the work of social scientists. Their expertise in a range of areas such as politics, economics, and culture has drawn them into the domain of public affairs in a number of ways. Social scientific knowledge is systematically derived, but it is also fundamentally interpretive and can shed new light on complex practical questions. Researchers have the ability to examine what appear on the surface to be isolated occurrences and to demonstrate how these are connected to one another and to larger societal changes. While they cannot predict the future, they can show where current trends are leading and suggest viable ways to respond in the present. Their conclusions are certainly not infallible, but have proven to be an integral component in creating new assessments of the modern world and are now an essential ingredient in the formation of public policy.

Although social scientists have become more involved in public affairs in recent years, they continue to be ambivalent about their role in this regard and tend to be divided in terms of how to approach their work as public intellectuals. A fundamental belief in their tradition is that it is important to maintain a healthy distance from politics in order to provide an evenhanded and objective assessment of its principal actors and institutions. From this perspective, when scholars are embedded in the ideas and activities of everyday life, they lose their ability to see the larger picture of the situation they are studying and can develop findings that support preconceived beliefs or goals. A contrasting position in the field is that virtually all social scientific investigations have some political dimensions to them, whether the researchers involved are aware of these or not. From this latter standpoint, while it may be convenient to characterize social scientists as set apart from the real world, they are unavoidably attached to it and, as such, have a responsibility to acknowledge these connections and take them into consideration in their own work.

This conflicting set of ideals places pressure on social scientists to engage in analysis from a neutral position while at the same time operating as integrated social actors. It raises difficult questions regarding the ethics of their profession and of their relationship to the political realm generally. Can they be both detached observers and public intellectuals at the same time, or are these two roles necessarily at odds with one another? What does it mean to be a public intellectual, and how does this relate to social research? What are some of the underlying issues involved in this debate, and how are these playing themselves out in the contemporary world?

The above questions are not entirely new but are part of an ongoing series of dilemmas social scientists have had to confront throughout modern history. The dominant perspectives in academia today did not arise in a vacuum but evolved in relation to changes in the constitution of society over time and as a function of the orientations and assumptions of its principal contributors. One can argue that these issues have been thoroughly addressed by past scholars and in more eloquent and insightful ways than has been done in recent years.

As a sociologist who has been grappling with these questions for quite some time now, I thought it would be enlightening to study this topic from a range of theoretical perspectives and with an eye toward some of the larger social implications involved. I could see that the conditions in academia were in many ways connected to the changes taking place in society broadly, and I felt it would be worthwhile to approach this investigation from a contextual standpoint. On the basis of this interest, I put together a study of some of the key thinkers in the social sciences, looking at the relationship between their observations about the trends of their time and their suggestions about how social scientists might proceed as public intellectuals in the face of these changes. I thought it would be valuable to discuss these ideas to see how they could inform the work of contemporary scholars operating in the midst of some very similar challenges in the field today.

Perhaps the greatest obstacles to designing a study of this nature are selecting the authors to be included in the discussion and deciding how to justify this determination. To facilitate this arduous and somewhat perilous task, I developed a series of criteria to serve as guides in the selection process. Chief among these was an interest in focusing on the work of scholars who devoted considerable attention in their writings to the ongoing rationalization of the institutional order and the implications of this trend in the arena of culture. I sought out those whose analyses centered on the growing interconnections between government, business, and academia and the influence of these ties on the direction and character of social scientific knowledge.

I also looked for authors who addressed the tension between democratic and authoritarian forces in modern society and the difficulties this tension presented for social scientists attempting to forge critical assessments of the dominant regimes in their respective milieus. My primary concern in this area was to consider the ways political and economic organizations can undermine the potential for democratic participation, and the bearing of this dynamic on the work of social scientists in the public realm.

I also sought out those who focused on issues associated with education and propaganda and on the relationship between scientific analysis and public opinion. I assessed the work of scholars who considered the ethical questions involved in attempting to shift public opinion and the ways social scientists could take on the dual role of being both a participant and an observer in the world of politics.

The authors who managed to survive this somewhat grueling list of constraints are among those who have made a substantial contribution to their fields and to the social sciences broadly. They include Max Weber, Thorstein Veblen, Karl Mannheim, Joseph Schumpeter, C. Wright Mills, John Kenneth Galbraith, and Pierre Bourdieu. Their analyses vary in a number of respects but also share some underlying themes, and their conclusions can be seen as providing the building blocks for an informed contemporary position on this topic.

Before entering into this investigation, I thought it would be helpful to review the foundations of early modern social thought on some of the issues involved to establish a starting framework for our current discussion. To that end, I begin the book with a chapter on the ideas of two nineteenth-century social thinkers, Auguste Comte and Henri de Saint-Simon. I do not present the work of Comte and Saint-Simon as an ideal to be applied in the present, but their formulations set the tone of this debate in the early stages of modernity and have acted as a principal foil against which more recent analyses have been framed. Many of the authors studied in this text developed their orientations in dialogue with these classical social philosophers, either refining their positions or opposing them outright, and therefore it seems appropriate to begin the book with an assessment of their work.

One will quickly see that the proposals of Comte and Saint-Simon are somewhat idealistic and a bit problematic in terms of their practical application. For instance, one of their principal suggestions is that the men of science, or the savants, be placed in positions of authority in the newly emerging social order. They believed that the superior knowledge of the savants entitled them to oversee the political and economic affairs of the state, thereby reducing errors in policy formation and providing moral guidance in the absence of a theological foundation. These aspirations grew out of their assumptions that the positive methods of science could produce universal truths about the nature of social phenomena and that a unified class of scientists would lead the Western world toward continually advancing forms of social organization in the future. Their recommendations were not accepted in their original form by subsequent thinkers but did inspire further inquiry into the questions of the relationship between social scientific knowledge and public affairs and of possible ways to bring these two worlds together.

The second chapter of the book turns to the writings of Max Weber, examining his understanding of the events in Europe in the early part of the twentieth century and his position on the political dimensions of social science. Weber offered an important contribution to social thought on this issue by contrasting the ethics of social science with the standard practices of politics. He observed a major transformation taking place in the West from traditional forms of economic and political organization to state-centered capitalism, and he characterized this change as part of the growing rationalization of society and the decline of individual autonomy. His primary concern regarding the influence of these trends on academic life highlighted the ongoing tendency of social scientists to be drawn into the logic of conventional knowledge. He observed their eagerness to hide behind the safety and security of institutional affiliations and considered the ways this interfered with their potential to develop new and enlightening analyses of the social order emerging around them. His writings helped clarify the relationship between social science and politics and continue to provide a rigorous theoretical framework for scholars wishing to avoid similar pitfalls in their own research.

Chapter 3 evaluates Thorstein Veblen's position on this subject and focuses on his conception of "the higher learning." Veblen wrote at roughly the same time as Weber but from the vantage point of the events unfolding in the United States. He is perhaps best known for his study of the elite in American society, *The Theory of the Leisure Class*, but throughout his writings, he examined the connections between the knowledge and material conditions of various social groups. Although he has been perceived erroneously as a utopian advocating the rise of the "engineers" in the management of the social order, Veblen actually rejected the idea that technical experts could assume a leadership position in the realm of politics and economy. He did not consider this a realistic possibility within the context of the ongoing trends of his time, but he did accept the premise that social scientists could significantly influence the course of history by virtue of their ability to shape the foundations of understanding in everyday life, and he developed an assessment of their public role from this perspective.

The fourth chapter of the book contrasts the opposing ideas of Karl Mannheim and Joseph Schumpeter on this topic and outlines their very different conclusions on the responsibilities of social scientists in the modern world. Mannheim witnessed the rise of Fascism in Germany and in Italy and raised serious doubts regarding the viability of laissez-faire principles to oppose this trend or act as an adequate guide for political decision making in the future. He characterized this transition as the decline of liberalism, by which he meant the gradual diminishing of open and free discussion of public issues and the eventual collapse of representative democracy. He recommended that social scientists intervene immediately and become directly involved in the task of managing public affairs, not only in the formation of policy objectives, but also in shaping the directions and focus of public opinion. Schumpeter, who also wrote during the years of the Nazi ascendancy, rejected the position that social scientists could provide any significant opposition to the ongoing deterioration of liberal values and practices. He suggested that social scientists were instead inclined to speed up the rationalization of society due to their narrow-minded vision of history and hostility to the capitalist order. The writings of these two authors, when viewed together, reveal some of the challenges of scholars living in the midst of the growing threat of authoritarianism and the consolidation of political power in the Western world.

Chapter 5 compares the work of C. Wright Mills and John Kenneth Galbraith, investigating the ways in which the events of the postwar world influenced their views on social science and politics. In the period following World War II, Mills and Galbraith examined the ties of business, government, and academia in the United States and addressed the ramifications of this arrangement in terms of a concern for individual liberty, democratic participation, and the development of long-term political and economic goals. Mills observed the impact of these changes on the university and formed a harsh critique of mainstream American social science. He sought to fashion an alternative approach to the study of society that could inform public officials as well as members of the larger population. Galbraith focused on the changing structure of the advanced industrial nations and observed a growing political leverage on the part of what he termed "the educational and scientific estate." He argued that as the task of policy formation grows increasingly technical and interdisciplinary in nature, political power becomes diffused, and this provides the opportunity for intellectuals to play a greater role in the creation of institutional knowledge and objectives. When taken together, the writings of Mills and Galbraith reveal the newer pressures facing academics in the postwar era and the ramifications of these pressures in terms of the potential of social scientists to approach their work in an independent manner.

The sixth chapter of the book examines the ideas of Pierre Bourdieu and his conception of the circumstances facing intellectuals in the later years of the twentieth century. Bourdieu also developed an analysis of the changing structure of advanced industrial society, and he focused on the ties between established frames of understanding and the conditions of their formation. He was particularly critical of the French academy and its tradition of eagerly accepting and abiding by the conclusions of accomplished scholars, regardless of the blatant inadequacies or inherent contradictions in their thinking. Bourdieu argued that the symbolic power of intellectuals enabled them to play a key role in supporting the current system of domination but also gave them the potential to transform this arrangement at a fundamental level. He presented his ideals to address the dilemmas facing social scientists and to suggest possible ways they might overcome these obstacles in the future.

In the final chapter of the book, I draw the connections between the work of these thinkers and more recent social transformations, building on the themes in their writing that continue to be relevant today. Their assessments of the economy, public opinion, democracy, and academia illustrate the ways in which ongoing institutional changes are related to the formation of prevailing beliefs and can shape the directions of society. Although the vast majority of social scientists tend to situate themselves within one or more of the respective traditions in their field, the few who manage to sidestep these limitations are in a better position to create alternatives to the central tenets of mainstream social thought. Of course, the members of this relatively small group are not the only ones capable of accomplishing such a goal. Social scientists on the whole have the potential to enhance the foundations of contemporary perspectives and establish new forms of understanding, even within the confines of today's relatively restrictive institutional environment.

Developing knowledge about the world and how to proceed in it is a task that entails more than simply gathering and conveying information. It means actively interpreting phenomena in a comprehensive, innovative, and enlightening way. The question of how to meet this challenge begins with an assessment of the agents involved in the formation of new knowledge. Are social scientists able to forge analyses that are relevant to the ongoing transformations taking place in the present? Can they effectively communicate these ideas to others outside their field? What are the forces they must contend with in doing so? Do their conclusions have any bearing on the future path of civilization? Hopefully, this book will shed some light on these and other issues that are so pressing in this rapidly changing and unpredictable age.

1

Knowledge and Politics in Early Modern Social Thought: Auguste Comte and Henri deRouvroy Saint-Simon

In the years following the French Revolution, many social philosophers were optimistic that the collapse of the feudal order would enable Western civilization to continue in its evolutionary progress toward enlightenment. The bonds of the *ancien régime* had been broken, and human beings were now free to create new forms of societal organization grounded in the principles of liberty, equality, and fraternity. This phase in French history saw a series of conflicts between the various groups vying for power in the wake of feudalism's demise. The rivalry between the Jacobins and the Girondins culminated in the temporary victory of Robespierre and the subsequent dictatorship of the Terror. The bloodshed of this period was then brought to a temporary close with Robespierre's execution and the establishment of the Directory. But the rapid climb to power of Napoleon Bonaparte, and his resulting military conquests, once again escalated the violence and undermined the stability of Europe in this intensely conflictual era.[1]

Theorists writing on the public role of the intellectual in this period developed analyses in response to what they perceived to be the perpetual chaos of their time. Henri de Saint-Simon and Auguste Comte were among the more influential of the early modern thinkers taking this approach. Their positions on this issue grew out of a concern to quell the organizational turmoil they observed in their own milieu. To them, the collapse of the *ancien régime* and its associated theological conceptions left a void in the new world that had not yet been filled. The disjointed framework that remained was no longer viable and lacked a unified set of political objectives, fostering a chaotic competition in the realm of public authority. They saw this disarray as the quintessential problem of their time and believed that the way to establish a more permanent stability would be to create an entirely new system of social organization, grounded in a theoretical orientation of a positivistic nature.[2]

Comte's and Saint-Simon's conceptions of the proper relationship of science and politics emerged within the context of these concerns, leading them to situate a quest for order at the center of their analyses and characterize the management of ideas as an essential component of European society's reorganization. The philosophical unity that had prevailed in the era of aristocratic rule was to them the basis of its strength as a stabilizing force, and they concluded that the formation of a new universal system of social thought would be crucial to building a new society. From this starting point, they developed the goal of forging a comprehensive body of knowledge designed to bring the prevailing unrest under control.

They set out to integrate the nascent ethos of scientific discovery into this newer philosophical system, hoping to establish a universal model that could serve as the basis for rational political and economic deliberation in the future. They were enthusiastic about recent accomplishments in the natural sciences and expected the scientific approach to carry over into the realm of social inquiry, providing a positive assessment of society and superseding the ill-formed conceptions of previous eras. The possibility of revealing new truths about the social world fostered a deep sense of optimism in these thinkers, and they sincerely believed that political decision making could be transformed into an exact science. They hoped that systematizing the formation of public policy would bring an end to ideological conflict and resolve the social problems caused by misguided convictions and poorly informed political judgments.[3]

The transition to modernity seemed to them to be an inherent step in the natural evolution of human social organization, moving from its primitive origins to a way of life in which civility and reason prevailed. To them, the older, savage military ways of conquest and fealty carried forward the traditions of mankind's barbarian past, furthering the practice of clan violence as a means of survival and interfering with the natural evolution of human progress. Yet Comte and Saint-Simon also believed that the feudal system offered an environment in which the seedlings of the new society could be nurtured, and they saw it as a valuable transitional step in the collective ascent of human civilization. Comte argued that although the traditions of the old regime inhibited the development of a more advanced way of life, a truly modern society could not have emerged directly from the earliest of human social arrangements. The formation of such an elaborate order required an intermediate social system capable of fostering complex ideas and providing the means through which a new structure of organization could evolve. He and Saint-Simon saw this period as a crude but necessary phase in human social evolution and believed that the industrialism of the turn of the century would eventually replace militarism as a way of life.[4]

These two social philosophers expected that the nation-state in the newer order would diminish in importance and eventually be overshadowed by a political and economic system of a much larger scale. This development would come about as a consequence of the fact that the modern form of social organization could only prosper in territorial units larger than those drawn on the basis of national divisions. From this point of view, industry naturally brings a greater range of groups into the fold, so that while it draws the various economic divisions of society together, it also facilitates a diffusion of authority, preventing the consolidation of power in the hands of any single faction. The budding system of industrial production in Europe at the turn of the century was itself an integrating force in that it brought together regions and peoples formerly in conflict with one another into a cooperative state, where each was essential to the functioning of the other. Less powerful groups that typically would have been overrun in the past were now more important to the survival of the system as a whole, and this prevented them from being marginalized or fully dominated.[5]

In contrast to the expectations of Comte and Saint-Simon, however, the events that followed the revolution did not unfold as smoothly as planned. Military conflict and nationalist sentiments persisted, reinvigorating the self-defeating traditions of an earlier time and further delaying the progress these thinkers anticipated. The continuing wars of Napoleon seemed to them to be a reversion to militarism and a reaffirming of the nation-state as the basis of social and economic organization in Europe. The ways of life typical of the feudal era were being carried over into the newer order, leading most Europeans to live within the confines of their previous cultural traditions and inhibiting the formation of a broad institutional reorganization.

Comte and Saint-Simon attributed this set of events to the influence of aristocrats remaining in power even after the transition to a new society had begun. Nations were still essentially governed by landowners, officers of the crown, ministers, and judges, in spite of their inability to provide competent leadership in a modern context. From the perspective of these theorists, a nation's leaders would always be despotic if chosen from among the nobility and the military. The solution to this problem was to reorganize society on the basis of a system in which the criteria for leadership paralleled the newer trends in science and industry.[6]

THE POSITIVE PHILOSOPHY

Comte's and Saint-Simon's conceptions of this emerging order developed in relation to their belief that the history of ideas in the West unfolded in a progressively advancing fashion, from a worldview grounded in theological principles to the more advanced but still limited knowledge of the metaphysical era. The turmoil associated with this transitional phase could be seen as rooted in the anarchy of competing theoretical orientations, each seeking to reorganize society in its own fashion. Although theological ideas were losing much of their influence in the modern industrial world, church leaders in this period continued to base their teachings on a faith in divine rule. Religious officials sought to reassert traditional forms of social organization characteristic of the feudal order and ignored the dramatic developments taking place in the consciousness and daily lives of believers. Saint-Simon and Comte saw this trend as indicative of the eventual transformation of religion and the rise of alternative perspectives throughout the world. They attributed the slow pace of this change to the persistence of past cultural practices and expected older beliefs to ultimately succumb to more modern conceptions based on science and reason.[7]

They also saw the metaphysical system of knowledge as inadequate in that it failed to provide a stable ideological foundation for the modern order. While its emphasis on critique did help to undermine the misguided beliefs of the feudal era, this philosophy was itself basically negative and unsuitable as a guide for political decision making. They conceded that this approach had gained popularity in recent years, but they pointed out that it remained speculative and relied on the strength of argumentation as evidence of validity. None of the positions characteristic of this form of knowledge could provide a solid starting point from which the new system of organization could grow. For instance, the metaphysical notion that each individual should be entitled to shape his or her own fate effectively challenged the legitimacy of monarchical authority. However, when applied as a principle in the formation of a new society, it could not resolve situations in which the rights of one individual conflicted with those of another. Its emphasis on freedom fostered a variety of competing political goals, furthering the extent of the chaos and preventing society from moving forward in a unified direction. Comte explained it in the following way:

> Regarded simply as a means of combating the theological system, the dogma in question favors the progress of the human mind. But it ceases to do so and loses all its value when conceived as a basis for the great social reorganization reserved for our epoch. It then becomes just as injurious as before it was useful, since it constitutes an obstacle to reorganization. Proclaiming the sovereignty of each individual reason, this doctrine in fact essentially tends to hinder the uniform establishment of any system of general ideas, without which nevertheless society cannot exist.[8]

Both Comte and Saint-Simon saw lawyers and judges as leftovers of the old order and discounted the potential of the courts to handle such disputes. They concluded that while the metaphysical system of knowledge provided a useful transitional ideology, it could not serve as a guiding ethos in the new

world. The realm of political ideology at this time seemed to them to be limited to a choice between a theological belief system that no longer applied
to the modern order and metaphysical knowledge that lacked the potential
to attain universality.

Comte and Saint-Simon saw the answer to this dilemma in the development of a positive philosophy, one that relied neither on the principle of divine rule nor on speculative argumentation. From the standpoint of the positive philosophy, all social phenomena are bound by invariable laws and
principles and based on an objective reality that exists independently of human experience. The goal of this form of inquiry would be to observe and
explain the historical trends of society, using empirical investigation and the
knowledge derived from previous studies. This approach would yield concrete and impartial results that were not subject to speculation or ideology.
The validity of these findings would rest on the dual foundation of systematic research and scientifically derived theory, yielding a positive account of
the events being analyzed and clarifying the ongoing developments of the
social order.[9]

They expected the systematic study of society to produce a universal set
of conclusions, "consolidating the whole into one body of homogeneous
doctrine" similar to the knowledge emerging in the natural sciences.[10] The
historical progression in the hard sciences such as chemistry or physics followed an evolutionary pattern from a variety of competing viewpoints that
were not systematically tested to a more unified model validated through scientific investigation. Social science would eventually follow the same course
of development, rising from a multifaceted and disjointed state of knowledge
to a universal and positivistic framework. It was slower in making the transition to a positive science than those fields assessing the physical world because society itself was so complex and therefore so difficult to understand
comprehensively.[11] Comte and Saint-Simon believed that it too would eventually follow the course established by its natural counterparts, in spite of
these obstacles.[12]

POLITICS AS A POSITIVE SCIENCE

Comte and Saint-Simon argued that just as the natural sciences developed
within the framework of an interest in serving humanity, the study of society
should also center its focus in the direction of public service. Their faith in
the ability of science to solve any problem in its path and their concern to
address the continuing chaos of their time led them to draw a connection between these two spheres and apply the techniques of systematic inquiry to
the world of politics. They believed that the problems of society could be addressed and eventually resolved through objective examination and analysis,

using scientific findings to formulate what would then be the "correct" course of political action.[13] While decisions of the past were the result of vague conjecture and speculation, this would no longer be the case under the auspices of the new system. The benefits of science would eliminate the uncertainties involved in the metaphysical administration of public affairs and would provide a solid grounding for politics. Saint-Simon characterized this position in a statement in *Le Politique*:

> We ought to acknowledge . . . that politics has been until now a conjectural science; that in the present state of knowledge, politics can perhaps be raised to the level of the positive sciences; . . . and that the social crisis in which the most advanced peoples of today are now engaged will not be totally terminated until this time when politics will be treated, cultivated and taught in the same way as physics, chemistry and physiology are taught today.[14]

Comte labeled this new orientation the "scientific doctrine of politics," arguing that the weaknesses and foibles of political bias would no longer interfere with the positive administration of modern society. Together, Comte and Saint-Simon articulated the view that objectifying the social order would offer the information that political leaders needed to make judgments that transcended ideological conviction, eliminating contention and debate in this realm and reducing the degree of conflict arising due to subjective differences. In the new system, the use of military force would be reduced as disputes of a political nature were gradually replaced by a reliance on the factual information of science. A common acceptance of the legitimacy of these findings would itself provide the basis for resolution, reconciling political differences and setting the course of action in an infallible way.[15]

Having declared the objectivity of this new doctrine, these theorists then proceeded to outline the underlying normative assumptions of such an approach. They argued that although the new science of politics would be substantiated by the certainty of empirical investigation, it would also require some ideological guidance, and they proceeded to offer their ideals in this regard. They believed a science of politics should be grounded in the assumption that the human species is distinct from all else in the natural world, and they characterized the primary goal of social research as one of finding the most effective way to act upon nature and modify it to the advantage of society. They further argued that inquiry must be designed to ensure that the exploitation of nature occurred in the most efficient and effective manner possible, speeding up the natural progression of human social organization. This form of investigation should seek, through observation and analysis, to better understand the evolution of the human race, to study past and present trends, and to adjust policy to accommodate inevitable future changes.[16] In this sense, researchers should determine the "real," predetermined path of history through the examination of social patterns, predicting the course of events in a positive manner. Policy decisions relying on this scientific analysis would then be compatible with natural developments and would yield a more stable and less disruptive environment. The overriding objective was to bring the new social system into harmony with the destiny of humankind. Doing so would facilitate the unfolding of progress while minimizing the shock of future change. Comte and Saint-Simon hoped this approach would be applied to ease the growing pains facing European civilization as it made the transition to modernity.[17]

The interconnectedness of the new order meant that poor judgment in the realm of politics could result in far more severe consequences than in the past and that grounding such decisions in the exactness of science was crucial to the future well-being of humanity. This set of circumstances required the formulation of a plan that relied on social science as its guide. The plan should make provisions for the exploitation of nature by industry as well as the activities designed to achieve justice. It was the means through which the rationality and predictive power of science could be used to more effectively guide society toward its natural ends. From the perspective of Comte and Saint-Simon, the plan could serve as an instrument of coordination in the formation of long-term projects created to address social ills and facilitate universal prosperity.[18]

Their belief in the guaranteed benefits of this approach led them to argue that, once established, the goals of the plan should supersede all other concerns. Cultural traditions, local customs, or familial mores were of little value if they contradicted the goals of the plan, and these matters should therefore yield to the more substantial requirements of society as a whole. Arguments based on metaphysical speculation or common understandings could not compete with the facts of science and should conform to its conclusions. Since the plan would be developed scientifically, its findings were innately valid and should be treated with the utmost sanctity, regardless of sentimental objections to the contrary.[19]

THE ROLE OF THE SAVANTS IN SOCIETAL MANAGEMENT

Comte and Saint-Simon saw the advance of civilization as inevitable and not likely to be deterred by any action designed to counter this trend. The emerging industrial order propelled history forward, and the new society would eventually flourish in spite of its current obstacles. Although such an improvement was destined to come about, it also required a degree of assistance to guarantee that the progress they expected would be achieved in the most effective and efficient manner possible. This guidance would be necessary to ensure that the new conceptual machinery was being used properly

and to the advantage of mankind. The group of individuals best able to fulfill
this role would naturally be the men of science, or the savants.

Comte and Saint-Simon proposed that the savants be given a leadership
position in the new society because of their advanced knowledge and training in "the system of intellectual habits of scientific thought."[20] As men of
science, they could communicate on the basis of a language that transcended national borders and were therefore not bound by local loyalties.
They were inclined to work together toward the same goal of developing
new factual knowledge about the world that could be applied universally.[21]
The savants understood the basic tenets of the scientific doctrine of politics
and were more likely to proceed in their investigations in a manner that embraced its fundamental objectives. In this sense, they were better able to
lead civilization in its proper direction than aristocratic leaders or the meta-
physicians. Saint-Simon stated this view quite explicitly: "A scientist, my
friends, is a man who foresees; it is because science provides the means to
predict that it is useful, and that scientists are superior to all other men."[22]
He and Comte concluded that, given the urgency of their current situation,
it would be "abnormal" to entrust this crucial responsibility to any group
other than the savants.

According to their proposed reorganization, public affairs should be managed by experts in each area of specialization. Matters of industry, for example, were of crucial importance to the stable functioning of the new order,
and the responsibility of overseeing this area should be entrusted to those
most familiar with its inner workings, the industrialists themselves. To Comte
and Saint-Simon, the industrialists were the skilled workers directly involved
in the production and distribution of goods and were therefore most qualified to act as the managers in this realm.[23] As experts in this capacity, they
could be entrusted to oversee all aspects of production, from the excavation
and supply of raw materials to the manufacturing and distribution of needed
goods.

Since the industrialists were crucial to the success of the new society, they
should be granted as much freedom as possible. The goal of the modern order was thus to liberate production, to free it of any restrictions that might inhibit its natural development.[24] Comte and Saint-Simon believed that uplift-
ing and sustaining industry was the primary task of this transitional phase
and that all political efforts should be organized to further this end. Activities
that contributed to the public good were inherently valuable, while those
that did not were potentially detrimental to the advance of civilization and
should be reduced or eliminated.[25]

Comte and Saint-Simon also argued that the new society required heightened supervision of the temporal sphere, including central coordination of
the industrial order. Their vision of a society with only a minimum of governmental intervention was thus moderated by a belief in the necessity of an

institutional arrangement involving the deliberate management of practical affairs. They attempted to reconcile the potential benefits of laissez-faire capitalism with the advantages of enlightened administration by articulating a vision of the new organizational framework for the industrial order that included both of these qualities.[26]

In an effort to work toward this goal, they proposed a sharp separation of authority between the practical and theoretical tasks involved in managing the new order. The distinction between these two spheres was to be clearly demarcated, with the industrialists given no hand in the affairs of theory and the savants not expected to participate in temporal matters. They sought to clearly define the set of responsibilities in each of these two areas to be certain that the savants were not too heavily restricted in their capacity to objectively foresee the necessary changes that would inevitably arise as civilization progressed. They argued that in the feudal era, the failure to fully develop this division of labor resulted in an inability of aristocratic leaders to understand the need for conceptual advance. Members of the clergy, whose task should have been to focus exclusively on spiritual issues, became too closely connected to the monarchical establishment and could not carry the state of knowledge about society to a higher level than that considered acceptable by the reigning authorities. In this arrangement, theologians were restricted by their affiliations to the ruling powers and unable to contribute to the development of knowledge without calling into question the legitimacy of the older system. The rigid structure of this form of organization prevented the further advance of ideas and delayed the progress of mankind.[27] Comte and Saint-Simon argued that binding the practical and theoretical responsibilities together in the modern era might again restrict the evolution of social thought at some point in the future by connecting the formation of knowledge to the established order. This could potentially force the savants to yield to the demands of industrial leaders rather than developing independent insight on the basis of objective investigation.[28]

Comte and Saint-Simon also endorsed this separation of authority on the grounds that the responsibilities of the savants were purely theoretical and should not involve the task of applying new discoveries to practical matters. From this perspective, some theories can be useful even though their relevance may not be immediately apparent in the present. Expecting scholars to demonstrate the applicability of every investigation in advance could interfere with their creative potential and limit the breadth of their intellectual imagination. They suggested that the connections between these two groups be maintained by a stratum of engineers specifically dedicated to this end. The task of the engineers would be to familiarize themselves with the ideas being generated in the theoretical world of science and develop new methods of applying these concepts in industry. They would then offer these potential applications to the industrialists, who could put them to use in the practical realm. Society would thus reap the benefit of new ideas without inhibiting their formation in the future.[29]

A NEW MORALITY FOR A NEW ORDER

Comte and Saint-Simon went beyond merely proposing that the savants be given the responsibility for developing new theoretical insights to inform the practical affairs of society. They also argued that the decline in legitimacy of the clergy left a spiritual void in the modern world, leaving an opportunity for a new authority to arise in its place. This leadership should be supplied by those who best understood the spirit of the new order. No group could accomplish this task as effectively as the savants. The former moral power of the church rested less on the superiority of its ideas than on its connections to the aristocracy. As new knowledge emerged, the church remained trapped in an outdated set of ethics that failed to take into account the newer circumstances of the modern world.[30]

Comte and Saint-Simon believed that just as the progression of civilization tended to follow a "natural" course of development, the human race could also be seen as having a natural morality. Moral questions were, from their point of view, not simply matters of conviction, but truths capable of being grounded in observation. The task of the savants in this regard should be to use systematic inquiry to discover the natural morality of mankind and develop a foundation of social ethics on the basis of this newfound insight.[31] Since scientific knowledge would produce a factual assessment of society, the morality that flowed from this knowledge would be infallible and thus impervious to metaphysical criticisms. They hoped that grounding the morality of the modern order in the tenets of science would eliminate the differences in moral positions that divided society and would reassert the natural and more beneficial course of human history.

From this perspective, the new order should be grounded in a set of "first principles" derived through scientific investigation.[32] Fundamental facts about the nature of mankind, discovered via social research, would provide the building blocks of a new moral foundation specifically suited to the industrial system. Principles devised scientifically were more closely connected to the way of life of the newer society and should therefore serve as the starting point in the creation of moral standards.[33]

Saint-Simon argued that the uniformity of knowledge established by the church in its most powerful years underscored the widespread acceptance of its morality, yielding a singularity of purpose and direction in the everyday world. As its followers began to splinter off into various religious sects, the foundation of its moral authority became diffused, weakening the influence of the church's doctrine as a stabilizing force. Both Saint-Simon and Comte believed that creating a single body of knowledge in the modern era would reestablish a universal set of moral guidelines and once again build a cohesive social order, in terms of its collective objectives and in day-to-day interactions. They allowed little room for deviations from this central norm and believed that a universal compliance to this standard would be essential to the continued survival of modern civilization. Comte presented this position in the following way:

> Hence the necessity for developing, by a special influence, the natural morality of man, in order, as much as possible, to bring the impulses of all within the limits required for the general harmony, by habituating them from childhood to a voluntary subordination of their personal interest to the common interest, and by constantly producing in active life, with necessary emphasis, the consideration of the social point of view.[34]

Since they did not envision a social order capable of functioning within the framework of a multiplicity of moral positions, they expected the new society to eventually adhere to a one-dimensional ethos as well. They gradually came to link the concept of "the natural tendency of humankind" with their own personal ideals, and sought to channel the course of human history in this direction.[35]

DEMOCRACY AND THE MASSES

These two theorists agreed that the abolition of the privilege of birth was acceptable because it did not interfere with what they considered to be the proper reorganization of society, but they rejected the notion of universal political equality since it meant placing the power of decision making in the hands of those who did not possess the knowledge or skills this responsibility required. They argued that as civilization advances, the division of labor increases, and this trend should extend to the realm of public affairs as well. The metaphysical principle of the sovereignty of the people worked well as a contrast to the notion of authority based on divine rule, but now that the power of the aristocracy had disintegrated, there was no longer any need to maintain this assertion in the new society. To them, political decision making in the modern era should be grounded in science, and most people did not operate in the calculating fashion needed to function at this level. They saw the average individual as incapable of understanding the world in an objective and impartial manner, and contended that only the savants could be entrusted to effectively carry out this highly complex endeavor.[36]

Comte and Saint-Simon also believed that most individuals did not have the education or the experience to make wise and well-informed political decisions. They contended that the men of science could develop a comprehensive knowledge of society that extended beyond the purview of the average individual. The casual observer could not achieve this depth of insight, and therefore a plan of reorganization based on such an expectation would be flawed. From their perspective, few are inclined to distinguish between short- and long-term consequences or between local concerns and those of a universal nature, and the tendency among the masses to give primacy to their own narrowly defined concerns would, if translated into politics, result in a failure to plan for the future and ultimately bring about a greater degree of conflict between competing ideologies and interests. Comte argued that most individuals have what he labeled "anti-social dispositions" in that they usually behave in a way that does not consider the broader implications of their actions. They are, he thought, unable to foresee the dangers of their own self-destructive tendencies. The work of the savants in forming a new moral order would be crucial as a counterbalance to this tendency and would place a form of control on the masses both in the realm of ideas and in the world of political decision making.[37]

Comte and Saint-Simon expected the vast majority of Europeans to accept this division of labor on the grounds that it was the most sensible arrangement possible in the modern era. They believed that addressing the bulk of the population directly on this subject would reveal the importance and necessity of placing savants in positions of power. Once made aware of the fact that the savants had the best interests of society as a whole at heart, most people would then accept their leadership and abide by their recommendations.[38]

Yet these authors also believed that to convince the masses of the righteousness of the authority of the savants, a large-scale system of education would be necessary. They pointed out that in the old order, the church conveyed the importance of maintaining a social perspective through regular services. This view was internalized by members of the congregation and became an integral component of the European belief system of that period. Comte and Saint-Simon contended that a universal moral guideline would also be necessary in the industrial period, and they proposed building a centralized system of education in order to achieve an internalizing influence of this magnitude.[39]

Comte argued that, in every society, notions of good and evil serve to guide people in their social interaction, and that this was true of the industrial order as well. The moral emptiness of the metaphysical era could be attributed to the lack of uniformly accepted beliefs. The new moral standards growing out of the work of the savants could be taught to individuals at an early age so that they would come to adopt a social perspective in their daily lives. This would elevate the lower classes by providing them with the proper philosophical orientation and moral guidance they needed in the new society.[40]

Comte and Saint-Simon suggested that the unfortunate but continuing use of force in the modern era emerged due to an overreliance on physical control as a means of maintaining order. In their view, violent repression could be effective only as a complement to spiritual guidance, and the process of educating the masses would better facilitate a protracted social harmony than an approach based on force alone. They did not believe that state violence could be completely eliminated in the new society, but they hoped that it would only be used as an adjunct to the management of ideas. In the words of Comte,

> Spiritual anarchy has preceded and engendered temporal anarchy. In the present epoch the social malady depends much more on the first than on the second cause. On the other hand an attentive study of the progress of civilization proves that the spiritual is now more completely prepared than the temporal reorganization of society. Thus our first efforts to terminate the revolutionary epoch should aim at reorganizing the spiritual power.[41]

Neither he nor Saint-Simon was concerned about the validity of the messages being promoted since these would be developed systematically by the savants and then passed down through a series of functionaries to the masses. Given that these social truths were formed using the basic tenets of science, the content of this material would be a direct reflection of reality and not subject to future criticism or debate. Their faith in the exactness of scientific knowledge prevented any such doubts from entering into their analyses, and they proceeded in purveying this educational ideal in a shroud of absolute certainty.[42]

THE PROPER ROLE OF KNOWLEDGE IN POLITICS

Enlightenment conceptions of the role of knowledge in politics emerged in the context of an air of optimism engendered by the new industrialism. Comte and Saint-Simon understood this period as an opportunity to apply the techniques of systematic investigation and analysis to the social world in the hope of creating a positive science of society. They saw science as an essential tool for social engineering and attempted to construct a theoretical framework of inquiry and political action that would best facilitate this end. The newer scientific approach to knowledge seemed to them to be capable of forging an understanding of the social world that could transcend interpretation and serve as the basis for flawless political decision making in the future.

In their eagerness to incorporate a rational system of inquiry into the political realm, they disregarded the possibility that forces other than an interest in the pursuit of objectivity might shape this new knowledge. They assumed a flow of influence from the theoretical to the temporal, expecting the stark reality of scientific findings to overpower any efforts to counter this arrangement. From their point of view, the revelations of factual information coupled with the demands of industrial development would naturally give rise to a social order in which new discoveries about the history of human civilization could be infused into the design of public policy. Although they expressed concern that the independence of intellectuals might be compromised by the practical requirements of established institutions, they expected science to ultimately overcome these pernicious influences and lead to the formation of politics organized on the basis of truth.

Their trust in the power of rational inquiry to predict the future course of events in an absolute fashion led them to assume that its conclusions would be unconditionally accepted in the realm of policy. The developments of science seemed from this standpoint to be outpacing other forms of knowledge, and this furthered their belief that a universal acceptance of the ethos of scientific discovery would necessarily evolve from the events of their day. Locked into this narrow vision of the social world, Comte and Saint-Simon saw the development of objective knowledge as a foregone conclusion and devoted their attention to the ways systematic inquiry could be used to most effectively benefit society. In their enthusiasm regarding the prospect of creating a science of politics, they failed to see the normative biases of their proposals and presented their own ideals as objective reflections of the real world.

Their image of the intellectual as a political leader stemmed from a romanticized vision of scientific knowledge as the saving grace of modern civilization. To them, the savants' expertise in its methods and goals rendered them the ideal contingent to fill the void in authority emerging with the fall of the feudal system. Their efforts to place the intellectual in a position of moral authority also grew out of this unflinching adherence to a belief in the imminent and necessary advance of social science in the new society. Their inability to imagine a society thriving without a unified moral grounding further solidified their conviction that the intellectual should assume this role in the modern world.

Comte and Saint-Simon believed that the savants could develop their knowledge in an independent manner, but they understood this independence to be a collective distancing of the world of social inquiry from any outside influences. They envisioned independent scholars as members of a unified class, working in conjunction with their peers to build a universal body of knowledge. While they favored the freedom of intellectual thought, they did not advocate extending this freedom to the level of the individual. They agreed that the philosophy of individualism played its part in helping to destabilize the legitimacy of the feudal order but concluded that it could not provide the foundation for a new society. Science was therefore a collective endeavor, grounded in empirical investigation and objective analysis. The savants were to be free of temporal concerns but would be bound by the conclusions and principles of investigation that had become standard in their field.

Although the ideas of these two social thinkers are untenable when held up to the light of present developments, their conceptions emerged without direct insight into the ways Western industrial society would evolve. They did not have the opportunity to witness the various changes that would occur over time and could only speculate as to the composition of society in the future. Later theorists had the advantage of being able to incorporate this crucial information into their own work and form analyses on the basis of new realities. Thus, the ideas of Comte and Saint-Simon were not rejected entirely but were reformulated on the basis of the specific developments unfolding throughout modernity. While their predictions regarding the future role of social science and the intellectual in modern society were inaccurate in many ways, the issues they raised nevertheless provided the starting point from which more recent variations have taken a lead.

NOTES

1. For more information on and analysis of the events surrounding the French Revolution, please see Georges Lefebvre, *The Coming of the French Revolution* (Princeton, NJ: Princeton University Press, 1988).

2. Comte and Saint-Simon disagreed on many issues; however, their ideas do overlap in a number of ways, and in this essay I primarily focus on their commonalities. I have addressed some of these differences in the endnotes as a way to clarify them for interested readers. Comte articulates his concerns regarding the ongoing anarchy of his time in his "Plan of the Scientific Operations Necessary for Reorganizing Society," reprinted in *On Intellectuals: Theoretical Studies, Case Studies*, ed. Phillip Rieff (Garden City, NY: Anchor Books, 1970), pp. 248–51. Saint-Simon expresses this view most clearly in *On the Reorganization of European Society*. Sections of this essay are reprinted in *The Political Thought of Saint-Simon*, ed. Ghita Ionescu (London: Oxford University Press, 1976), pp. 83–98.

3. For Comte's view on this, please see Comte, "Plan of the Scientific Operations," in Rieff, *On Intellectuals*, pp. 248–69. Saint-Simon outlines this position in *Letters from an Inhabitant of Geneva to His Contemporaries*, in Ionescu, *Political Thought*, pp. 65–81.

4. Comte, "Plan of the Scientific Operations," in Rieff, *On Intellectuals*, pp. 257–60.

5. Saint-Simon asserted this view throughout much of his writing, but he was most explicit in *Industry*, reprinted in Ionescu, *Political Thought*, pp. 98–128. Comte also stated this position in *Our Social Anarchy and Its Sources*, sections of which are reprinted in Rieff, *On Intellectuals*, pp. 248–49.

6. For more on Saint Simon's view of the ways science and industry would work together to facilitate the development of an integrated social order, please see

Richard Swedberg, "Saint-Simon's Vision of a United Europe," *Archives Européennes de Sociologie* 35, no. 1, 1994, pp. 145–69.

7. This is one of the key differences between the views of Comte and Saint-Simon. Comte expected older, theological conceptions of the world to eventually fade and be replaced by a secular orientation grounded in the principles of science. Saint-Simon was a firm believer in God, and explicitly stated this in a letter he wrote to his nephew (Ionescu, *Political Thought*, p. 82). He argued that it was of the utmost importance that a religious framework underscore the new philosophy, grounded in the essentially Christian principle that "men should treat one another as brothers" (Saint-Simon, *The New Christianity*, in Ionescu, *Political Thought*, p. 210). In the new order, this principle would be stated in the following way: "Religion should guide society towards the great goal of the most rapid improvement possible in the lot of the poorest class . . . it should organize itself in the way most suited to allow it to achieve this great end" (Saint-Simon, *The New Christianity*, p. 210). Saint-Simon stated that the versions of Christianity practiced in his day were "heresies" sustained only by the perpetuation of misunderstanding and physical force. These, he argued, should be replaced by a perspective that recognized the fundamental principles stated above and that accepted the new knowledge being generated by science. For more on his position on this issue, please see Saint-Simon, *The New Christianity*, in Ionescu, *Political Thought*, pp. 204–18.

8. Comte quoted in Rieff, *On Intellectuals*, pp. 249–50. Comte's major contributions to social thought are thoroughly examined in the seminal work by Lewis Coser, *Masters of Sociological Thought: Ideas in Historical and Social Context*, second edition (New York: Harcourt Brace Jovanovich, 1977). Coser also analyzes the work of other authors reviewed in this text, including Max Weber, Thorstein Veblen, and Karl Mannheim.

9. Comte outlines this position in a three-volume set of writings entitled *System of Positive Polity* (London: Longmans, Green, and Co., 1875). This extensive collection was translated and condensed by Harriet Martineau under the title *The Positive Philosophy of Auguste Comte* (London: George Bell & Sons, 1896).

10. Comte quoted in Rieff, *On Intellectuals*, p. 235.

11. Comte, *The Positive Philosophy of Auguste Comte*, p. 7.

12. Richard Emge argues that one could characterize Saint-Simon as among the principal founders of the ideas behind the sociology of knowledge in that he focused on the relationship between the material world and the realm of ideas. Although he encouraged intellectuals to strive for independence, Saint-Simon was also aware of the profound influence the conditions of their work could have on their perspectives. For more on this interpretation of Saint-Simon, please see Richard Martinus Emge, "Saint-Simon and the Sociology of Knowledge and Science," *Kolner Zeitschrift fur Soziologie und Sozialpsychologie*, Supplement 22, 1980, pp. 317–34.

13. Comte in Rieff, *On Intellectuals*, pp. 262–64.

14. Selections from *Le Politique* can be found in Ionescu, *Political Thought*, pp. 189–90.

15. Comte very clearly states his position on this issue in *The Positive Philosophy*, pp. 15–18. Others interpret Comte as recognizing the interpretive dimensions of science. For more on this perspective, see Julien Freund, "La Politique d'Auguste Comte,"

Revue Philosophique de la France et de l'Etranger 110, no. 4, October–December 1985, pp. 461–87.

16. Although they rejected the varieties of sectarian Christianity of this period, Comte and Saint-Simon held on to the belief that the primary purpose of the natural world is to serve mankind. They incorporated this assumption into the doctrine of politics, positing that all social research begin with a view of nature as existing for the sake of benefiting humanity.

17. This is an underlying theme in the work of both Comte and Saint-Simon, but explicit examples of their positions on this issue can be found in Comte's "Plan of the Scientific Operations," in Rieff, *On Intellectuals*, pp. 262–66, and Saint-Simon's *Letters from an Inhabitant of Geneva*, in Ionescu, *Political Thought*, pp. 65–81.

18. Comte, "Plan of the Scientific Operations," in Rieff, *On Intellectuals*, pp. 262–66, and Saint-Simon, *Letters from an Inhabitant of Geneva*, in Ionescu, *Political Thought*, pp. 65–81.

19. Comte, "Plan of the Scientific Operations," in Rieff, *On Intellectuals*, pp. 262–66, and Saint-Simon, *Letters from an Inhabitant of Geneva*, in Ionescu, *Political Thought*, pp. 65–81.

20. Comte quoted in Rieff, *On Intellectuals*, p. 253.

21. Ionescu, *Political Thought*, p. 68.

22. Saint-Simon quoted in Ionescu, *Political Thought*, p. 76.

23. Comte states his position on this in Rieff, *On Intellectuals*, pp. 253–54. Saint-Simon outlines his view most clearly in *The Catechism of the Industrialists*, reprinted in Ionescu, *Political Thought*, pp. 182–203. Saint-Simon initially included the laborers working in the factories in his definition of the industrialists, arguing that their knowledge in this regard was useful and therefore as important to society as that of the industrial managers. He assumed that the potential differences in interest between the owners and the workers in industrial facilities would be resolved by virtue of their common objective in continuing the task of production. Toward the end of his career, Saint-Simon recognized that these divisions were not so easily resolved, and he became somewhat disillusioned with the prospect of a universal harmony in the industrial world.

24. Saint-Simon drew a distinction between the producers and the idlers, characterizing the producers as individuals whose activities contributed to the common goal of furthering industrial production and the idlers as those who did nothing to this end. The landowners, officers of the crown, ministers, and judges were no longer integral to the functioning of the new order. Saint-Simon held that the loss of the producers would be devastating to the country, while the loss of the idlers would result in only a sentimental sadness but would cause no lasting political damage to the state. He went as far as to list the actual names of members of the royal family who would not be missed if they were suddenly no longer around, and he was arrested by the French police for publishing this sentiment. Unfortunately for him, while he was in custody, the Duc de Berry, one of the men on Saint-Simon's list, was killed by a radical named Louvel. Saint-Simon was later tried and found guilty of subversion, but was acquitted on appeal.

25. While they embraced the notion of useful work, their orientations differed from the utilitarian perspective in the sense that they did not see the course of events in a society as the result of the sum of individual interests, but as related to cultural

traditions and the structure of institutional arrangements. In this regard, their positions were much more closely aligned with that of the French collectivist tradition, later adopted by Tocqueville and Durkheim. Nevertheless, their enthusiasm regarding the benefits of a large-scale system of industrial production paralleled the utilitarian ideal that placed a value on useful work. See Saint-Simon, *Industry*, in Ionescu, *Political Thought*, pp. 99–128, and Comte in Rieff, *On Intellectuals*, pp. 281 and 282.

26. This is one of the main differences between the formulations of Comte and Saint-Simon on the one hand and those of the classical liberal tradition on the other. While classical liberals tended to favor the uninhibited development of industry, Comte and Saint-Simon argued that the goals of production far outweighed the importance of ownership. They maintained that property should be owned as well as managed by an educated elite, as this would allow for the more efficient organization of industry. See Saint-Simon, *On the Reorganization of European Society*, in Ionescu, *Political Thought*, pp. 83–98, and Comte, in Rieff, *On Intellectuals*, pp. 253–54.

27. Comte was much more concerned about the separation of authority than Saint-Simon was. The latter expected the industrialists and the scientists to work together in the administration of society. Each would have their own respective responsibilities, but they would pool their knowledge in establishing the plan.

28. Saint-Simon, *On the Reorganization of European Society*, reprinted in Ionescu, *Political Thought*, pp. 85–98.

29. Comte, in Rieff, *On Intellectuals*, pp. 252. Saint-Simon in Ionescu, *Political Thought*, p. 81.

30. Saint-Simon, Ionescu, *Political Thought*, pp. 204–218. In his assessment of Comte, Gaetano Congi builds on the interpretation of H. Gouhier, who suggested that Comte's work can be seen as "religious positivism," meant to serve as a new belief system to replace what Comte considered to be the older, outdated, religious dogma of his time. For more on this view, please see Gaetano Congi, "Sociology and the Social Question in Auguste Comte," *Sociologia e Ricerca Sociale* 18, no. 52, 1997, pp. 24–64.

31. Rieff, *On Intellectuals*, p. 277.

32. Comte disagreed with Saint-Simon that the development of an industrial order would necessarily lead to the proper moral reorganization of society. Comte held that one should not be so enthusiastic about the advantages of an industrial state as to assume that this force could, of its own accord, yield a proper spiritual reorganization. He argued that every form of organization, including industrial society, has sources of disorder and that the appropriate moral influence could be developed only on the basis of scientific inquiry. He saw the modern industrial system as yielding a weak and fluctuating moral code which, if left to its own accord, would lead to a situation in which the most powerful elements of society would dominate the less powerful. Although he agreed with Saint-Simon that the period of military conquest would most likely be dissolved by the new industrial order, he believed that allowing temporal institutions to unfold in a laissez-faire manner would lead to an environment where "might makes right," rather than one in which the principles of a newer, scientifically grounded morality could reign.

33. While Saint-Simon agreed with Comte that a universally accepted set of first principles would be a prerequisite to a stable temporal order, he did not accept the latter's contention that these principles could be derived via scientific inquiry alone.

Although he was an outspoken critic of the Catholic and Protestant churches of his time, he nevertheless argued that the fundamental principle of Christianity could be ultimately beneficial to the new order. In his view, the church had lost sight of the basis of Christianity that professed that each individual should love others as though they were his brothers. This principle, while fundamental to the teachings of Christ, was no longer an integral part of the church doctrine, and the focus had shifted away from it to other insignificant and petty concerns serving to divide humankind rather than to bring it together. From this starting point, the remaining moral and ethical principles could be derived, providing the theoretical underpinning for what Saint-Simon labeled the New Christianity. Once people began to see each other as brothers, they would no longer accept the conditions of the poor as inevitable and would feel compelled to take action to remedy their deplorable situation. The system of industrial production acted to advance this newer form of morality as it brought an ever-increasing number of individuals into its sphere of influence. The interconnectedness of the industrial system facilitated an interdependence that led people to work together and develop a sense of mutual respect, just as the basic principle of the New Christianity professed.

34. Comte, "Plan of the Scientific Operations," in Rieff, *On Intellectuals*, p. 277.

35. Rieff, *On Intellectuals*, p. 280.

36. Rieff, *On Intellectuals*, p. 275.

37. Comte, in Rieff, *On Intellectuals*, pp. 282–85. Jean-Paul Frick argues that although Comte largely rejected the principles of democracy, his concept of power does have some democratic dimensions to it. From this perspective, Comte's goal of developing a science of politics was grounded in an interest in creating a more just society, in which the concerns of the larger population would be more readily addressed. Frick maintains that Comte wanted to bring science into the equation to lessen the instability caused by fluctuations in public opinion and despotic rule, and therefore benefit the social whole. For more on this interpretation, please see Jean-Paul Frick, "The Question of Power in Auguste Comte's Theory and the Significance of His Political Philosophy," *Revue Philosophique de la France et de l'Etranger* 113, no. 3, July–September, 1988, pp. 273–301.

38. Saint-Simon actually wrote a long essay directly addressing the larger population of France, explaining why the savants were naturally the best suited to be given the responsibility of managing the new order. See *Letters from an Inhabitant of Geneva*, pp. 76–81.

39. Saint-Simon, *The New Christianity*, in Ionescu, *Political Thought*, pp. 204–18. Comte, "Plan of the Scientific Operations," in Rieff, *On Intellectuals*, p. 282.

40. Comte, "Plan of the Scientific Operations," in Rieff, *On Intellectuals*, pp. 252 and 253.

41. Comte, "Plan of the Scientific Operations," in Rieff, *On Intellectuals*, pp. 252 and 253.

42. This interpretation of Comte's position differs significantly from that of Juliette Grange. Her view is that Comte believed that scientific research did not yield absolute knowledge but could identify regularities or patterns that could then be characterized as laws, with the understanding that they would be revised with the advent of new findings. For more on this position, please see Juliette Grange, *La Philosophie d'Auguste Comte: Science, Politique, Religion* (Paris: Presses Universitaires de France, 1996).

2

Max Weber: Social Science and Politics in the Transition to State Capitalism

The conceptions of Comte and Saint-Simon regarding the scientist's public role may have provided a suitable starting point for social thought on this question in the early stages of modernity, but the changes accompanying the rise of state capitalism in the beginning of the twentieth century demanded the formation of new and more subtle analyses. Theorists writing in the midst of this transition were faced with the reality that the predictions of these earlier thinkers had not materialized as expected. The social sciences had not produced universal laws on the nature of human interaction, policy formation was not grounded in scientific calculation, and intellectuals had not formed a unified stratum working collectively toward an enlightened ideal. Many of the older cultural traditions and values still predominated, not only influencing the ideas and perceptions of members of the broader population, but also informing the decisions of political and economic leaders. Public policy continued to be created in terms of narrow worldviews and on the basis of national and ethnic loyalties. The premodern tradition of resorting to military conflict in the face of regional disagreements defined the political landscape of the Western nations, and theological conceptions of human existence still overshadowed secular interpretations of the social world. Although the techniques of science and industry had become effective tools in shaping the character of modern life, notions of how to use this newfound power emulated earlier modes of understanding and failed to adequately address the complexities of the newer society.

Max Weber developed his assessment of knowledge and politics in the context of this large-scale transformation, considering the ways in which social scientists had chosen to respond to this set of circumstances and evaluating the implications of their reaction in terms of decision-making trends at

21

the national and international levels. He could see that while the ideals of the early modern thinkers on this subject were limited and not applicable to the existing social order, the statements and actions of academic intellectuals had nevertheless become influential in the realm of government. Weber sought to describe the developments he saw unfolding in his time as a way to offer insight into the importance of the social scientist's role in the political arena, and to outline his ideal on this question.

Weber's analyses are grounded in his concern regarding the autonomy of the individual and the restrictive nature of the authoritarian and bureaucratic institutions emerging in the early twentieth century. He characterized Germany in this post-Bismarckian period as undergoing a transition from leadership based on the strength of charismatic and principled authority to the more mechanized "leaderless" democracy of advanced industrial society. This series of changes seemed to him to be indicative of the increasing rationalization of Western civilization and the strengthening of the "iron cage" of state-centered capitalism. He cited the mechanization of the party system in Germany as an example of this trend; in this system, the selection of public officials took place on the basis of a candidate's conformity to a strictly defined party platform rather than an ability to fulfill the essential requirements of a political leader. Weber argued that although charismatic leadership was an essential component of democratic politics in the twentieth century, the party system as it existed in Germany prior to World War I was antithetical to the selection of strong leaders grounded in a firm set of political convictions. He was troubled by the realization that candidates of this kind usually fell prey to the requirements of the party machine, leaving only a collection of bureaucratically minded conformists in key positions of authority.[1] Sound leadership involved a willingness to challenge conventional wisdom and address public issues with a broad view of the changes taking place on a national and global scale. While Weber was not optimistic that this tendency toward bureaucratization and poor decision making could be altered, he nonetheless offered his suggestions regarding the proper role of intellectuals in the public arena to address these concerns.

Weber's emphasis on the political was directly related to his view of the nature of German politics in this period, in which leaders had the power to manage the affairs of the nation without giving careful consideration to the forces of business. The sluggish nature of the German government in making the transition from an imperial to a parliamentary order enabled officials to act with less deference to outside influences, but it also distanced them from the rapidly changing circumstances evolving both within and beyond the country's borders. Weber wrung his hands in dismay over the arrogance of the kaiser in the period leading up to the war and as the intellectuals of his day hid behind the protective wall of officialdom rather than provide the informed guidance he thought they should offer in such a crucial time.[2]

He viewed the routinization of political decision making as a dangerous trend emerging in part as a result of the lack of leadership among public officials and their reluctance to intelligently address the urgent problems facing Germany and its neighbors in this period.[3] Although Weber's analyses differed sharply from those of Comte and Saint-Simon, he echoed their concerns regarding the need for enlightened leadership within the auspices of the modern political order. He believed that decision making required a sense of the long-term implications of any political action as well as an informed understanding of the ends to which leaders might aspire, but unlike the earlier theorists, he did not assume that an intellectual stratum could manage public affairs in a calculating fashion.[4] His insight into the intellectualist rationalization associated with the rise of state capitalism led him to see the inherent flaws of such an arrangement, and he hoped to offer a more refined set of suggestions as to the possible ways systematically gathered knowledge could contribute to policy formation.

Weber expressed concern regarding the future of Western civilization, but he did not characterize the drift toward rationalization as necessarily inevitable. He assumed social scientists would be capable of influencing future events in the West and sought to provide a series of guidelines they might use to act in a responsible and effective manner to confront this and other problematic trends unfolding in this time.[5]

Weber approached the question of the public role of social scientists in two ways. The first emphasized their potential to aid in the interpretation and analysis of social issues, and the second centered on what he considered to be the ethics of those involved in politics. He suggested that these two areas of endeavor remain somewhat separated, so that the proper work of one would not interfere with that of the other, but he also suggested ways the two could strengthen one another in the long run.[6]

Within this framework, social scientists engaged in research had a responsibility to limit the extent to which their own personal or political views influenced the focus and character of their investigations. While systematically derived findings might ultimately enable political actors to more effectively achieve their goals, it was not the task of researchers to use inquiry as a means to reach predetermined political ends. Their responsibility was to facilitate a broad understanding of their topic of study and develop the knowledge needed by leaders to address policy issues in an informed manner.[7]

In contrast to this role, the task of the political intellectual involved entering more fully into the domain of public life while still retaining some connections to the discussions and debates of scientific inquiry. Weber expected social scientists acting in this capacity to have a firm knowledge of recent developments in their field as well as the ability to infuse this insight into the often backhanded and deceptive milieu of politics. He respected scholars in each of these two spheres but saw the ethics of science as distinct from those of politics and sought to lay out the differences in a clear fashion.

THE ROLE OF THE SOCIAL SCIENTIST IN PUBLIC AFFAIRS

Weber disdained what he called the "technical" approach to political decision making. He saw this approach as a mode of problem solving in which the ends are assumed to be given and the actor simply chooses the most effective means to achieve these ends. He argued that in politics, the ends are not always clear but emerge as a result of the continuous playing out of conflicting ideological positions of competing groups with a limited potential for compatibility.[8] These differences in orientation necessarily place politics in the democratic realm, where the tension between conflicting goals is at the root of policy formation. Weber attempted to show that, in a liberal democracy, the process of conflict resolution involves an interaction between leaders and their constituents. Within this framework, important issues do not simply arise spontaneously from the concerns of the population but grow out of the actions of smaller agenda-oriented groups. Political hopefuls align themselves with a core constituency, develop a set of positions, and then appeal to the larger population for support. Once elected, they are restricted in their ability to act freely due to the external pressures imposed upon them, but they are ultimately required to make decisions on the basis of their own insight, knowledge, and convictions.[9]

To Weber, social inquiry could play a key role in this endeavor via its potential to help political actors "gain clarity" in their understanding of the situation at hand. He saw social inquiry as providing the means through which one could identify and assess the ideas behind a given way of thinking and reveal these ideas to the holders of such a view as well as to their opponents. Analysis could be used in this sense to critically examine the value judgments serving as the foundation for political and administrative decisions. Weber did not assume that social scientists could determine the validity of political convictions or prove one set of commitments superior to others. He did, however, take the position that their work could help to expose the underlying preconceptions of a given set of political aspirations and present these preconceptions in a more concrete and bare form. He argued that this approach provided a way to examine values in the absence of the objectives with which they are intertwined and a way to directly assess the core ideological foundations of competing political positions.[10] A key goal of social science from this perspective is to enable political actors to more acutely comprehend the basis of their own convictions as well as those of others, and possibly reevaluate the policies associated with these views.

Weber also argued that social inquiry could help to reveal the potential consequences of a projected policy and assess whether a given means for achieving the desired end is appropriate. He qualified this assertion, stating that while research can identify the trends of a particular period, it cannot predict the future course of events in an absolute way. He understood that the consequences of political actions often stray significantly from the original intentions of the actors involved, and he argued that "the final result of political action regularly stands in completely inadequate and often even paradoxical relation to its original meaning."[11] From Weber's point of view, while social scientific evaluation can offer insight into the likely outcomes of a planned action, it can only do so within the range of predictability characteristic of the realm of human affairs. He saw the historical tendency of political actions gone awry, but he held fast to the belief that inasmuch as it is possible to assess the feasibility of political objectives, social science is best able to succeed at this task.[12]

He also suggested that social inquiry could critically evaluate the ends themselves using formal logic. From Weber's point of view, social scientists could assess the "internal consistency" of a set of goals. He observed political enthusiasts naively romanticizing the image of the society they hoped to create, often disregarding many of the negative aspects of their ideal. Weber turned to social science to challenge these delusions and build an enlightened perspective among policy makers. He hoped that by offering insight into the ideological foundations of policy positions and considering the likely consequences of their implementation, social scientists could help leaders better understand the circumstances at hand and act in a more informed manner than they might in the absence of such findings.[13] According to Weber,

> the scientific treatment of value-judgments may not only understand and empathically analyze (*nacherleben*) the desired ends and the ideals which underlie them; it can also "judge" them critically. This criticism can of course have only a dialectical character, i.e., it can be no more than a formal logical judgment of historically given value-judgments and ideas, a testing of the ideals according to the postulate of the internal *consistency* of the desired end. It can, insofar as it sets itself this goal, aid the acting willing person in attaining self-clarification concerning the final axioms from which his desired ends are derived. It can assist him in becoming aware of the ultimate standards of value which he does not make explicit to himself or which he must presuppose in order to be logical. The elevation of these ultimate standards, which are manifested in concrete value judgments, to the level of explicitness is the utmost that the scientific treatment of value-judgments can do without entering into the realm of speculation. As to whether the person expressing these value-judgments should adhere to these ultimate standards is his personal affair; it involves will and conscience, not empirical knowledge.[14]

Weber recommended drawing a connection between the world of social science and that of political decision making, but he emphasized the point that policy could not be formed on this basis alone. Only willing political actors with the requisite conviction and authority could accomplish this task. "An empirical science cannot tell anyone what he should do but rather what he can do."[15] To Weber, politicians could not fully rely on the advice of experts to weave their way through the variety of dilemmas they confronted regularly. They could draw on this knowledge as a source of information and guidance but were required to balance their decisions with contextual factors and pragmatic concerns.

In spite of his faith in the ability of social inquiry to act as an aid to policy-making, Weber subscribed to the belief that this could be done within the context of a democratically organized polity. He did not favor democratic forms of organization on the basis of their inherent merit and saw many reasons to rebuke the theoretical assumptions underlying their use, but he supported the notion of democracy on the grounds that it could act as a counterforce to the rationalizing tendencies of the party machine.[16] In his view, it could produce leaders capable of managing the huge bureaucratic structures characteristic of the modern era and provide a means through which their actions could be kept in check. He saw voters as unable to fully participate in the many complex matters of policy facing parliament on a regular basis and gave little credence to direct democracy, but he argued that public officials should be limited by the boundaries of a representative democracy in which they would be judged not on the basis of each decision but on the sum of their accomplishments while in office.[17]

In response to the seemingly paradoxical dilemma of whether to base policy decisions on democratic participation or on the rule of experts, Weber attempted to carve out a middle ground relying on representative democracy as well as the information and analysis drawn from social research. He did not seek to place the responsibility of policymaking in the hands of an intellectual elite but suggested that inquiry could provide the guidance needed by elected officials, who could then set policy with the benefit of this insight.[18]

At the crux of Weber's ideal is his belief in the importance of working toward an objective social science. He recognized that scientists could not fully eliminate their own biases and that interpretation was essential to deciphering the "facts" in this type of inquiry. Yet he insisted that scientists had an obligation to tenaciously strive for accuracy, in spite of this potential fallibility: "[The possibility of bias] . . . proves nothing against the duty of searching for the truth."[19] He was critical of the young scholars of his day who, upon learning of the interpretive nature of scientific knowledge, were quick to jump to the conclusion that the pursuit of objectivity was a futile task altogether. Weber saw this position as somewhat naive and indicative of a poor understanding of the complex nature of knowledge itself. He contended that although value judgments are central to any investigation, social science does have the potential to shed new light on important issues by virtue of its critical and systematic orientation. He recognized that it is grounded in a normative set of assumptions and made no pretense that this foundation somehow transcended values, but he also argued that investigators could operate within the confines of these norms while at the same time gaining insight into their subject matter, without engaging in self-deception or nearsightedness.[20]

Weber did not embrace the notion of relativism in the social sciences, but he claimed that while "factual knowledge" was within the realm of interpretation, it could be seen as the result of an effort to minimize the extent to which value judgments played a role in its formation. He held this view of knowledge to be in sharp contrast to conclusions developed in a persuasive manner by researchers operating from the point of view of an advocacy position. Weber argued that social scientists have an obligation to search for and reveal the relevant facts of their inquiry, including those that might serve as evidence to undermine their own political orientation or goals. These "facts" do not constitute absolute truth or reality itself but can reveal more about the social order than inquiry in which little effort is made to reduce normativity. The task of the social scientist operating from this perspective is to engage in an unrelenting quest for understanding in spite of the epistemological obstacles involved.[21]

Weber extended this call for neutrality into his analysis of higher education, arguing that university professors had an obligation to refrain from bringing their own political leanings into the classroom. He understood that political issues were often an important part of the curriculum in the social sciences and did not suggest limiting these discussions, but he maintained that it was inappropriate for professors to try to push students toward one political orientation or another.

> To the prophet and the demagogue, it is said: "Go your ways out into the streets and speak openly to the world," that is, speak where criticism is possible. In the lecture room we stand opposite our audience, and it has to remain silent. I deem it irresponsible to exploit the circumstance that for the sake of their career the students have to attend a teacher's course while there is nobody present to oppose him with criticism. The task of the teacher is to serve the students with his knowledge and scientific experience and not to imprint upon them his personal political views.[22]

Weber observed some of his colleagues attempting to use the podium as a means through which to promote their own political ideals and defend their positions on the basis of what they claimed were scientifically derived conclusions, and he argued that this sort of presentation was misleading since political questions cannot be fully separated from value judgments and are essentially a matter of personal conviction. From Weber's perspective, a central task of higher education is to broaden the perspectives of students and help them to make informed political assessments. Scholars who focus their energies on corralling students into their own value system are not living up to this fundamental principle.[23]

In assessing the larger goals of social science, Weber emphasized its potential to facilitate a deeper understanding of the social world. He was aware of the distinction between linear and circular views of human social life, and he raised the question, does death have any meaning for modern mankind? He reiterated Tolstoy's argument that since the lives of modern civilized individuals are only minute components in the larger structure of an ever-progressing history, they never see the concluding finale in which the sum of their work reaches its ultimate destination. Instead, they are forced to be content with the knowledge that they contributed their small part to this great scheme. Weber remarked that Tolstoy valued the sense of finality a premodern human being could experience in having come full circle in death, and Weber demonstrated his empathy with this viewpoint. He then challenged Tolstoy's claim that the value of science lies only in what it can provide to the larger collection of shared knowledge and stressed instead its ability to foster new insight into the world in the present. To Weber, social inquiry can serve not only as a means to work toward the long-term goals of modernity but also as a contributor to personal or collective enlightenment in a more immediate sense. He understood its limitations, but he continued to emphasize the value of the modern scientific perspective on this basis rather than placing it on a par with other forms of knowledge.[24]

THE ETHICS OF THE POLITICAL INTELLECTUAL

While Weber expected the social scientist to strive for objectivity and withhold personal value judgments, he drew quite a different set of standards in assessing the role of the intellectual involved in politics. He understood that social scientists were a part of the world of opinion and conviction, and did not suggest that they shy away from this in favor of a full-fledged retreat into the ivory tower. Instead, he recommended that those entering the public realm acknowledge the characteristic qualities of modern politics and take the steps necessary to act effectively in this milieu.[25]

Weber's framework centered on the question of ethics in this setting and underscored his distinction between what he called the "ethic of ultimate ends" and the "ethic of responsibility." He outlined the differences between these two and reflected on the implications of employing them in the realm of modern politics.[26] The ethic of ultimate ends is one in which individuals pursue an ideal goal in a dogmatic way, failing to account for the consequences of their actions. "If an action of good intent leads to bad results, then in the actor's eyes, not he but the world . . . is responsible for the evil."[27] Intellectuals following this mode of thinking are susceptible to advocating action deemed to be working toward a meritorious end, in spite of the negatives involved in achieving this end and the possibility that such an action might not bring about this end. Such intellectuals are, in Weber's assessment, naive idealists, failing to pursue a reasoned approach to politics. He was particularly critical of the intellectuals during World War I who sought to extend the conflict on the basis of their hope to bring about socialism, neglecting the evidence that prolonging the war would undoubtedly fail to accomplish this goal. Weber sought to show that following the ethic of ultimate ends in this fashion could blind intellectuals to the realities of the situation at hand and possibly exacerbate the very set of circumstances they sought to improve.[28]

In contrast to this approach to political decision making, Weber proposed the ethic of responsibility, in which intellectuals consider the consequences of the actions they recommend as well as the ends they seek. Following this ethic means striving to reach an ideal set of objectives, but with an awareness of the harm this pursuit might bring and a willingness to adjust one's position in relation to the unique circumstances of each situation. To Weber, this orientation involved weighing the benefits of a projected policy against its pitfalls and taking a pragmatic stance in the effort to achieve measured success rather than risk complete failure.[29]

He also pointed out that following the ethic of responsibility in an absolute fashion could lead intellectuals to be overcompromising of their own values. Resting too securely on the assumption that politics is necessarily a matter of compromise could further push the decision maker into the realm of bureaucratic routine, where the opportunity for contestation and pursuing one's convictions are so thoroughly overshadowed that they become meaningless.

His solution to this apparent dilemma was to suggest that the proper task of political actors is to seek a balance between these two sets of ethics and retain an element of idealism even when the situation seems to demand compromise. Weber proposed that public intellectuals develop and sustain their own convictions, not in a naive way, but in full view of the consequences of their actions and with an awareness of the need for informed decision making, even in the face of the enigmatic and unpredictable challenges of modern politics.[30]

Weber saw that some scholars more closely aligned themselves with the established order, relinquishing their convictions so thoroughly that they reduced themselves to mere supporters of the "up and coming powers." He refrained from labeling members of this cast as intellectuals and instead referred to them as the literati or intelligentsia. He bitterly rejected the establishmentarian attitudes of the Prussian literati of his time, arguing that they typically looked to the views of others in developing their analyses and avoided deviating too far from their peers so as to remain within the inner circle of policy advisors. This strengthened the validity of conventional thought, regardless of its glaring internal contradictions or its failure to adequately address pressing political issues.[31]

He also criticized the tendency of the intelligentsia to contribute to the bureaucratization of politics by approaching questions of public policy in a narrow and technical fashion. He saw the intelligentsia as career professionals trained in a specific area of policy and assessing each issue from the point of view of their own specialization. This reduced their ability to understand the larger implications of their actions and perpetuated the poor decision making characteristic of the German leadership in the period leading up to World War I. Although experienced in political affairs, the intelligentsia were not devoted to any set of long-term goals other than an interest in preserving their own positions in the official hierarchy, and they developed their conclusions accordingly. He saw them as operating behind the scenes, managing public policy in a bureaucratic fashion, while elected political leaders acted as ceremonial figureheads. This arrangement heightened the technical effectiveness of an administration, but prevented its leaders from acting decisively and with a broad view of the issues facing the nation.[32] "The future belongs to bureaucratization, and it is evident that in this regard the literati pursue their calling—to provide a salvo of applause to the up-and-coming powers—just as they did in the age of laissez-faire, both times with the same naïveté."[33]

In his analysis of the ancient Roman and Chinese bureaucracies, Weber saw that once these became firmly entrenched, they remained in place until the larger society and its corresponding social structure collapsed. He contended that although they were constraining and inflexible, their strength relative to any other form of political organization ensured their continued dominance.[34] The modern form of bureaucracy was even more "escape-proof" than its premodern counterparts due to its highly rationalized organizational structure and its elaborate division of labor.[35] The myopic vision of the literati and their mechanistic approach to the management of public affairs further cemented the hold of modern bureaucracy on all those living within its reach. Weber went as far as to suggest that the fate of individuality would lie in the outcome of the struggle between intellectuals acting independently and the more narrow, technically inclined intelligentsia weaving their way through the mazes of officialdom.[36]

His dissatisfaction with the policies of the German government prior to and during World War I led him to appeal to the social scientists of his day to act on the basis of the evidence before them. He recognized the limitations of their power in the political realm and was aware of the growing influence of party politics, but he persisted in his effort to challenge these trends and urged his colleagues to sustain their ideological independence. Weber could see that leadership in the modern world required a degree of savvy not common in the scientifically inclined, but he hoped that social scientists in the public realm would draw on systematically derived knowledge in forming their positions and in conveying them to others. He understood that there would be instances where politicians might attempt to employ the findings of science in choosing the course of action they wished to pursue but run into opposition on the part of conflicting actors and institutions. Under these circumstances, the best they could do is to accept their limited control over the situation and strive to work toward their informed goals, even in the face of these ongoing pressures.[37]

SOCIAL SCIENTISTS AND POLITICS IN STATE CAPITALISM

Weber rejected the belief of the early modern thinkers that politics could be made into an objective science in the service of societal advancement. He called into question the suggestion that scientists be placed in positions of power by virtue of their allegedly superior wisdom or their ability to transcend culturally narrow ideological orientations. Yet he accepted the more fundamental notion that scientific knowledge could be of value in the modern order and sought to fashion a new understanding of its role in this context.

Weber transformed the ideals of his predecessors in relation to the changes taking place in the West, particularly those involving the advance of the state in governing the activities of the market. His assessment of the ways a machine-like organization of politics restricted the autonomy of the individual and interfered with the potential for insightful decision making directly challenged the claims of Comte and Saint-Simon that such an arrangement would necessarily yield beneficial ends. Their optimism with respect to the potential of a scientifically oriented leadership blinded them to the idea that the goals of politics are less technical questions than they are a function of norms and values. Weber's analysis brought these conceptual weaknesses to the fore and provided the basis for a more balanced view of the social scientist's public role. His suggestion that they strive to retain a broad understanding of the trends of their time and avoid the easy descent into narrow specialization offered a middle ground between positivism and relativism, while at the same time facilitating a level of integration between the worlds of social science and public affairs.

Weber was aware of the unique histories of other regions of the world and relied on this insight to form his analyses of politics, but he grounded his positions on scientific inquiry in the specific set of circumstances unfolding in his own milieu. Although writing in the early stages of the transition to state capitalism, he saw that the growing connections between the economic and political orders of the industrial era had already limited the potential for insightful, long-term policy making. He observed experienced political leaders and their advisors being replaced by teams of experts, and argued that this institutional shift would likely shape the course of modern society as the newly formed bureaucracies continued to flourish.

Weber's writings on this issue illustrate the larger point that the emergence of state capitalism demanded a greater degree of conformity on the part of social scientists to the institutional pressures they faced.[38] He understood that in this environment, they would have to tenaciously struggle to retain their independence and resist the inclination to hide behind the security of professional affiliations or traditional social analyses. Although he was not optimistic about the future directions of Western civilization, Weber maintained that social scientists had a responsibility to engage in broad-minded, independent inquiry and to offer their analyses to others in the hope that their work could contribute to personal or collective enlightenment, and he developed his own conclusions within the framework of this ideal.

NOTES

1. Weber outlined his views on the ethics of politics most clearly in his essay "Politics as a Vocation," in *From Max Weber: Essays in Sociology*, ed. Hans Gerth and C. Wright Mills (New York: Oxford University Press, 1958).

2. For more on Weber's view of politics during this time, please see his essay "Political Concerns," in *From Max Weber*, pp. 32–44.

3. Weber discussed the rationalization of politics throughout much of his writing, but prominent examples can be found in "Bureaucracy and Political Leadership," *Economy and Society: An Outline of Interpretive Sociology*, trans. Guenther Roth and Claus Wittich (Berkeley: University of California Press, 1978), pp. 1393–1416.

4. An overview of his ethics of the social scientist can be found in Weber, "Science as a Vocation," in *From Max Weber*, pp. 129–56.

5. Weber, "Science as a Vocation."

6. In the two essays "Science as a Vocation" and "Politics as a Vocation," Weber outlines two sets of ethics for those in each of these two fields.

7. Weber expresses his position on this in "Science as a Vocation."

8. Weber, "Politics as a Vocation," in *From Max Weber*.

9. Weber, "Science as a Vocation," p. 125.

10. Weber, "Objectivity in Social Science and Social Policy," in *The Methodology of the Social Sciences*, trans. and ed. Edward Shils and Henry Finch (New York: Free Press, 1949), p. 54.

11. Weber, "Politics as a Vocation," p. 117.

12. Weber, "Science as a Vocation," p. 150–56.

13. Weber, "Science as a Vocation," p. 151.

14. Weber, "Objectivity in Social Science," p. 54.

15. Weber, "Objectivity in Social Science," p. 54.

16. Peter Breiner offers an in-depth assessment of Weber's ideas on democratic politics, arguing that while Weber saw direct democracy as problematic in many respects, he nevertheless sought to articulate a viable theoretical framework for participatory democracy. Please see Peter Breiner, *Max Weber and Democratic Politics* (Ithaca, NY: Cornell University Press, 1996).

17. Max Weber, "Domination and Legitimacy," in *Economy and Society*, p. 949. For more on Weber's position on the question of direct versus representative democracy, please see Anthony Giddens, *Politics and Sociology in the Thought of Max Weber* (London: Macmillan, 1972), pp. 16–25.

18. David Beetham offers a clear assessment of Weber's view on this issue in "Social Science and Political Practice," in *Max Weber and the Theory of Modern Politics* (London: Allen & Unwin, 1974).

19. Weber, "Science as a Vocation," p. 146.

20. Weber outlined this view in his essay "Objectivity in Social Science and Social Policy." For more on his position on this topic, please see Susan Hekman, "Max Weber and Post-Positivist Social Theory," in *The Barbarism of Reason: Max Weber and the Twilight of Enlightenment*, ed. Asher Horowitz and Terry Maley (Toronto: University of Toronto Press, 1994), pp. 267–86.

21. Richard Wellen offers some insight into Weber's work on this question, arguing that Weber understood the interpretive nature of social scientific inquiry but did not accept the presuppositions of positivism or relativism. Wellen suggests reading Weber's position as a call for intellectual integrity. Please see Richard Wellen, "The Politics of Intellectual Integrity," *Max Weber Studies* 2, no. 1, November, 2001, pp. 81–101.

22. Weber, "Science as a Vocation," p. 146.

23. Weber articulates this perspective in "Science as a Vocation," pp. 145–48. Mark Weaver points out that one of Weber's main goals in taking this position is to stress the importance of helping students to develop the critical thinking skills they need to make sound political judgments on their own. For more on this issue, please see Mark Weaver, "Weber's Critique of Advocacy in the Classroom: Critical Thinking and Civic Education," *Political Science and Politics* 31, 1998, pp. 799–801.

24. Weber, "Science as a Vocation," pp. 139–56.

25. Weber, "Politics as a Vocation," pp. 115–28.

26. Weber, "Politics as a Vocation," pp. 120–28.

27. Weber, "Politics as a Vocation," p. 121.

28. Weber, "Politics as a Vocation," pp. 121–22.

29. Weber, "Politics as a Vocation," pp. 120–28.

30. Weber, "Politics as a Vocation," pp. 120–28.

31. Max Weber, "Bureaucratization and the Naïveté of the Literati," in *Economy and Society*, vol. 3, pp. 1399–1403.

32. Weber, "Bureaucratization and the Naïveté of the Literati."

33. Weber, "Bureaucratization and the Naïveté of the Literati," p. 1401.

34. Weber's views on the Roman and Chinese bureaucracies can be found in "Bureaucratization and the Naïveté of the Literati," p. 1401.

35. For the modern bureaucracy as "escape-proof," see Weber, "Bureaucratization and the Naïveté of the Literati," p. 1401.

36. Ahmad Sadri, *Max Weber's Sociology of Intellectuals* (New York: Oxford University Press, 1992), p. 73. Sadri offers a very interesting and insightful interpretation of Weber's view of intellectuals and argues that Weber's analyses often involved the attempt to articulate a balance between apparently incompatible perspectives. Examples of this in Weber's work include the tension between the ethic of ultimate ends and the ethic of responsibility, and the distinction between objectivity and subjectivity.

37. Weber, "Politics as a Vocation," pp. 127–28. Guenther Roth and Wolfgang Schluchter argue that while Weber expressed his concern regarding the ongoing rationalization of modern society, he also took the position that history is unpredictable and that the future could bring unexpected changes. For more on this and other aspects of Weber's work, please see Guenther Roth and Wolfgang Schluchter, *Max Weber's Vision of History: Ethics and Methods* (Berkeley: University of California Press, 1979).

38. Alan Scott offers an interesting critique of Weber's claims regarding the universality of the constraints placed on social scientists. Scott argues that social scientists are perhaps not as restricted as Weber suggested and that they are in many ways capable of taking on an entrepreneurial role in their work. For more on this analysis, please see Alan Scott, "Between Autonomy and Responsibility: Max Weber on Scholars, Academics and Intellectuals," in *Intellectuals in Politics: From the Dreyfus Affair to Salman Rushdie*, ed. Jeremy Jennings and Anthony Kemp-Welch (London: Routledge, 1997), pp. 45–64.

3

Thorstein Veblen: The Social Scientist as Innovative Thinker

As the tremors of industrial expansion shook the political infrastructure of the European nations, the growth of capitalism in the United States gave rise to a qualitatively new form of political economy. The lack of a preexisting institutional order, a substantial flow of immigrant labor, and vast tracts of undeveloped territory in the United States created an ideal opportunity for the newer system to thrive. In this setting, business and industry encountered a great deal of freedom to expand and develop, and commerce quickly became a powerful force in shaping the political landscape. American governmental institutions in turn provided the support needed to facilitate this rapid growth, and by the early 1900s, the United States had become a major player in the world economy in terms of both finance and trade.

As an economist and social thinker writing in the midst of these changes, Thorstein Veblen fixed his gaze on the relationship between economic trends, culture, and public affairs, and considered the role of scientific knowledge in this context. In contrast to Weber, Veblen did not focus his attention on politics or political leaders when addressing this region of the world.[1] To him, the power of leadership in the United States resided in the hands of businessmen who controlled the financial markets. Veblen argued that any attempt to understand the underlying forces of politics in this setting should begin with an assessment of the ways business institutions influenced the direction and character of government in the early twentieth century. He saw that in this period, the investment bankers, or "absentee owners," had gained the upper hand over corporate business via their ability to control capital investment. Corporations involved in production that failed to yield a high level of return risked losing their financial support and were forced to adjust their practices to meet the demands of investors.[2]

Veblen pointed out that as these developments unfolded, the technological complexity of industry had advanced rapidly, speeding up the production of goods and raising the efficiency of their distribution to a level capable of meeting the material needs of a greater number of people. The prospect of a satiated market threatened to bring down prices and reduce profits, which led investors to turn to the power of the state to protect their interests. Trade regulations, tariffs, price controls, and other industry guidelines emerged as a result of this involvement and diminished the threat to profits facing the corporate managers of production, ultimately providing a more stable investment environment for the absentee owners.[3]

Thus, Veblen did not treat business and government as separate entities but framed them as components of an integrated institutional order. While Weber viewed the emergence of large private corporations as a necessary counterforce to the growth of the bureaucracies of government, Veblen saw these as powerful institutions working in concert with one another. The state machine, from the latter's point of view, grew in proportion to the demands of finance and industry and became more elaborate as the threat to profits increased. The rising complexity of industry and its subsequent growth in productive capacity demanded new regulations to ensure the security of investment capital. The state became the proper means through which to achieve this goal and maintain the stability of traditional economic arrangements. The result, from Veblen's point of view, was a gross mismanagement of resources and human labor, and a significant degree of waste in the form of the doubling of productive facilities and money spent on extraneous ends such as public relations and product advertising. He saw this mismanagement and waste occurring at a time when the techniques of production required to meet the basic material needs of the broader population were readily available but largely ignored by the political and economic leaders in a position to employ them.[4]

Although he perceived this situation to be problematic in many respects, Veblen did not conclude that the solution was to draw on the knowledge of science to rationalize the social order as suggested by Comte and Saint-Simon. He conceded that the emergence of state-centered capitalism in the West did lead to advances in the technology of production in the short term, but he also argued that it gave rise to the development of a commercial and bureaucratic apparatus of a monolithic nature, headed by leaders with narrow and often ideologically charged perspectives. He recognized that a growing reliance on scientific findings in the formation of policy had played a part in this transition, but he also saw the naïveté in romanticizing the Comtean notion of building a science of politics, and he devoted the latter portion of his writings to subtly expressing his discontent with the particular character of science as it evolved in the industrial nations during this period in history. He empathized with the fervor of thinkers who hoped that a more reasoned approach to politics might arise in the United States, but he ultimately concluded that such an arrangement would be unlikely to occur in the near future.[5]

To Veblen, the only way·this type of change could arise would be through the displacement of the business leadership and its financially based institutions in government. He considered the possibility that the mismanagement of industry by the absentee owners might lead to an eventual collapse of the existing economy, but he also believed that even in the event of such a fall, there was little chance a form of administration would emerge other than one based on market principles. He grounded this contention on the fundamental point that any group attempting to overthrow capitalism must be capable of managing the industrial system, which was a huge technical task including the allocation and distribution of resources and material goods, the coordination of productive facilities, the supervision of workers, and the maintenance of an unending host of practical issues on a global scale. The only group remotely capable of doing this would be the specialists in industry themselves, those holding the joint stock of technical knowledge, or, as he called them, the engineers. To demonstrate the improbability that the engineers could accomplish this task, he considered a hypothetical situation in which they manage to realize their advantageous position and unite to overthrow the "captains of finance," taking on the responsibility of political and economic administration. He maintained that although the engineers were the only possible contenders for this new position of authority, their ability to fulfill this role was embarrassingly insufficient. Rather than acting as a united, class-conscious group capable of collectively managing the industrial order, the engineers were a passive and individualistic lot, with a "commercialized frame of mind," content to be "the obedient employees of businessmen."[6]

> By settled habit the technicians, the engineers and industrial experts, are a harmless and docile sort, well fed on the whole, and somewhat placidly content with the "full dinner-pail" which the lieutenants of the Vested Interests habitually allow them. It is true, they constitute the indispensable General Staff of that industrial system which feeds the Vested Interests; but hitherto at least, they have had nothing to say in the planning and direction of this industrial system, except as employees in the pay of the financiers. They have hitherto been quite unreflectingly content to work piecemeal, without much of an understanding among themselves, unreservedly doing job-work for the Vested Interests; and they have without much reflection lent themselves and their technical powers freely to the obstructive tactics of the captains of industry; all the while that the training which makes them technicians is but a specialized extension of that joint stock of technical knowledge that has been carried forward out of the past by the community at large.[7]

Veblen also argued that the mind-set of most Americans led them to be distrustful of authority figures other than those tied to the free-market orientation of business. They saw any opposition to this perspective as indicative of an affinity with a more repressive and establishmentarian viewpoint and as paralleling the notion that public matters could be organized in a planned fashion. Veblen argued that the favorable image of the businessman and the principles of laissez-faire in American culture further diminished the possibility that the engineers could rise to this level of leadership.[8] He viewed this set of circumstances as both the product of advanced capitalism and the means through which its continued survival was ensured.[9]

SCIENCE AND PUBLIC POLICY

Veblen's criticism of the institutional order in the United States stemmed in part from his doubt that a political economy of this magnitude could ever be brought into the domain of reasoned control. A key component of this skepticism grew out of his views regarding the limitations of science as a form of inquiry. He pointed out that the underlying principles of the sciences were themselves based on a set of assumptions that could not be validated in a matter-of-fact way. While Weber suggested that scientists accept these starting assumptions in spite of their interpretive foundations, Veblen took the position that this element of uncertainty called into question their legitimacy at a fundamental level. Rather than take the leap of faith needed to endorse the credibility of traditional scientific knowledge, he chose to highlight the extent to which its preconceptions were unexamined, and he emphasized its socially constructed nature.[10]

Veblen argued that knowledge is closely tied to the underlying "habits of thought" of its purveyors, where the manner in which information is understood can vary radically from one orientation to the next. He saw the habits of thought of a given culture as central to the ways in which ideas are created and maintained in the minds of its members, and he claimed that preconceived schemes of categorizing information provide the initial medium through which experience is understood and everyday perceptions are formed. To Veblen, the modern scientific perspective is no different from other types of knowledge in that it is also tied to a particular orientation and grounded in an initial set of starting assumptions. He isolated and critically examined these fundamental beliefs as a way to further elaborate what he perceived to be its inherent shortcomings.[11]

His earliest challenge to the grounding of modern science lies in his critique of Kant's conception of inductive reasoning, in which the findings derived in the study of one set of circumstances are thought to be generalizable in the form of conclusions about the world on a broad level. He argued that a central weakness of this logic is that it presumes the existence of a consistent set of relations in all circumstances, leaving aside the possibility of variation from one situation to the next.[12] Veblen saw modern scientists in this light, as relentlessly searching for laws and formulas that could be applied universally while leaving out aspects of their topic that failed to fit neatly into the models they proposed.

As an example of this, he cited the underlying belief of the scientists of his day that all of life tended in the direction of advancing complexity, moving from a simple to a refined state. This view manifested itself in the assertion that human beings, if left to their own intuitive tendencies, would necessarily develop increasingly elaborate forms of social organization over time, moving from the lower culture of the primitive to the higher or more intricate relations of civilized mankind. He applied this critique to the Hegelian notion that human knowledge could develop ever-higher states of consciousness through the dialectical exchange of ideas. Veblen argued that one form of consciousness can only be considered "higher" than another on the basis of a normative point of view, and he characterized this fundamental belief as centered in the habits of thought characteristic of the West in this period.

Veblen's critique of scientific knowledge led him to question the validity of its standing in the modern order. Rather than hoping to elevate it to the status of a guiding reference, he sought to understand how this metaphysically grounded mode of inquiry achieved the prominence it did in the West. To Veblen, the early modern utilitarian principles and the rise of industrial capitalism helped shape the state of technology in this period and legitimate the underlying preconceptions of scientific inquiry. He argued that the tendency of modern scientists to perceive external objects as things and the notion that the relations between these things could be best understood in terms of cause and effect were reflective of the image of the worker producing a finished article of trade. Object relations perceived within this framework are assumed to exist in a manner similar to the process of manufacturing, in which the cause is seen to "produce" the effect.[13] In Veblen's eyes, this was a particularly mechanistic understanding of causation in that each object is thought to exist in isolation from the other, incapable of change in the absence of some external influence. Scientists operating from this perspective are therefore inclined to break down their object of study into distinct, measurable components, seeking to identify the patterned relationships between them. This interferes with their potential to grasp the more subtle dimensions of their subject matter or develop analyses of a comprehensive or integrated nature.

Veblen saw the principles of science as defined in relation to the market, where the demand that findings be of "merchantable" value led researchers to frame their investigations in terms readily understood and appreciated by businessmen. The business emphasis on monetary value in the form of income and expenditure gave rise to a system of accounting that required the use of numerical tabulation and statistical analysis. Scientific findings presented in a format paralleling that of pecuniary accountancy were more compatible with this mode of thought than those offered in qualitative or literary terms, and resonated with the self-image of the businessman as dealing with the practical matters of modern life. Scientists seeking the approval or the financial backing of business enterprises or their partners in government approached research accordingly, engaging in studies that could be presented in a concrete fashion and organizing their inquiry from the outset to accommodate institutional objectives.[14]

As a form of knowledge that followed in the footsteps of industry and business, science became a means through which the goals of these two spheres could be realized. Veblen contended that this type of inquiry provided the kind of information sought after in the machine age, attracting the attention of the technologists and their business-oriented financial supporters. Industry leaders welcomed data that could be used to reduce the costs of production or facilitate the distribution of a product, and they subsequently promoted the importance of science, not only as a means to serve these ends, but also as a universal benefit to the whole of modern society. From Veblen's point of view, the rise in the prominence of science was a function not of its inherent superiority but of the constraints and expectations of a culture that valued the workings of the machine and the principles of business.

> The modern technology is of an impersonal, matter-of-fact character in an un-exampled degree, and the accountancy of modern business management is also of an extremely dispassionate and impartially exacting nature. It results that the modern learning is of a similarly matter-of-fact, mechanistic complexion, and it similarly leans on statistically dispassionate tests and formulations. Whereas it may fairly be said that the personal equation once—in the days of scholastic learning—was the central and decisive factor in the systematization of knowledge, it is equally fair to say that in later time no effort is spared to eliminate all bias of personality from the technique or the results of science or scholarship. It is the "dry light of science" that is always in request, and great pains are taken to exclude all color of sentimentality.[15]

As the standard assumptions and approaches of scientific investigation shifted to match these normative perceptions, it came to be seen as the most effective way to learn about the world in a useful and productive manner.[16]

Veblen extended this critique to social science, arguing that its interpretive qualities limited its ability to provide a solid grounding for policy formation in the modern world. He criticized the work of scholars who claimed to be operating at an objective level, pointing out that many of them demonstrated a lack of insight into the nature of their own biases.[17] He observed researchers organizing and presenting data in a matter-of-fact way while unwittingly conforming to the contemporary fashions of thought in their respective fields. Veblen suggested that the prospect of comprehensively managing the societal order would require a form of knowledge that was all-inclusive and infallible. The value-laden and inherently subjective character of social science rendered it largely unsuitable for such a task.[18]

The irony of Veblen's analysis is that although he refuted the notion that social science could serve as a direct guide to political decision making, he did see it as capable of bringing an element of reason to the emerging trends in the modern world. He sought to show that social science could be of a personal and reflective nature, capable of producing new and valuable assessments of the social order. Social scientists may not be in a position to herald the objectivity of their findings, but they are able to offer an enlightened view of the world that is consciously embedded in a normative orientation. Veblen saw social science as capable of broadening human understanding in a manner similar to the work of the artist, where the image created is meant to be not an exact representation of reality but an expression of a deeply held personal viewpoint or uncommon observation. His own writings are conventionally situated within the domain of social science, but they can also be read as a statement of his underlying convictions and philosophical sentiments about the world, particularly aspects of it he saw as misguided or unjust. Veblen characterized social science as the opportunity to open the door to new ways of seeing the world and conveying those images to others.[19] His critique of it in this respect was not an outright rejection of the drive to learn about the world and act on the basis of this knowledge, but of the specific directions this form of inquiry had taken in the West.

THE HIGHER LEARNING

Although Veblen rejected the belief that modern society could be managed in a rational manner by technical experts forming public policy on the basis of scientific analyses, he did consider the possibility that scholars might influence historical trends in a more subtle fashion, over an extended period of time. He argued that every culture has its own version of an esoteric or theoretical body of knowledge that is developed and maintained by a select group of intellectuals operating within the framework of that social order. The ideas and beliefs of this group are typically held in high esteem by members of that culture. In the West, the locus of this knowledge tended to be in the university, where abstract conceptions of the world are most frequently discussed and debated.[20] Veblen saw this knowledge as very important and hoped that intellectuals in academia would also recognize the extent to which their work could have a fundamental impact on the underlying framework of social thought and perhaps, in turn, on the course of history.

Veblen advocated the idea of engaging in research on the basis of "idle curiosity," in which a fundamental passion to learn about a given topic on the part of the researcher provides the primary motivation to pursue the investigation. He saw idle curiosity not as something one learns over time but as an innate human drive. It could be seen, for instance, in the desire of the young to seek out new knowledge about their surrounding milieu without any express purpose in mind other than an interest in satisfying this urge. To Veblen, research organized on this basis is more likely to transcend the boundaries of conventional thought in one's field and produce qualitatively new conceptions of the everyday world.[21]

As one quickly comes to see when reading Veblen, his enthusiasm for a set of goals is usually offset by a very pervasive skepticism that such goals could ever be realized. In this case, the admiration he expressed for idle curiosity was strongly held in check by his belief that the emphasis on practicality in Western society would be extremely difficult to overcome.

> The intellectual predilection—the idle curiosity—abides and asserts itself when other pursuits of a more temporal but more immediately urgent kind leave men free to take stock of the ulterior ends and values of life; whereas the transient interests, preoccupation with ways and means of life, are urgent and immediate, and employ men's thought and energy through the greater share of their life. The question of material ways and means, and the detail requirements of the day's work, are forever at hand and forever contest the claims of any avowed ulterior end; and by force of unremitting habituation the current competitive system of acquisition and expenditure induces in all classes such a bias as leads them to overrate ways and means as contrasted with the ends which these ways and means are in some sense designed to serve.[22]

Veblen maintained that utilitarian and business principles had penetrated the university system, infusing it with the notion that the only knowledge of any worth was that which demonstrated its immediate usefulness in everyday life. While the utilitarian perspective emphasized practicality as an extension of the idea that expert knowledge could be used to advance civilization to new heights, business-minded entrepreneurs saw the value of this knowledge in its potential to assist in the goal of strengthening the economy and raising profits. Veblen argued that this conception of science corrupted the character of higher learning by requiring researchers to outline their practical goals prior to an investigation, locking them into a predetermined range of objectives and limiting the diversity of their findings.[23] He saw that scholars motivated by idle curiosity had the distinct advantage of being able to detach their inquiry from this requirement and were better able to seek out new discoveries and creatively interpret that which they chose to study.

From his point of view, the act of pursuing knowledge in the hope of achieving a set of clearly defined ends guides research down a narrow and well-trodden path and can blind the investigator to interpretive possibilities outside this framework.

Veblen's critique of the efforts to link these two forms of inquiry should not be seen as an indication of his failure to recognize the value of practical knowledge. On the contrary, he pointed to its fundamental importance as a means of securing the well-being of the larger population in an industrial society. As one who devoted much of his attention to industrial matters, Veblen recognized the worth of this endeavor and emphasized its significance in his own analyses. Technical research, from his vantage point, played a key role in sustaining the productive apparatus by providing the information needed to organize and carry out its objectives. To Veblen, practical knowledge was itself corrupted by an effort to connect it to higher learning in that, under this arrangement, technical researchers were required to characterize and approach their work as though it were of a theoretical nature, and this requirement pulled them away from the more practical aspects of their study. He understood the crucial need for this form of knowledge but argued that binding it to the abstract dimensions of social thought interfered with its quality and effectiveness.[24]

His suggestion that higher learning be pursued in the manner of an idle curiosity also stems from his observation that social scientists are inclined to develop new interpretations of their subject within the framework of older ideas. He saw the social analyses of his contemporaries as reflecting those of a previous era and not well suited to explain the newer set of circumstances unfolding around them. In his view, social scientists typically reinforced the same set of assumptions, preconceptions, biases, and beliefs as their predecessors and failed to offer anything genuinely new or uniquely revealing. Veblen argued that as young scholars are drawn into the circle of the old, they are educated in the logic of established perspectives and tend to see the world from within the confines of these limitations. Even those who seek to escape the conforming pressures of this arrangement are reined in as the ideas they create are folded into the main body of knowledge in their field. When these ideas are drawn too far outside traditional boundaries, they are either rejected altogether or reconfigured to more closely resemble earlier patterns, leading new frames of understanding to remain closely connected to those that preceded them.[25]

Veblen also acknowledged that not all new ideas fail to become established. He noted that genuinely novel positions rarely break through the confines of conventional thought and that scholars who offer substantial contributions to the development of alternative theories are typically cordoned off in the margins of their respective fields. However, he also argued that thinkers who are less securely grounded in the norms and traditions of a given culture have historically been more effective in stepping outside the points of view consonant with those traditions. Intellectuals in the margins have the advantage of being able to more readily remove themselves from the elements of the society they are studying and are therefore in a much better position to offer innovative analyses than those who are more fully embedded in that milieu.[26]

Veblen's focus on the imitative qualities of scholarly knowledge underscored his claims that economic trends and social patterns are closely connected to the foundation of everyday belief and that significant change could occur at this fundamental level. He did not expect the analyses of intellectuals to single-handedly bring about large-scale societal transformations, but his sense of the precarious nature of the modern social order led him to consider the possibilities that might emerge as a consequence of its faltering or collapse. He suggested that the future character of the West would be influenced by perspectives that were at one time unpopular or out of synch with conventional thought, and he favored a standard of scholarship among social scientists that highlighted their position in developing these newer orientations.[27] Veblen thus saw the foremost task of social scientists as one of selecting topics of study on the basis of their own curiosity, their own scholarly interests, and a passion for independence. He thought they should do this without attempting to achieve a predetermined objective, but with an awareness of the potential of their ideas to provide alternative forms of understanding in the future.[28]

THE PUBLIC ROLE OF THE SOCIAL SCIENTIST

Veblen observed early in the twentieth century that state intervention in the market served to maintain the efficacy of the price system in spite of its inherent contradictions, but he also foresaw the limitations of this temporary solution and recognized the dilemmas involved in the long-term effort to rationalize the spheres of politics and economy. Rather than building a sustainable system of social organization, this approach ironically fostered new and more pervasive forms of irrationality.

Veblen felt that social scientists could play a key role in addressing this ongoing irony by virtue of their ability to redefine conventional thinking, but he expected institutional pressures to limit the extent to which they could approach their work in a critical or self-directed fashion. The requirement that researchers meet practical demands and fit their analyses into the rubric of accepted knowledge reduces the possibility that they can break away from outmoded habits of thought and develop unique and creative insight into the social world.

Veblen's analysis of this issue reflects neither the hopes of a utopian optimist advocating a revolution of the technicians nor the misgivings of a terminal pessimist forecasting the ultimate doom of humanity. He believed that the future course of civilization is not predictable and that unforeseen change could occur at any time, in spite of existing trends. In his view, social scientists have the potential to shape an uncertain future, but not as the technical managers of the new order. The locus of their influence lies in the world of ideas. Veblen's critique can thus be read as a call to social scientists to think beyond the realm of their respective traditions, to challenge obsolete claims, and to develop incisive and enlightening interpretations of the ongoing dynamics of public affairs. While this may mean operating in the margins of public debate on key social issues in the present, history has shown that this is the place where new forms of understanding begin.

NOTES

1. Veblen did draw this distinction in his analyses of other regions of the world. In his work *Imperial Germany and the Industrial Revolution* (London: Macmillan, 1915), he offers an in-depth examination of the ways political institutions shaped the directions of German society at the turn of the century. That he did not specifically evaluate the institutions of government in the United States at this time should be read as an indication of the power he attributed to business in the realm of public affairs.

2. Thorstein Veblen, *The Theory of Business Enterprise* (New York: Scribner, 1932; orig. pub. 1904), pp. 268–74.

3. Thorstein Veblen, *Absentee Ownership and Business Enterprise in Recent Times* (New York: Augustus Kelly, 1964; orig. pub. 1923).

4. Thorstein Veblen, *The Engineers and the Price System* (New York: Harcourt, Brace & World, 1963; orig. pub. 1921).

5. Veblen, *The Engineers*, pp. 162–69.

6. Veblen, *The Engineers*, pp. 151–52. Veblen's position on this subject has been an ongoing source of controversy among scholars for many years. He has been attacked by some authors who claim that *The Engineers and the Price System* is a clear example of his endorsement of technocratic elitism. Early holders of this view, such as David Riesman (1953) and Daniel Bell (1963), tended to read *The Engineers* as an indication of Veblen's hopes that a special class of experts would assume a revolutionary role, eventually acquiring a level of political power sufficient to control society's productive institutions. This view was challenged by others who saw a contradiction between this interpretation of *The Engineers* and the seemingly anarchist tendencies typical of Veblen's earlier writings. Bernard Rosenberg (1953) and H. J. Hodder (1956) pointed to Veblen's antipathy toward centrally coordinated institutions and argued that his position was much more complex than one would gather based on a superficial reading of *The Engineers* alone. In their view, Veblen addressed the tension, as he

saw it, between the dangers of authoritarian institutional restraint and the problems arising in an industrial system subject to the direction of the "captains of finance." De bate continued on this question into the 1980s and 1990s via the writings of Donald Stabile (1988), Malcolm Rutherford (1992), and Rick Tilman (1972, 1992, 1996). While Rutherford and Stabile argue that Veblen did, in fact, see the engineers as a potentially revolutionary class and sought to direct his work to that class, Tilman (1996) refutes this, pointing out that Veblen's ideas and values were based on traditions that opposed the views he seems to be endorsing in *The Engineers*. Tilman concludes with the suggestion that Veblen might be thought of as a "radical conservative" who favored large-scale changes in the structure of the major political and economic institutions in Western societies but believed that such changes would most likely never take place, and further believed that if they did occur, they might not bring about the results originally intended. For more on this debate, please see David Riesman, "The Social and Psychological Setting of Veblen's Economic Theory," *Journal of Economic History* 13, no. 4, Fall, 1953, pp. 449–61; Daniel Bell, "Veblen and the Technocrats: On the Engineers and the Price System," *The Winding Passage: Essays and Sociological Journeys 1960–1980* (Cambridge, MA: Harvard University Press, 1980), pp. 69–90; Bernard Rosenberg, "A Clarification of Some Veblenian Concepts," *American Journal of Economics and Sociology* 12, no. 2, January, 1953, pp. 179–87; H. J. Hodder, "Political Ideas of Thorstein Veblen," *Canadian Journal of Economics and Political Science* 22, August, 1956, pp. 347–57; Donald Stabile, "Veblen's Analysis of Social Movements: Bellamyites, Workers, and Engineers," *Journal of Economic Issues* 22, no. 1, March, 1988, pp. 211–26; Malcolm Rutherford, "Thorstein Veblen and the Problem of the Engineers," *International Review of Sociology*, new series, 2, no. 3, 1992, pp. 125–50; Rick Tilman, "Veblen's Ideal Political Economy and Its Critics," *American Journal of Economics and Sociology* 31, 1972, pp. 307–17; Rick Tilman, *Thorstein Veblen and His Critics, 1891–1963: Conservative, Liberal, and Radical Perspectives* (Princeton, NJ: Princeton University Press, 1992); Rick Tilman, "Veblen and the Industrial Republic: The Path to the Future," in *The Intellectual Legacy of Thorstein Veblen* (Westport, CT; London: Greenwood, 1996), pp. 167–97.

7. Veblen, *The Engineers*, pp. 135–36.

8. Veblen, *The Engineers*, pp. 167–69.

9. For an interesting and enlightening interpretation of Veblen's larger theoretical perspective, please see Stephen Edgell, *Veblen in Perspective: His Life and Thought* (London: M. E. Sharpe, 2001).

10. Thorstein Veblen, "The Place of Science in Modern Civilization," in *The Place of Science in Modern Civilization and Other Essays* (New Brunswick, NJ: Transaction, 1989; orig. pub. 1906), pp. 1–31.

11. Veblen, "Place of Science."

12. Thorstein Veblen, "Kant's Critique of Judgement," in *Essays in Our Changing Order*, ed. Leon Ardzrooni (New York: Augustus Kelly, 1964; orig. pub. 1884), pp. 175–93.

13. Thorstein Veblen, *The Instinct of Workmanship and the State of the Industrial Arts* (New Brunswick, NJ: Transaction, 1990; orig. pub. 1914), pp. 263–68.

14. Thorstein Veblen, *The Higher Learning in America* (New Brunswick, NJ: Transaction, 1993; orig. pub. 1918).

15. Veblen, *Higher Learning*, p. 5.

16. Veblen, "Place of Science," pp. 1–31.

17. An example of this can be found in his essay entitled "The Technology of the Predatory Culture," in *The Instinct of Workmanship and the State of the Industrial Arts* (New Brunswick, NJ: Transaction, 1990; orig. pub. 1914), p. 141, in which he comments on the work of "the Eugenicals, whose labors," he argues, "are no doubt to be taken for all they are worth."

18. Veblen, *Higher Learning*, pp. 1–3.

19. Veblen, *Higher Learning*. Arthur Vidich (1994) argues that Veblen's analysis of the higher learning continues to be relevant in more recent times and is particularly incisive with regard to the practices of the American university system. For more on this topic, please see Arthur Vidich, "The Higher Learning in America in Veblen's Time and Our Own," *International Journal of Politics, Culture, and Society* 7, 1994, pp. 639–68.

20. Veblen, *Higher Learning*.

21. Veblen, *Higher Learning*, pp. 33–36.

22. Veblen, *Higher Learning*, p. 33.

23. Veblen, *Higher Learning*, p. 33.

24. Veblen, *Higher Learning*, pp. 20–23.

25. Veblen, *Higher Learning*, pp. 20–23. John Patrick Diggins offers an insightful assessment of Veblen's position on this subject in *The Bard of Savagery: Thorstein Veblen and Modern Social Theory* (New York: Seabury, 1978).

26. Veblen, "Place of Science."

27. Veblen expressed his concerns regarding the tendency of German intellectuals during World War I to defend the authoritarian government in place at the time. He saw that Germany had yet to make the transition to a modern order and maintained that its lingering imperialism could be indicative of a potentially dangerous situation in the future. His ability to foresee the volatile nature of this arrangement led Colin Loader and Rick Tilman to assess his approach to inquiry and consider its value as a forecasting method. For more on this, please see Colin Loader and Rick Tilman, "Thorstein Veblen's Analysis of German Intellectualism: Institutionalism as a Forecasting Method," *American Journal of Economics and Sociology* 54, no. 3, July, 1995, pp. 339–55.

28. Veblen, *Higher Learning*, p. 41.

4

Karl Mannheim and Joseph Schumpeter: Social Science, Intellectuals, and Politics in an Age of Declining Liberalism

In the period following World War I, a series of economic and political changes undermined the stability of national governments in the West. Financial entrepreneurs in the United States borrowed extensively to invest in what seemed to them to be an endlessly expanding market that would yield continually rising returns. Lending institutions distributed commercial loans at an escalating pace, and corporate leaders pursued increasingly risky but lucrative business practices. After a period of unprecedented economic growth, the stock market crash of 1929 brought this expansion to a grinding halt. Investors who had borrowed extensively could not repay their debt, and the banks closed their doors, leaving the majority of consumers unable to meet their ongoing financial needs.

The repercussions of this crash extended to Europe and other nations around the world. Without sustained financial support from the United States, Germany was unable to continue its war reparations to France, and the relations between these two European nations further deteriorated. The rise of Nazism and Fascism exacerbated tensions around the globe and undermined the potential for a peaceful coexistence among the Western powers. The result was a reaffirmation of ethnic divisions, the expansion of nationalist propaganda, and a resurgence in the preparations for war.[1] Theorists observing this transformation revised the analyses of their predecessors and considered the public role of the intellectual from within the context of these increasingly unstable conditions.

Karl Mannheim witnessed the events in Germany during the years of the faltering Weimar Republic and the Nazi rise to power. As a left-leaning intellectual and outspoken critic of Fascism, he was forced to flee to England in 1933, and he continued his work at the London School of Economics. The drift toward Fascism in Europe played a significant role in transforming his outlook from the reserved orientation of the traditional social scientist to the impassioned and prescriptive approach of the intellectual activist, seeking to formulate solutions to a dire crisis.[2]

Mannheim's experience in Germany during the early stages of the Nazi ascendancy led him to see these events as indicative of the gradual deterioration of liberal democracy in the West. He did not perceive this change as a temporary deviation from the traditions of the past, but as evidence of a more fundamental decline of the principles and conditions of bourgeois capitalism. To him, the early modern ideals of laissez-faire economics could no longer lift the West out of its predicament. The growth of Fascism and Communism signified a potentially dangerous trend in the direction of increasingly repressive forms of political control. He feared that this pattern would continue to spread if not addressed in a direct and confrontational manner, and he sought to lay the groundwork for what he termed a "third way"—an alternative to the apparent choice between the free market on the one hand and totalitarian modes of government on the other. His prescriptions regarding the proper place of social science in the political sphere emerged in relation to this dilemma.[3]

Joseph Schumpeter also witnessed these events firsthand, initially as a lecturer in Vienna and later as a professor of economics at the University of Bonn. His grounding in matters of economy led him to understand this transition in relation to changes in capitalism on a global scale. In 1927, he emigrated to the United States and accepted a position in economics at Harvard University, where he further pursued this critique.[4]

Schumpeter also formed his assessment of social science in relation to the ongoing trends of his time, but he interpreted this period very differently than did Mannheim. In his view, the market crash and ensuing depression were not indications of the demise of laissez-faire capitalism but examples of the natural ebb and flow of the free-market system. He argued that the West could more effectively pull itself out of this crisis if the economy were unimpeded by rigid regulation than it could under the auspices of the New Deal, and he questioned the belief that controls of this variety would preserve individual autonomy. To Schumpeter, the growth of totalitarian regimes in Europe did not emerge as the result of inadequate government involvement but as the result of the ill-formed policies of intervention of an increasingly regimented and rationalized system of public administration.[5]

While these two thinkers addressed many of the same themes as those before them, they recognized that circumstances had fundamentally changed from the time of Weber and Veblen, and they developed social analyses from within this newer context. Their views on the public role of the social scientist grew out of the concerns they formed in observing the events of this unusually tumultuous period.

MANNHEIM: THE NECESSITY OF PLANNING

Mannheim grounded his outlook in the observation that the forces of industry had uprooted many people from the tightly knit networks of association in their own provincial communities and funneled them into crowded urban areas, where they tended to be less connected to the others around them. This transformation stripped them of the orienting frameworks in their previous social environments and left them increasingly vulnerable to the emotionally driven and persuasive appeals of divergent political groups. The messages circulating in this context tended to be limited in their perspicacity and designed to promote the goals of one faction or another. The result was that many people in this setting were not well informed about political issues and typically fashioned their perspectives in terms of insular concerns, with a narrow view of the events unfolding at that time.[6]

Mannheim argued that the newer techniques of propaganda pushed public opinion in volatile and erratic directions and increased the pressure on political leaders to pursue shortsighted and often irrational policies. In this environment, the marketplace of ideas was no longer an even playing field where opponents could expect open debate to yield fair and balanced conclusions. Propaganda tied the hands of public officials attempting to act on the basis of reasoned judgment and gave a greater level of legitimacy to groups seeking to exploit these dynamics in the service of their own self-centered objectives.[7]

He also observed that developments in communication, transportation, and finance had further integrated what had previously been relatively independent regions of trade and commerce. Mannheim argued that this interconnectedness rendered the new order more fragile and subject to disruption than in the past. Poorly conceived policies in one region could now unravel the stability of another, reverberating throughout the global economy. In this setting, the integrity and reliability of political decisions are more significant, and a lack of coordination at the level of public administration could lead to devastating repercussions in the future.[8]

> In many respects, it is true, modern society is much more flexible than earlier societies since, owing to technological advances, it has greater reserves at its disposal. Thus, for example, certain critics of capitalism never thought that it could possibly support such gigantic armies of unemployed for so many years. On the other hand, the interdependence of all its parts makes the modern order much more sensitive than a simpler form of economic organization. Indeed, the more minutely the individual parts of a large mechanism fit into one another, and the more closely the single elements are bound up together, the more serious are the repercussions of even the slightest disturbance. In a well-organized railway, for instance, the effects of an accident are more far-reaching than they were in the stagecoach system of transport, where accidents and dislocation

were taken for granted from the very beginning. In the more or less simple economy of pre-war Russia hundreds of thousands and even millions could die of starvation without causing maladjustments in the rest of the world. In contrast with this, in the world economy of the present day over-production in one market becomes the misfortune of other markets. The political insanity of one country determines the fate of others, and the brutal, impulsive, emotional outbursts of the masses in action signify a catastrophe for a whole society and even for the entire world, since the interdependence of the modern social organism transmits the effects of every maladjustment with increased intensity.[9]

Mannheim lamented the reluctance of liberal-minded politicians to accept the fact that a fundamental structural change had taken place in the West, and he believed that a dangerous drift toward authoritarianism would likely envelope the remaining democracies if this tradition of inaction continued. In the newer order, political matters could no longer be left to fate but required careful and deliberate intervention, based on a consciously formed set of values and ideals. Political leaders and public institutions were under a new obligation to become directly involved in managing the directions of society, including not only the economy but the social and cultural spheres as well.[10]

SCHUMPETER: THE PROBLEMS OF PLANNING

Schumpeter agreed with the viewpoint that a structural change had taken place in the West and that politics had become increasingly subject to the emotional fluctuations of public opinion, but he did not conclude in the face of these developments that the only wise option would be to strive toward a more deliberate and rational ordering of the economic and social worlds. He argued that the laissez-faire approach to capitalism was not in itself flawed and that under the proper circumstances, it was capable of bringing about a greater range of benefits than could be gained from a planned society. He saw the tendency toward rational control as evidence of a march toward socialism, one that was likely to occur anyway, given existing trends, but also one that he did not care to join.[11]

To Schumpeter, the drift toward socialism was unfolding independently of the influence of any single actor or group. The efforts of social thinkers and political activists to further rationalize the social order were, in his view, misguided attempts to artificially speed up this progression. It was rooted in an eagerness to rush ahead into a form of existence that was likely to arrive eventually and would, in any case, yield highly undesirable results. His distaste for what he perceived to be the outcome of this transition stemmed from his contempt for the mundane, bureaucratic, and controlling nature of a comprehensively organized social order. Such a society, although more efficient and stable in many respects, would also be repressive in a way that few understood.[12]

He agreed that a planned economy would enable leaders to more effectively reach their practical goals, but believed that this success would come at a great cost. While the concerted effort to push Western civilization in this direction might reduce uncertainty and volatility by coordinating various components of the social order, it would also unavoidably lead to a greater centralization of authority, heightened repression, and a loss of individual autonomy. Control of the economy does not in itself pose a great risk to personal freedom, but regulations of this nature can gradually weave their way into the social realm, reducing the range of options available to the individual on a more personal level in the long run.[13]

Schumpeter suggested that in the liberal democracies of the West, decisions affecting the broader population were not purely political questions but a function of trends in the business world as well. Although managing the economy in a systematic fashion might reduce the complexities and conflicts typical of a laissez-faire order, it would also likely undermine the innovative spirit of the entrepreneur. In this sense, the value of entrepreneurial activity could be found in its tendency to foster new forms of organization and bring previously unimagined possibilities into the lives of the average individual. Under the weight of growing administrative and bureaucratic requirements, creativity and invention invariably suffer. Progress takes on an impersonal and manufactured quality. It is no longer the result of the heartfelt and impassioned actions of the self-motivated entrepreneur but the product of the routinized behavior of the specialized office worker, seeking to achieve predictable results. The attempt to fully rationalize the social order undermines the potential of capitalism to produce a fulfilling existence for most individuals and leaves in its wake a mechanized, predictable, and static way of life.[14]

> Technological progress is increasingly becoming the business of teams of trained specialists who turn out what is required and make it work in predictable ways. The romance of earlier commercial adventure is rapidly wearing away, because so many more things can be strictly calculated that had of old to be visualized in a flash of genius.[15]

Schumpeter accepted the view that these efforts were to a great extent grounded in a concern to improve the situation of the poor, and he did not advocate abandoning the needs of this sector to promote economic growth. He did challenge the view, however, that the ideal way to address this problem was through economic incentives and constraints. Adjustments to the economy tended to have a disruptive influence on capitalism itself, and this tinkering impaired its ability to enhance the prosperity of the social whole. He believed that the issue of poverty should be approached politically, meaning in ways that provided assistance where needed, without interfering with the mechanism of the market to achieve this end. In his view, adhering to laissez-faire principles did not necessarily imply that basic human concerns should be ignored but meant intervening in ways that did not dampen the ability of the free-market to raise the standard of living of society on a broader level.[16]

MANNHEIM: ON KNOWLEDGE AND POLITICS

Mannheim agreed that society was becoming increasingly rationalized, and he addressed this issue by drawing a distinction between "functional" and "substantial" rationality. In the social world, functional rationalization involves the formation of a regimented and mechanistic system of organization, leaving little room for the human dimensions of everyday life such as intuition and emotion. Substantial rationality, on the other hand, is grounded in a concern to expand understanding and engage in practices on the basis of a sober assessment of the world. Mannheim argued that while recent history in the West showed a growing reliance on functional rationality and had indeed suffered as a result, the response to this trend should not be to reject rationality of all types, but to augment the level of substantial rationality in the existing order. He pointed out that in the early modern era, entrepreneurs and a relatively independent intelligentsia helped to build and maintain substantial rationality by developing a historical view of contemporary events and adhering to a sense of fairness and the pursuit of reason. The recent advance of functional rationalization posed a threat to modern civilization in that it inhibited the extent to which reasoned judgment could serve as a guide in public affairs.[17]

To Mannheim, the events of the interwar period undermined the notion that civilization would automatically advance from one generation to the next. The growing support of totalitarian regimes demonstrated that confusion and mythology did not simply fade away with the mere passage of time. These trends called for a conscious effort to strengthen the realm of substantial rationality in society through a renewed pursuit of fairness and reason. His investigation into the relationship of knowledge and politics can thus be seen as an effort to provide the intellectual foundations for this quest.[18]

One of the central weaknesses of traditional social science from Mannheim's point of view was its contemplative and formal nature. Researchers employing this perspective routinely strive to understand the world in ways that are ahistorical and not bound by cultural limitations. The goal in this tradition is to develop a model of one's subject matter that can be strengthened over time through observation and analysis. Mannheim understood the positivist notion of scientific knowledge to be of this variety, framing the world in absolute terms and rejecting metaphysical or interpretive conclusions. He contended that this outlook grew out of the utilitarian point of view, where the social world is seen as made up of objects interacting with one another on the basis of fixed natural laws. Within the logic of this framework, the only knowledge of significant value is that which can be applied to practical matters in the service of the betterment of humankind.[19]

Mannheim argued that the positivist leanings of traditional social science limited its ability to provide the means through which to grasp the subjective nature of human interaction. Designed to rise above cultural variation, this form of inquiry typically disregards the more subtle aspects of the social order, including the meanings people attribute to their actions. He conceded that there is an appeal associated with the prospect of uncovering information of a transcendent quality but argued that the attempt to gather such data necessarily involves filtering out key dimensions of the reality one is studying. Researchers examining the social world from this perspective intentionally abandon their personal mode of understanding and replace it with one that is foreign to living experience. Mannheim found it ironic that while social scientists justified this orientation on the grounds that it facilitated the expansion of knowledge, the actual result was to limit the insight of observers approaching investigations in this manner.[20]

He contended that the definitions and categories that positivist researchers employ in their analyses are culturally specific and are thus selective and circumscribed. In this sense, all social inquiry is based on a set of a priori assumptions, whether the investigators involved are aware of them or not. The notion that one can bypass these limitations is fundamentally flawed and can give social scientists the idea that their conclusions are inherently superior to those of others. This undermines the value of alternative forms of inquiry, and enhances the influence of functional rationality in the social world.[21]

> No one denies the possibility of empirical research nor does anyone maintain that facts do not exist. (Nothing seems more incorrect to us than an illusionist theory of knowledge.) We, too, appeal to "facts" for our proof, but the question of the nature of facts is in itself a considerable problem. They exist for the mind always in an intellectual and social context. That they can be understood and formulated implies already the existence of a conceptual apparatus. And if this conceptual apparatus is the same for all the members of a group, the presuppositions (i.e., the possible social and intellectual values), which underlie the individual concepts, never become perceptible.[22]

Mannheim sought to point out that although social scientific knowledge is grounded in systematic investigation and capable of revealing important "truths" about the social world, it nevertheless could not transcend the culturally specific norms and values of the scholars in each of its traditions.

Building on the work of Weber, Mannheim contrasted social scientific knowledge with what he termed "political knowledge," or a mode of understanding that entails bringing together information from a variety of spheres, such as the practical and subjective elements of everyday life. Often expected to make crucial decisions within a limited period of time, political leaders must look at their milieu in an informal way, relying on personal experience and acumen. They must have a range of information at their disposal, including knowledge of history, of traditional laws and legal norms, and of the common tendencies of key actors. These constraints require them to focus more intently on the tangible conditions of the current situation rather than viewing it solely in the abstract. Political knowledge is thus typically oriented to provide the analyses politicians need to meet their immediate responsibilities.[23]

Mannheim argued that while political knowledge is valuable in developing an understanding of the practical components of a situation, it is also limited in that it is usually bound to a specific philosophical orientation. The bearers of political knowledge are often less interested in developing a broad understanding of their subject matter than in finding information that can be used to support a predetermined set of objectives. Political knowledge is, in this sense, the knowledge of a fighting group. It is the knowledge of factions, of revolutionaries, and of political parties. Those involved in forming political knowledge cannot simply accept any and all evidence arising from their investigations. The narrowness of their perspective tends to push them in a dogmatic direction and limits their ability to acknowledge aspects of the situation that fail to conform to the goals of the groups they represent.[24]

Although Mannheim recognized the weaknesses of these two approaches, he did not see this as an indication of the elusive nature of knowledge itself. He proposed drawing on the strengths of each in an effort to bring them together to form a more comprehensive understanding of the social world. His goal in this sense was to supplement the contemplative character of scientific inquiry with the inherently intuitive and practical focus of political knowledge. Rather than shun aspects of social thought that are outside the sphere of rational logic, the task of seeking a broader perspective involves drawing these into the investigation. This should be done in a way that does not limit the resulting perspective, but enhances it.[25]

Mannheim suggested that the effort to develop a broad view begin with a sociological attitude toward the study of knowledge, one that examines human consciousness in relation to the circumstances of the groups involved. The observer relying on this method can then draw connections between the underlying foundations of experience and the consciousness of social actors, examining the different ways people come to understand their world, how these views achieve salience, and how they are broken down or transformed. This mode of inquiry enables the researcher to assess a perspective as growing out of a given context, rather than viewing it in isolation. It can shed light on the nature of consciousness in ways that the positivist methods of social research typically fail to do. Mannheim saw this approach as capable of bringing matters of interpretation and meaning into the realm of social inquiry, without limiting the orientation of the researcher or favoring one perspective over another.[26]

As in the case of Weber, Mannheim rejected the Comtean suggestion that social science serve as a guide to policy in a positive sense, but he did believe that a comprehensive assessment of social trends could provide leaders with the insight they needed to proceed in an informed manner. He contended that the new order required the intentional and thorough management of public affairs, and that knowledge of this sort could serve to rein in previously uncontrolled factors, including aspects of society formerly left unaddressed, such as culture and consciousness. His goal in this respect was to rely on this understanding to redirect the social forces threatening the survival of Western liberal traditions, particularly reasoned justice and democratic participation. To Mannheim, political leaders could no longer simply accept the unfolding events of their day as matters of fate, but were required to actively direct societal change in an effort to work against the advance of authoritarianism, in all its forms.[27]

SCHUMPETER: THE FALLIBILITY OF SCIENTIFIC KNOWLEDGE

Schumpeter also saw the early modern scientific model as growing out of the orientation of the utilitarian component of bourgeois liberal thought, and he agreed with Mannheim that in its narrow and positivist form, it could offer little insight into the subtleties of social life. He added that this orientation actually originated prior to the transition to modernity and only became dominant in the context of the rationalizing tendencies of capitalism itself. Yet rather than take the position that this model be broadened to overcome its limitations as Mannheim suggested, Schumpeter pointed to its weaknesses and challenged the idea that this form of knowledge should serve as a guide in forming policy. He did not doubt that a science of politics could be established or that it might actually enhance the ability of a central authority to manage public affairs, but he questioned the wisdom involved in deliberately seeking to create a scenario of this nature.[28]

Schumpeter observed that underlying the logic of planning was a fundamental belief in the predictive capacity of scientific knowledge. Researchers operating from this perspective typically perceive their assessments to be of a higher caliber than those developed on the basis of experience or intuition. This presumed superiority can give decision makers a sense of confidence that the consequences of their actions will lead to the predictions as spelled out in the plan. Schumpeter pointed out, however, that history has repeatedly demonstrated the inability of systematically based policy directives to withstand the test of practical application. He cited the attempts of the early modern utilitarians to apply the findings of scientific inquiry to political decisions in the early stages of the bourgeois liberal order. Only after recurring failures to achieve their objectives did the insight of their conservative critics become apparent to them. Schumpeter argued that seasoned political leaders are less likely to place this level of trust in the findings of science. Their awareness of the unpredictable consequences of policy leads them to be much more cautious in this respect.[29]

Schumpeter also maintained that the attempt to rationalize politics tends to reinforce existing patterns of organization, leaving less room for change than is possible in a system grounded in the principles of laissez-faire. Planning for the future on the basis of this knowledge might indeed create a more stable society in the short term, but it also fosters stagnation at an institutional level, even in the face of a desperate need for change. Once an infrastructure is established to maintain the stability of the existing order, society's potential to adapt to unexpected developments is significantly diminished, and older systems are perpetually reproduced. Schumpeter cited the inability of the Soviet bureaucracy to adapt to the rapidly changing circumstances in the period leading up to World War II as evidence of this phenomenon and argued that its institutional structure would likely interfere with the state's capacity to reform itself in the future. He was skeptical of the idea that bureaucratically organized governments could meet the unexpected challenges they would face as the global economy continued to undergo major transformations.[30]

Schumpeter also questioned the assumption that a society is something that can be transformed at will. From the point of view of the planning enthusiast, once the conditions of a given social order become evident and the ideal policies are envisioned, the final step of implementing the plan is merely a matter of logistics. Schumpeter argued that this reasoning fails to acknowledge the structural nature of social change and projects a malleable quality on what is essentially an unpredictable and fluid network of social relations. He cited the eagerness of some intellectuals to institute socialism in the United States during the Great Depression and noted that this effort failed in part because the existing social order in this country had not yet developed the infrastructure needed to accommodate a system of planning. He suggested that one can speak of the "maturity" of a given society—meaning the extent to which it has become sufficiently complex in its organizational structure—and develop a sense of which regions might be able to make this transition successfully. Nations that are not structurally able to accommodate a predetermined ideal are less likely to succumb to the interventionist efforts of political actors, regardless of the nature of their objectives.[31]

This leads to Schumpeter's larger point that the underlying logic of traditional social science fails to consider the historically specific character of its subject matter. The idea that one series of events can be used as a guide in the analysis of another assumes a degree of consistency that does not necessarily exist. The attempt to draw comparisons across historical and temporal boundaries illustrates the extent to which the framework of the mathematico-scientific model penetrated the realm of traditional social inquiry. To Schumpeter, this practice is merely an extension of the utilitarian faith in the ability of the human sciences to yield increasingly universal conclusions about the social world, culminating in the development of a single mode of understanding that can be applied in all time periods and in all regions of the world.[32]

> Few will deny . . . that in the cases of logic, mathematics, and physics the influence of ideological bias does not extend beyond that choice of problems and approaches, that is to say, that the sociological interpretation does not, at least for the last two or three centuries, challenge the "objective truth" of the findings. This "objective truth" may be, and currently is being, challenged on other grounds but not on the ground that a given proposition is true only with reference to the social location of the men who formulated it. To some extent at least, this favorable situation may be accounted for by the fact that logic, mathematics, physics and so on deal with experience that is largely invariant to the observer's social location and practically invariant to historical change: for capitalist and proletarian, a falling stone looks alike. The social sciences do not share this advantage. It is possible, or so it seems, to challenge their findings not only on all the grounds on which the propositions of all sciences may be challenged, but also on the additional one that they cannot convey more than a writer's class affiliations and that, without reference to such class affiliations, there is no room for the categories of true or false, hence for the conception of "scientific advance" at all.[33]

He concluded that the best a science of society could do is to examine the existing trends of a given social order and reveal the broader tendencies of that region and period. The appropriate role of inquiry, from this point of view, is not to guide people toward specific ends but to present pieces of analyses as food for thought. Assessments of the social world could, in this sense, be developed without the expectation that they serve as a means to achieving a predetermined objective.[34]

MANNHEIM: INTELLECTUALS AND PLANNING

Mannheim recognized the dangers involved in the attempt to manage the social order but believed that measures of this sort were necessary to address the structural changes taking place in this period. To him, the consolidation of power occurring in the West would proceed with or without the principles of planning, and the inclination to refrain from taking difficult steps on the basis of this fear would be, in effect, handing over power to regimes of a totalitarian variety. Continued inaction further limited the chances that institutional coordination could serve as a means to secure political freedom and justice in the future. He hoped to facilitate the implementation of a planned order in the remaining democracies rather than allow them to fall into the hands of dictatorial elements.[35]

In an effort to address these concerns, he outlined the ways a planned society might be created in the West. He realized that merely heralding the value of comprehensive knowledge was itself insufficient as a grounding for such a goal, and sought to more concretely link the abstract world of ideas to the practical and demanding arena of politics. A central problem of this endeavor involved defining the group that could best develop this knowledge. His contention that consciousness flowed directly from one's class background led him to doubt that individuals attached to a specific socioeconomic group would be capable of developing the broader outlook necessary to build such a synthesis.[36]

He believed that in the modern era, intellectuals best fit this requirement due to the diversity of their background and philosophical orientation. Whereas in the early stages of modernity they constituted a relatively unified stratum of thinkers representing the interests and perspectives of the upper classes, they had more recently managed to free themselves of these ties and create variegated and contrasting conceptual formulations. In this environment, intellectuals regularly encountered the challenges of open-ended critique and no longer simply defended the status quo.[37]

Mannheim argued that even in the face of this diversity, intellectuals as a group possessed the potential to assert a common underlying set of social values. He saw a degree of consistency in their convictions and argued that this grew out of their experiences in the realm of education. To him, the spirit of competition in the world of ideas demonstrated the fact that most of them shared an interest in the Enlightenment goal of achieving continually higher levels of collective consciousness. One characteristic uniting intellectuals in this respect was a concern to expose the weaknesses in poorly conceived arguments and infuse this ongoing debate with new forms of insight. Even the skeptics, he argued, pursued this objective as they questioned the conclusions of the positivists. This was a central strength of intellectual discussion: its collective seeking of a keen understanding of the social world. Mannheim believed that the unique position of intellectuals in the contemporary order enabled them to better appreciate the variety of conflicting forces of society while at the same time maintaining a critical stance in the interest of achieving a broader perspective.[38]

Mannheim's concern that the industrial nations had become too fragmented politically led him to encourage intellectuals to work toward reducing these differences, not by attempting to impose a uniform outlook on the whole of society, but by relying on methods of critique to challenge the inadequacies and biases of narrowly defined perspectives. He attributed the growing gap between divergent orientations to the ability of extremists to escape challenges to their unsupported claims. The Fascists and the Communists succeeded in this by relying on propaganda to avoid facing the weaknesses of their viewpoints. Without having to confront the scrutiny of intellectual criticisms, they were better able to draw the support of larger segments of the population for their political programs. Mannheim argued that intellectuals have a responsibility to question the legitimacy of unsubstantiated ideas and offer constructive alternatives as a way to elevate the level of public discourse on key social issues. He thought they could accomplish this in a variety of ways, including joining competing groups with the intention of acting as a moderating force, and guiding political discussions toward more open-minded understandings of the problems they sought to address.[39]

Mannheim conceded that their lack of attachment to any particular social class rendered intellectuals prone to an insecurity with respect to their role as guides in the realm of consciousness. As outsiders, they are not fully connected to the variety of narrow perspectives circulating in the larger society and are likely to conclude that they have no business interfering with the ideas of others. He countered this concern with the argument that it is their very position as outsiders that enables them to develop new modes of understanding and broad ways of seeing the world, and that only by overcoming these inhibitions can they meet this crucial need in the new order.[40]

SCHUMPETER: THE LIMITED VISION OF THE INTELLECTUAL

Schumpeter did not see intellectuals as capable of transcending narrow perspectives, and he expressed grave doubts that they could develop knowledge of any value or utility in public affairs. He pointed out that, in the late modern era, the abundant availability of educational opportunity and the incentives to raise one's social status led to a rapid rise in the number of intellectuals as a class. This expansion was not met, however, with a parallel increase in the institutional positions available to them in the social order. Many were unemployed or working in a capacity that did not meet their expectations, leaving them displeased with their own social situation.

The result was a smoldering hostility among members of this group toward the existing order. This translated into a tendency to be critical of modern institutions, with a particular emphasis on the evils of capitalism. Schumpeter argued that their dissatisfaction led them to view the market mechanism negatively, often blaming it for many of the problems they observed. While in the feudal era, intellectuals traditionally focused on discrete aspects of the social order, the pattern in the contemporary intellectual world was to find fault with the system as a whole. The resulting conclusions were often of a grand and all-encompassing nature, advocating widespread change through reform or revolution. To Schumpeter, this was an indication of the intellectuals' failure to recognize the structural component of social change and of their naïveté in political matters. Their hostility toward capitalism prevented them from being able to comprehend modern society from the point of view of the larger picture and kept them in the dark with regard to the strengths of this economic system.[41]

Yet in spite of their limitations, intellectuals tended to see themselves as operating at a higher level than others, developing superior analyses and offering new and revealing insight into the world at large. They were inclined to present their arguments as based on rational and objective foundations, and as unfettered by the mundane and confused world of everyday life. Schumpeter contended that this facade of objectivity quickly broke down when intellectuals faced ideas that challenged their sensibilities. His own work involved presenting controversial positions in a straightforward and mundane fashion, and he was intrigued by the harsh and emotional responses this approach would often invoke from colleagues claiming to be detached from their material. He observed that challenging these positions directly exposed their underlying subjective nature.[42]

Schumpeter saw this happening as a result of capitalism itself, arguing that its rationalizing tendencies undermined the strength of earlier intellectual traditions. In the feudal era, these traditions acted as a check against the proliferation of poorly conceived analyses. Social assessments could not rise in stature due to their alleged connection to systematic calculation, but only by drawing on the long-standing and time-tested conceptions of those preceding them. He argued that in more recent times, this moderating force had been stripped away, enabling inane perspectives to gain legitimacy by projecting an image of being grounded in the precepts of scientific thought. He did not see earlier analyses as necessarily superior to all others, but suggested that conclusions known to be foolish from the point of view of seasoned public officials were often given sincere consideration by leaders in the new order. No longer bound by these limitations, modern intellectuals could offer their opinions under the guise of science, engaging in deceptive, ideological wrangling and lowering the standards of scholarly debate.[43]

Although uninformed and misguided in their judgments, intellectuals managed to retain a degree of influence among members of the larger population. In Schumpeter's view, the average person lacked the information needed to challenge the assertions of intellectuals and frequently accepted unsubstantiated claims about the social world, provided that they resonated with the tenets of popular belief. Intellectuals aware of this tendency could use it to their advantage, whether to promote the objectives of a given political program or simply to advance their own career interests. The abundant availability of intellectual messages in the form of books and other media further extended the reach of low-level ideas into the world of everyday knowledge.

Schumpeter raised the point that in times of economic downturn, uneducated people were likely to harbor a sense of dissatisfaction with their lot. He also argued that the alienating character of industrial society tended to isolate individuals and fill them with a nagging sense of insecurity about their future. He suggested that these difficulties alone were insufficient to produce a sustained hostility toward the system of capitalism as a whole. Such an antipathy required exposure to the one-sided and anticapitalist analyses of intellectuals to become a significant influence.

> Of course, the hostility of the intellectual group—amounting to moral disapproval of the capitalist order—is one thing, and the general hostile atmosphere which surrounds the capitalist engine is another thing. The latter is the really significant phenomenon; and it is not simply the product of the former but flows partly from independent sources, some of which have been mentioned before; so far as it does, it is raw material for the intellectual group to work on.[44]

While capitalism actually facilitated an ongoing improvement in the material conditions of everyday life, the incremental nature of these gains led many to take them for granted, and the focus of intellectuals on isolated problems drew popular attention toward the negatives of this mode of existence. This placed an undue pressure on political leaders to succumb to ill-conceived demands in order to stay in power, regardless of the consequences involved in doing so. Politicians failing to follow this protocol were attacked politically and eventually replaced, catalyzing the trend toward rigid economic controls and advancing the transition toward socialism.

Although intellectuals rarely entered into positions of leadership themselves, Schumpeter pointed out that they had become plentiful behind the scenes as experts in areas of political advising, speech writing, and public relations. Their work in this capacity enabled them to influence the character of policy by infusing it with their own rationally oriented assumptions of the world. This initial framework carried over into the conclusions they developed, and gradually redefined social issues in terms that were well suited to their ideological agenda. Their naïveté with regard to the long-term consequences of policy making led them to formulate banal prescriptions that, when put into practice, often yielded abysmal failures.

Yet in spite of all this, Schumpeter did not suggest that intellectuals themselves held the capacity to shape the broader trends of history. Instead, they were merely acting out their part in the changing social order as it unfolded in response to the rationalizing tendencies of capitalism. He summarized the significance of their role in ushering in the age of socialism as that of "a midwife's assistant," not a crucial actor, but one available to help in the event of unexpected problems.[45]

MANNHEIM: POLITICS AND PLANNING

Mannheim's optimistic view of intellectuals stemmed from the scenes of desperation he saw emerging in the West. He sought to form a viable response to these events and sustain his mission of social reconstruction, in spite of its inherent risks. He did not accept the prospect of trends continuing as they had in his lifetime, and he held little confidence in the actions of political leaders to offer effective solutions to this ongoing predicament. While his hopes prevented him from seeing the ideological nature of his proposals, nowhere was his idealism as great as in his writings on the question of morality in political planning.[46]

To Mannheim the current crisis was, at its core, a crisis of morality. Innovation and technical mastery over the forces of nature had reshaped the material world with startling speed, but the collective capacity of society to resolve moral issues in this new milieu had not kept pace. New circumstances continually arose as a result of these structural changes, but little progress had been made in developing values that enabled competing groups to co-exist peacefully and productively. This situation required a new social philosophy, one that could offer a firm grounding for the newer order. From this point of view, the goal of raising the moral standards of civilization requires a conscious effort, not only in creating relevant principles, but also in implementing them on a large scale.[47]

Mannheim believed that most citizens were not capable of developing the broad principles needed to bring about this harmony. Their day-to-day concerns compelled them to focus on immediate needs and prevented them from stepping back to see the larger moral problems of society as a whole. He considered members of the upper classes to be less burdened by short-term worries, but he feared that their financial and political interests might bias their moral framework and prevent them from being able to develop an all-inclusive social philosophy. He again turned to the intellectuals to take on this responsibility and expected them to rise above the demands of personal or petty interests to seek a fair and just social order. Mannheim appealed to them to develop these higher principles and offered some suggestions as to how they might work toward this end.[48]

Although he was a firm believer in the ability of a comprehensive viewpoint to provide valuable information into the workings of a social order, Mannheim rejected the idea that this type of knowledge could serve as a viable way to resolve moral dilemmas. He echoed Weber's claim that political choices were matters of conviction and were not reducible to systematic formulae. Yet he also contended that while knowledge of this nature could not spell out the proper set of moral standards for a society of its own accord, it could offer information that the principled observer might use toward this end. To Mannheim, a comprehensive orientation could serve as a means through which to develop insight into important cultural questions and demonstrate the range of morals that would be appropriate in a given setting. Political actors could then promote these standards to help nurture a sense of social responsibility among members of that culture and foster an enlightened harmony in society as a whole.[49]

Mannheim's interest in the specifics of local norms and traditions grew out of his belief that a moral philosophy suited to the new order should be both universal and particular in character. He sought to integrate existing elements of local culture into this newer set of standards and suggested that intellectuals form this philosophy at least in part on the basis of democratic principles. Drawing input from a variety of different groups would ideally prevent this philosophy from being too removed from the reality of contemporary social life. It would provide the means to form an orientation that resonated with the ideals of a broad segment of the population and would better facilitate the social integration needed in this time of growing division.[50]

He sought to avoid placing too much emphasis on the importance of local input and to ensure that this new grounding did not shift with the fluctuations in sentiment occurring at the level of public opinion. Mannheim believed that relying too heavily on consensus would connect the foundation of the new social order to the varying perspectives of competing groups and potentially undermine its stability. He suggested supplementing this collection of local views with a general set of principles to provide a relatively consistent starting framework.[51]

Yet the question remained, how would the more universal aspects of this new social philosophy be formed? Having demonstrated the limitations of both social inquiry and the consensus approach, Mannheim turned to an unexpected arena to fulfill this need: the world of religion. He suggested that for this new morality to be genuine, it would need to be of a spiritual variety. It would have to touch the individual at a level so deep that the validity of its truth would be seen as transcending scrutiny. The attempts of leaders in the Soviet Union to infuse socialism with a religious quality failed precisely for this reason. It involved relying on what was essentially an intellectually oriented philosophy to inspire emotional and heartfelt convictions among members of the populace. Its tangible and pragmatic character precluded the possibility that it could generate the awe or wonder characteristic of a belief in the inherent superiority of a distant, mysterious, and all-powerful God.[52]

Mannheim repeatedly stated that he did not advocate imposing a uniform creed on all members of society but sought to invoke a broad sense of the common underlying sentiments in the varieties of religious experience. He saw this manifesting itself in a range of unique and diverse cultural traditions and hoped that the newer orientation could be grounded in the fundamental values of "decency, mutual help, honesty, and social justice."[53] He did not seek to build this set of principles within the framework of existing religious practices but planned to draw on the general spirit of goodwill that underscored them. This, he argued, would help to nurture the spiritual integration of distinct social groups while at the same time connecting the new order to a balanced and influential set of moral principles.

> Although the different forms of religious substance coexist very often in society at large and have their proper share in the spiritualization of life, together they form a dynamic entity and in one historical period everything may depend on the intensity of personal experience and in another on the vitality of fellowship or tradition. The survival of Democracy depends on whether it is able to become not only a clearing-house of ideas and incentives but also a creator of a new vision, socially and spiritually, a vision of a better future which will give a lead to the peoples rising against universal aggression.[54]

In his effort to form the conceptual framework for a new spirituality, Mannheim argued that the goal should be to teach values to members of society in ways that would ultimately facilitate a more stable, compassionate, and well-organized social order. He suggested that the new beliefs be disseminated at an institutional level, through education and, if necessary, through the persuasive techniques of propaganda. Yet he also emphasized the point that these messages should defend the importance of individual freedom, a respect for cultures different from one's own, and the value of reason. From his perspective, the effort to manage public opinion was already taking place in the West and had become the standard course of action of political leaders in the remaining democracies, though few were willing to admit it. He pointed out that these techniques were readily available to groups willing to use them to their own strategic advantage, as the Fascists did to promote an ideology of hatred and misunderstanding. If liberal-minded government leaders failed to accept this reality, their interests, concerns, and values could be cast into the margins indefinitely.[55]

Mannheim believed that intellectuals might do this of their own accord through the spoken and written word, but he also expected the new social philosophy to be spread broadly and systematically. He did not suggest—as did Comte and Saint-Simon—that intellectuals assume this responsibility as a class, but argued that those who filled this role should have, at the very least, an intellectual foundation. From his point of view, this task should be handled at the level of government institutions, to ensure that values developed in the intellectual realm reached a significant percentage of the populace.[56]

He admitted that this task placed a high degree of authority in the hands of only a few public officials, but he hoped that a system of checks and balances would restrict their ability to use this power in an authoritarian or oppressive manner. The question that kept haunting Mannheim in this regard was, if the planners obtained the authority to provide the foundation of the new order, then who would supervise them? He phrased this in his words as the question, "Who plans the planners?" He realized that even with a system of checks and balances in place, the possibility existed that this privilege might be abused to the point where existing leaders prevented anyone outside their circle from acquiring a significant level of political power.[57] What steps could be taken to guarantee that this would not happen in the future? Although he struggled with this question extensively in his later years, he never managed to find a resolution that met his own standards of critique.[58]

SCHUMPETER: POLITICAL LEADERSHIP

Schumpeter rejected the notion that an allegedly superior social morality developed by intellectuals should be spread via mass education and the techniques of propaganda. The notion of controlling consciousness was, to him, an affront to human dignity and likely to yield even greater forms of oppression in the future. He rejected the belief that the best way to liberate human consciousness was to guide it, and he used a satirical writing style to expose the absurdity of this proposition. He agreed that the management of ideas had become more common in his lifetime, but he did not see this as a justification to engage in such a practice. The attempt to mold public opinion was yet another example of the continuing rationalization of the social order, a trend he detested but felt powerless to overcome.[59]

Schumpeter believed that meddling in the realm of consciousness was dangerous in that it could lead to a narrowing and dulling of human understanding to the point of insipid conformity. Creativity and innovation were among the qualities he valued most, and taking steps to interfere with these offended his sensibilities. Closing in on the consciousness of the young was particularly offensive in that it not only narrowed the outlook of future generations but also had a numbing and homogenizing influence on the population over time. He pointed out that the Soviet system of education involved rigidly controlling the content and orientation of classroom material in order to promote a favorable attitude in the upcoming generation toward the issue of factory discipline. The goal in this case was to deliberately infuse the larger practical concerns of planners into the curriculum of the schools. The new bearers of this orientation would then carry on the tradition of striving to maintain what was essentially a routine and mechanistic existence. Schumpeter expected few objections to be raised to this sort of repression, arguing that children being instructed in the universal value of practicality would eventually grow into adults lacking an understanding of its objectionable nature. Once the ball of mind control was rolling, he argued, there was little anyone could do to stop it in the future.[60]

Schumpeter was fundamentally opposed to the idea that a central authority could use propaganda toward the benefit of society as a whole. He challenged the notion that a universal "common good" could be defined in absolute terms, and he pointed to the wide range of ideals this phrase might invoke. Mannheim's assertion that a set of universal values could contribute to an overarching social philosophy presumed the existence of a compatibility between social groups that did not exist in the real world. At the root of this image was the unstated assumption that rationally oriented planners have a better sense of the actual interests of a society than do members of the population themselves. Underlying this logic is the belief that rational thinking should dominate the orientations of all individuals and that those who do not see its inherent superiority simply have not attained the enlightenment of the rational thinker. From this perspective, propaganda should be used to reveal to the masses the ideals they would seek if their consciousness were of a higher level.

Schumpeter perceived democratic politics to be inherently competitive, with different factions continually fighting for the attention and support of the larger public.[61] He concurred with Mannheim's view that political knowledge is necessarily limited in terms of its orientation but rejected the belief that it could become broader by tying it to the ethos of social science. The essentially competitive character of democratic politics prevents any single party from developing this expanded perspective. Schumpeter dismissed the possibility that a faction finding itself in a position of authority would voluntarily limit its own power or endorse ideas other than those facilitating its preferred agenda. From his point of view, such an expectation fails to understand the essence of democratic politics itself.[62]

Schumpeter's lack of faith in the ability of propaganda to yield beneficial ends also stems from his belief that political leaders are, at their core, incapable of acting on the basis of a higher morality. Public officials in a democratic order are inclined to engage in favoritism and behind-the-scenes deal making, working to protect their own interests and enhance their personal egos. They are required in many ways to follow a Machiavellian set of standards, not only to ensure their own survival, but to promote the success of their political goals. In this light, the expectation that an existing leader would voluntarily take action to secure the development of an open-minded orientation is naive at best, and borders on the utopian.

Schumpeter concluded that political decision making is ultimately of an "extra-rational" nature and cannot be completely controlled by the forces of reason. The trend toward rationalization may have successfully inhibited the creativity and innovation of the entrepreneur, but it failed to eliminate the influence of popular emotion in politics and economy. Leadership, in this sense, requires more than just intellectual or scientific knowledge. It involves relying on a sense of the ways unpredictable elements in a given situation might unfold in the face of new policies, and taking action that may not conform to the ideological demands of a consistent moral philosophy in order to achieve a desired set of goals. Without a clear view of the irrational and unpredictable forces of politics, the intellectual is likely to remain in the dark on these issues and continue to form narrow-minded and obtuse policy recommendations.[63]

THE NEW PUBLIC ROLE OF INTELLECTUALS

In the midst of the large-scale changes taking place in the 1930s and 1940s, the goals of Auguste Comte and Henri de Saint-Simon surfaced once again—albeit in an altered form—in the work of Karl Mannheim. Mannheim sought to revive some of the original ideals of these thinkers in spite of his awareness of the problems involved in the attempt to apply systematically derived knowledge in the management of the social world. His affinity with Weber, although pronounced in many respects, was also tinged with a sense of urgency in the face of what he perceived to be the final opportunity to preserve the freedoms of the liberal era. His view of the events in the Soviet Union, Germany, and Italy as indicative of a larger and more permanent structural transition led him to conclude that such horrors would also befall the remaining Western nations unless appropriate steps were taken to prevent this from happening. That he modified this view somewhat after living in England indicates the extent to which his initial positions were grounded in the particular circumstances of German politics and culture. His tendency to extrapolate from the German case to the whole of Western civilization, and his assumption of a continuity among different societies, underscored his belief in the need for such drastic measures.

His view of the trends in this period served as the basis for his affinity with planning. This approach to leadership was, to him, the only alternative to the pervasive downward spiral of irrationality and domination spreading throughout the globe. Although his ideas were at times deeply optimistic and ideological, Mannheim nevertheless provided a valuable contribution to social thought on this subject in that he revealed some of its central ironies. He showed that while the ideology of laissez-faire was, of its own accord, unable to provide the basis for long-term decision making in the new order, the logic of planning also suffered from fundamental contradictions. His sincere desire to develop an internally consistent and comprehensive proposal for a planned order led him to take the steps needed to achieve such a goal. This degree of thoroughness ultimately led him to confront the dilemmas involved in answering the question, who plans the planners? It exposed the limitations of the belief that politics can be brought under the realm of scientific management and more fully articulated the paradoxes inherent in the attempt to connect political administration to the knowledge of the intellectual. His critique did not emanate from the point of view of the skeptic or the sophist but from that of a rational thinker, seeking to ground politics in the power of reason.

Schumpeter's contribution differed from Mannheim's in its assertion that while the rationalization of the social and economic orders could be a more effective way to organize society, it would also strip away the vitality, freedom, and sense of vision that had been the hallmark of laissez-faire capitalism in the previous two centuries. His concern regarding the growth of bureaucratic and authoritarian forms of leadership led him to develop an analysis that challenged intellectuals to more seriously consider the consequences of the goals they so idealistically pursued. Yet rather than appeal to their sensibilities, Schumpeter merely presented his observations in a matter-of-fact manner, pointing to the ways these trends would likely play themselves out. His images of the shock brigades, the intellectual repression, and the control of public opinion as paving the way for a more stable and unified social order revealed the dark side of socialism lying at the end of this quest.

He ultimately saw intellectuals as little more than a nuisance, unworthy of the respect and authority accorded them by politicians and the public alike. His view of them as dilettantes who lacked the knowledge or capacity to wisely engage in political matters turned the vision of the early Enlightenment thinkers on its head. It undermined the assertion that politics could be reduced to a science, or that society would benefit from the attempt to bring an allegedly higher consciousness to the realm of decision making. Schumpeter reminded the rationalists of the unpredictable nature of human beings and scoffed at past efforts to engage in this form of planning. He identified the folly associated with these endeavors but also demonstrated his belief that a more rigid order would likely plague humanity in the future, regardless of the actions of intellectuals.

Taken together, the work of these two authors highlights the issue of the increasingly public nature of politics in this period. They saw political factions becoming more deeply entrenched in the logic of their own narrow beliefs and witnessed propagandistic appeals drawing the emotions of national populations to polar extremes. They illustrated the ways these trends deteriorated the interconnections of social groups on a large scale and undermined the stability of public opinion. While they clearly disagreed regarding the proper response to this newer set of circumstances, their shared focus on this aspect of society brought the role of the public to the fore. In the newer order, any attempt to consider the relationship of knowledge and politics was now required to include the dynamic and ever-present force of popular sentiment as a key component of public administration. Policy could no longer be formed behind closed doors within the framework of earlier traditions, but fluctuated with the views of a nation's citizenry. While in the past, public opinion only occasionally surfaced as an independent force of social change, it now served as an integral component of the everyday routine of politics and significantly altered the nature of policy formation in the newer order.

In this light, the assessments of these two social thinkers revealed a new role for the intellectual in public affairs. In addition to providing the analyses and insight needed in the realm of policy making, intellectuals also had begun to assume the position of liaison between academic knowledge and public opinion. Their involvement ranged from the social scientist attempting to observe and analyze economic trends to the political advisor suggesting new ways to formulate policy. Working on behalf of the established order, intellectuals now applied their skills to strengthen existing institutions, but they also acted as critics seeking to bring about institutional reform. In whatever capacity they found themselves to be involved, intellectuals had become deeply enmeshed in the connections between leaders and the led.

This new arrangement was both promising and threatening in that while it presented the opportunity to bring together the worlds of knowledge and politics, it also afforded intellectuals an avenue of approach to the halls of political power. The hope that higher levels of understanding might infuse international politics with an element of wisdom contrasted the reality of intellectual analyses as subject to the whims and idiosyncrasies of less-esteemed forms of inquiry. Mannheim and Schumpeter highlighted these developments to draw the attention of intellectuals to their new role and challenge them to meet its obligations in the years to come.

NOTES

1. For a more thorough description of these events, please see Francis L. Carsten, *The Rise of Fascism* (Berkeley: University of California Press, 1980), and Derek H. Aldcroft, *From Versailles to Wall Street, 1919–1929* (Berkeley: University of California Press, 1977).

2. Lewis Coser (1977) observed this shift in Mannheim's orientation, arguing that, in his later work, Mannheim became a *"sociologue engagé,"* abandoning a more reserved, scholarly approach in favor of one advocating planning and social reorganization.

Coser argues that although Mannheim repeatedly expressed his appreciation of democratic values, he failed to show how a viable democracy can be preserved in a society guided by a planning elite. He suggests that Mannheim discussed the compatibility of these two assertions in an ambiguous manner and did not provide a clear explanation of how such a coexistence would be possible. Please see Lewis A. Coser, *Masters of Sociological Thought: Ideas in Historical and Social Context*, second edition (New York: Harcourt Brace Jovanovich, 1977). Colin Loader (1985) also developed an overview of Mannheim's social thought, seeing it as moving through a series of stages, where each stage is a synthesis (the "cultural-philosophical synthesis," the "political synthesis," and "the synthesis of democratic planning"). Although Loader sees Mannheim's thought as going through these various stages, he nevertheless characterizes it as exhibiting an underlying continuity, with an emphasis on the question of the orientation of the individual in the modern world. For more on this, please see Colin Loader, *The Intellectual Development of Karl Mannheim* (Cambridge: Cambridge University Press, 1985). Also, for a very clear overview of Mannheim's life and work, please see David Kettler, Volker Meja, and Nico Stehr, *Karl Mannheim* (London: Tavistock, 1984).

3. For more on his assessment of these trends, please see Karl Mannheim, *Man and Society in an Age of Reconstruction* (New York: Harcourt, Brace & World, 1940), pp. 3–35. Also see David Kettler and Volker Meja, *Karl Mannheim and the Crisis of Liberalism: The Secret of These New Times* (New Brunswick, NJ: Transaction, 1995).

4. Robert Loring Allen (1991) provides a very detailed and gripping biography of Schumpeter. He also examines some of Schumpeter's major contributions to economic and social thought. Please see Robert Loring Allen, *Opening Doors: The Life and Work of Joseph Schumpeter* (New Brunswick, NJ: Transaction, 1991). Richard Swedberg (1991) also offers an interesting and enlightening biography of Schumpeter and examination of his ideas. Please see Richard Swedberg, *Joseph Schumpeter: His Life and Work* (Princeton, NJ: Princeton University Press; Oxford: Polity Press, 1991).

5. Harry Dahms provides a solid overview of Schumpeter's primary contributions to social and economic thought, arguing that Schumpeter's work can be read as highlighting three forms of rationalization unfolding throughout the history of modern capitalist society: (1) competitive, entrepreneurial capitalism; (2) corporate managerial capitalism; and (3) the rise of socialism. For more on this assessment of Schumpeter's work, please see Harry F. Dahms, "From Creative Action to the Social Rationalization of the Economy: Joseph Schumpeter's Social Theory," *Sociological Theory* 13, no. 1, March, 1995, pp. 1–13.

6. Mannheim, *Man and Society*, p. 59.

7. Mannheim, *Man and Society*, p. 73.

8. Mannheim, *Man and Society*, pp. 50–52.

9. Mannheim, *Man and Society*, p. 50.

10. Mannheim, *Man and Society*, p. 113. David Kettler, Volker Meja, and Nico Stehr (1990) argue that Mannheim ultimately sought to defend the underlying principles of the liberal tradition. Please see David Kettler, Volker Meja, and Nico Stehr, "Rationalizing the Irrational: Karl Mannheim and the Besetting Sin of German Intellectuals," *American Journal of Sociology* 95, no. 6, May, 1990, pp. 1441–73.

11. Joseph Schumpeter, *Capitalism, Socialism, and Democracy* (New York: Harper & Row, 1962), p. 299.

12. Randall Collins (1986) examines the work of both Weber and Schumpeter on this topic, arguing that the writings of these two authors can be read as contributing to a deeper understanding of contemporary capitalism. Please see Randall Collins, "Weber and Schumpeter: Toward a General Sociology of Capitalism," in *Weberian Sociological Theory* (Cambridge: Cambridge University Press, 1986). Jürgen Osterhammel also compares the perspectives of Weber and Schumpeter in "Varieties of Social Economics: Joseph Schumpeter and Max Weber," in *Max Weber and His Contemporaries*, ed. Wolfgang J. Mommsen and Jürgen Osterhammel (London: Allen & Unwin, 1987).

13. Schumpeter, *Capitalism, Socialism, and Democracy*, p. 214.

14. Eduard März (1991) offers an in-depth examination and overview of Schumpeter's contribution to social and economic thought. He points out that Schumpeter's primary focus was on the long-term influences of capitalism, such as the ways larger corporations take over and squeeze out smaller family-owned businesses. Schumpeter argued that this trend has a destabilizing effect, creates new forms of insecurity, and ultimately contributes to the rationalization of the social order. For more on this analysis, please see Eduard März, *Joseph Schumpeter: Scholar, Teacher, and Politician* (New Haven, CT: Yale University Press, 1991).

15. Schumpeter, *Capitalism, Socialism, and Democracy*, p. 132.

16. Schumpeter, *Capitalism, Socialism, and Democracy*, p. 127.

17. Mannheim, *Man and Society*, pp. 58–60.

18. Alan Scott (1987) argues that the focus on Mannheim's sociology of knowledge and hermeneutic orientation can lead one to miss the point that his most fundamental concern was the defense of Enlightenment concepts such as reason as a balance to the fragmentation of ideas associated with modernity. Please see Alan Scott, "Politics and Method in Mannheim's 'Ideology and Utopia,'" *Sociology* 21, no. 1, February, 1987, pp. 41–54.

19. Karl Mannheim, *Ideology and Utopia: An Introduction to the Sociology of Knowledge* (New York: Harcourt, Brace & World, 1968; orig. pub. 1936), pp. 147–50.

20. Mannheim, *Ideology and Utopia*, p. 151.

21. Mannheim, *Ideology and Utopia*, pp. 92–103.

22. Mannheim, *Ideology and Utopia*, p. 102.

23. Mannheim, *Ideology and Utopia*, p. 152.

24. Mannheim, *Ideology and Utopia*, pp. 109–91.

25. Mannheim, *Ideology and Utopia*, p. 240.

26. Mannheim, *Ideology and Utopia*, pp. 140–69.

27. Mannheim, *Man and Society*, p. 138. David Kettler, Nico Stehr, and Volker Meja (1987) draw on the work of Mannheim to address some of the dilemmas associated with the idea of developing a science of politics, and they also focus on the issue of relativism in the political sphere. Please see David Kettler, Nico Stehr, and Volker Meja, "Is a Science of Politics Possible? The View From Mannheim," *Society* 24, no. 3, March–April, 1987, pp. 76–82.

28. Schumpeter, *Capitalism, Socialism, and Democracy*, pp. 124–25.

29. Schumpeter, *Capitalism, Socialism, and Democracy*, p. 295.

30. Schumpeter, *Capitalism, Socialism, and Democracy*, pp. 198–200. For more on Schumpeter's social and economic views, please see Yuichi Shionoya and Mark Perlman, eds., *Schumpeter in the History of Ideas* (Ann Arbor: University of Michigan

Press, 1994). Also see John Bellamy Foster, "The Political Economy of Joseph Schumpeter: A Theory of Capitalist Development and Decline," *Studies in Political Economy* 15, Fall, 1984, pp. 5–42.

31. Schumpeter, *Capitalism, Socialism, and Democracy*, p. 295.

32. Schumpeter outlines this position most explicitly in the essay "Science and Ideology," *American Economic Review* 39, no. 2, March, 1949, pp. 345–59. Reprinted in *Essays of Joseph A. Schumpeter*, ed. Richard V. Clemence (Cambridge, MA: Addison-Wesley, 1951).

33. Schumpeter, "Science and Ideology," p. 350.

34. Schumpeter, *Capitalism, Socialism, and Democracy*, p. 416.

35. Mannheim, *Man and Society*, pp. 1–52.

36. Mannheim, *Man and Society*, p. 217.

37. Colin Loader (1997) points out that Mannheim's view of intellectuals stemmed from his a priori assertion that there are many varying interests and perspectives in the realm of culture. Intellectuals are free-floating in the sense that their connections to the everyday world are partial and multifaceted. Loader argues that this interpretation of intellectuals renders them unable to act as a coherent political group. For more on this analysis, please see Colin Loader, "Free Floating: The Intelligentsia in the Work of Alfred Weber and Karl Mannheim," *German Studies Review* 20, no. 2, May, 1997, pp. 217–34. Hans Speier (1988) argued that the notion of free-floating intellectuals is problematic in the sense that intellectuals are tied in many ways to the practical realities of everyday life. Please see Hans Speier, "Mannheim as a Sociologist of Knowledge," *International Journal of Politics, Culture, and Society* 2, no. 1, Fall, 1988, pp. 81–94. For more on Mannheim's view on the question of intellectuals and planning, see *Freedom, Power, and Democratic Planning*, edited by E. K. Bramstedt and Hans Gerth (London: Routledge & Kegan Paul, 1951). This is a collection of essays written by Mannheim during the latter portion of his career but compiled posthumously.

38. Mannheim, *Man and Society*, p. 64. David Kettler (2002) argues that when drawing on the work of Weber and Mannheim, one can see that the primary task of intellectuals involves facilitating informed and enlightened discussion of social issues. Please see David Kettler, "Political Education for a Polity of Dissensus: Karl Mannheim and the Legacy of Max Weber," *European Journal of Political Theory* 1, no. 1, July, 2002, pp. 31–51.

39. Mannheim, *Man and Society*, p. 365.

40. On Mannheim's position regarding intellectuals as outsiders, see the introduction to Mannheim, *Freedom, Power, and Democratic Planning*.

41. Schumpeter, *Capitalism, Socialism, and Democracy*, pp. 145–55. Mayer Zald and John McCarthy (1975) argue that Schumpeter observed that in a market-based economy, the bourgeois class is forced to facilitate a minimal level of freedom in order to accomplish its own goals with respect to trade and commerce. As a result, it is tolerant of the freedoms that intellectuals require to develop their critiques of society. Zald and McCarthy review Schumpeter's claim that the rising employment of intellectuals in the educational apparatus and other institutionally supported positions is likely to produce abundant criticism of capitalism and that sporadic periods of unemployment could exacerbate their tendency to foment unrest. Zald and McCarthy suggest that such unrest could lead to eventual policy changes, and they proceed to

theorize the ways to restore a critical attitude among contemporary intellectuals to better facilitate such change. For more on this view of Schumpeter, please see Mayer Zald and John McCarthy, "Organizational Intellectuals and the Criticism of Society," *Social Service Review* 49, no. 3, September, 1975, pp. 344–62. Eduard März (1991) offers a different interpretation of Schumpeter's position on this issue, outlining his distinction between the creative entrepreneur and the technically oriented "managerial team." In this account, bureaucratization in the sphere of production takes place as the spontaneous and independent actions of the creative entrepreneur are slowly replaced by the rational and calculating decisions of the managers of a boardroom. Schumpeter saw this process as an example of the gradual encroachment of socialism into the capitalist order, taking place independently of any deliberate or concerted action on the part of intellectuals. In this sense, the forces of the productive system are themselves instrumental in bringing about the rationalization of the economy, and the conscious attempt to direct such a system misunderstands this fundamental trend. März then outlines Schumpeter's assessment of these changes and notes specifically his point that the superiority of such a system is not guaranteed, thus suggesting that Schumpeter did not have an optimistic view of this inherent tendency of capitalism, nor did he endorse, as Zald and McCarthy assume, the attempt on the part of intellectuals to rationally manage the productive apparatus. For more on this issue, please see Eduard März, "Schumpeter's Vienna," in *Joseph Schumpeter: Scholar, Teacher, Politician*, pp. 99–113.

42. Schumpeter, *Capitalism, Socialism, and Democracy*, p. 144.

43. Schumpeter, *Capitalism, Socialism, and Democracy*, p. 124.

44. Schumpeter, *Capitalism, Socialism, and Democracy*, p. 153.

45. Schumpeter, *Capitalism, Socialism, and Democracy*, p. 413.

46. Toward the end of his career Mannheim brought together a group of intellectuals with the goal of attempting to guide society on the basis of a united vision. This group had very little political power and did not have a significant impact on the direction of political events. Emil Oestereicher (1985) argues that Mannheim's effort on this front stemmed from his rather idealistic hopes with regard to the future directions of politics. Oestereicher maintains that it was Mannheim's weak analysis of modern industrial society that fueled his misguided solutions. From Oestereicher's point of view, Mannheim feared the democratization of society, seeing a link between it and the gradual deterioration of an established set of standards for the elite, which contributed to the massification of cultural life and paved the way for the rise of Fascism. Mannheim sought to effect a "revolution from above" in which a united intelligentsia would persuade the ruling class to accept their more humane vision of a planned society. These relatively naive and romantic ideas failed both in their assessment of the issues of his day and in their ability to offer a realistic vision of the future. For more on this view, please see Emil Oestereicher, "Politics, Class, and the Socially Unattached Intellectual: A Re-Examination of Mannheim's Thesis," *State, Culture and Society* 1, no. 3, Spring, 1985, pp. 209–24. Colin Loader challenges this critique, arguing that Mannheim did in fact seek to preserve a democratic order and that he was not resistant to social change. In Loader's view, Mannheim believed that a new monopolistic stage had been ushered in by the war and that a previous reliance on what Loader labels "unreflexive traditionalism" could no longer serve as the foundation for the social order. Mannheim's attempt to consciously reorganize society grew out of

his drive to counterbalance the tendencies toward Fascism he saw surfacing all around him. At the center of his mission to restore democracy was the effort to build an enlightened, responsible citizenry, capable of seeing through the appeals of demagogues and resisting the drift toward irrationalism that had become so common in the years leading up to the war. Loader argues that Mannheim sought to promote the sort of change that would guard against disorientation and insecurity, and this meant actively engaging in a conscious intellectual effort to guide human affairs. For more on this interpretation of Mannheim, please see Colin Loader, *The Intellectual Development of Karl Mannheim*.

47. Karl Mannheim, *Diagnosis of Our Time* (New York: Oxford University Press, 1944; orig. pub. 1943), pp. 113–15.

48. Mannheim, *Freedom, Power, and Democratic Planning*, p. 129.

49. Mannheim, *Diagnosis of Our Time*, pp. 113–33.

50. Mannheim, *Ideology and Utopia*, p. 143.

51. Mannheim, *Diagnosis of Our Time*, pp. 147–56.

52. Mannheim, *Diagnosis of Our Time*, pp. 135–44.

53. Mannheim, *Diagnosis of Our Time*, p. 119. He seems to contradict himself here in that while he claimed to be advocating the development of a broader religious perspective, he frequently used the word "Christian" to describe this. See pages 115–30 for examples of this.

54. Mannheim, *Diagnosis of Our Time*, pp. 140–41.

55. Mannheim, *Freedom, Power, and Democratic Planning*, pp. 35, 138–40. Lewis Coser (1977) criticized Mannheim's attempt to formulate a theory of propaganda designed to direct the social psychology of the individual away from the tendency to be susceptible to mass appeals. This attempt, along with Mannheim's suggestion to organize the selection of political leaders in a scientific manner, led Coser to suggest that Mannheim's formulations had become "flabby" and brought him "in dangerous proximity to the ghost of Auguste Comte." Please see Lewis A. Coser, *Masters of Sociological Thought*, pp. 440–41.

56. Mannheim, *Freedom, Power, and Democratic Planning*, p. 140.

57. Mannheim, *Freedom, Power, and Democratic Planning*, p. 263.

58. Mannheim devotes quite a bit of attention to this issue in *Freedom, Power, and Democratic Planning*.

59. Schumpeter, *Capitalism, Socialism, and Democracy*, p. 154.

60. Schumpeter, *Capitalism, Socialism, and Democracy*, p. 151.

61. John Medearis examines Schumpeter's ideas on democracy and argues that while most scholars are familiar with his theory of democracy as competition among elites, few are aware of his notion of democracy as a potentially radicalizing force that can lead to socialism. Medearis argues that Schumpeter sought to develop a theoretical orientation that could serve to challenge this latter prospect and enable a select group of elites to ward off this possibility. For more on this aspect of Schumpeter's work, please see John Medearis, *Joseph Schumpeter's Two Theories of Democracy* (Cambridge, MA: Harvard University Press, 2001).

62. Schumpeter, *Capitalism, Socialism, and Democracy*, p. 154.

63. Schumpeter, *Capitalism, Socialism, and Democracy*, pp. 150–55.

5

C. Wright Mills and John Kenneth Galbraith: Institutions, Social Science, and the Role of Intellectuals in the New Industrial State

The end of World War II and the fall of the authoritarian regimes in Germany, Italy, and Japan seemed to many in the West to be an indication that human civilization was once again on the path to a civil and democratic order. The Fascists had been defeated, and the wave of ignorance and irrationalism marking this phase in history had lost its earlier momentum. This optimism fueled a spirit of consensus among policy makers, industry leaders, and voters in the United States that translated into an eagerness to work cooperatively in the postwar renewal effort.

Members of the academic community hoped that scientific work would play an important role in shaping the events of this historical period. Research funding was plentiful and grew as the rapid pace of change raised more questions than it did answers. Business leaders and federal policy makers sought to develop new ways to achieve their goals and appealed to the universities to assist them in this effort. The result was a rising call for large-scale research projects, and departments in the social and natural sciences grew quickly to meet this demand.

Many scholars enthusiastically welcomed these changes, and, of course, others viewed them a bit more skeptically. C. Wright Mills and John Kenneth Galbraith were among those who questioned the logic and directions of the new institutional order. They critically appraised the prevailing perspectives circulating in the academy at this time and sought to articulate a broader vision for the future of intellectuals, social science, and public policy.

C. Wright Mills was perhaps one of the most outspoken critics of the institutional developments in the United States following the war. He remained in the ideological margins of the discipline throughout much of his career and developed a reputation for speaking out against what he considered to be the simplified and conformist analyses of his colleagues. While a lecturer at Columbia University, Mills openly attacked many of the ideas championed by scholars in his home institution, and lambasted intellectuals in the United States and abroad for habitually defending the ideologies of the leading nations in the Cold War. He emphasized the undemocratic nature of politics in the industrialized world and scrutinized the hierarchical organization of authority that had surfaced in the United States in the 1950s. To him, the exigencies of war and the resulting consolidation of national institutions concentrated the power of decision making in the hands of a few select leaders in the military, business, and political spheres. His view of the role of social science in this context was one that centered on the ways it could challenge the apparent oligopoly of power emerging in this period.[1]

Galbraith's experience as an economist at Harvard University and ambassador to India with the Kennedy administration enabled him to form a more intimate view of the workings of powerful economic and political institutions in the United States and around the world. He did not echo Mills' claim that decision making had fallen into the hands of a select few. Instead, he took the position that the internal structure of the new institutional order had become a significant factor in shaping public policy at the national and international levels. From his vantage point, the changes that had taken place during the war significantly altered power relations in the new industrial state, and this realignment afforded intellectuals an avenue of influence they did not have in the past.[2]

Although the perspectives of these two thinkers differed significantly from one another regarding the organization of industrial society in the postwar era, their mutual focus on the connections between knowledge and power shed new light on the question of the public role of the intellectual in the context of these ongoing transformations.

C. WRIGHT MILLS: THE POWER ELITE

The deterioration of liberal values and practices observed by Mannheim and Schumpeter prior to and during World War II had, in Mills' view, further crystallized as the postwar societal order unfolded. From his vantage point, although the outcome of the war had brought about the end of the overtly authoritarian regimes of the sort witnessed in Germany and Italy, the trend toward liberal decline continued during the 1950s. Nations in the West still retained elements of the liberal tradition but were drifting toward increasingly restrictive forms of political organization under the guise of representative democracy. Rather than foster the open exchange of ideas in which enlightened citizens had the ability to shape the course of political events, the newer institutional structure tended to limit the boundaries of public debate. Mills saw this as the disintegration of genuine publics and a shift toward mass society. He argued that most people in this setting were not well informed regarding the nature of their predicament and lacked an awareness of the steps needed to improve their lot. The range of viable voter alternatives diminished as the positions of the leading parties drifted toward an increasingly uniform orientation, and this convergence further reduced the potential for meaningful democratic participation on a large scale.[3]

Mills observed that in each period of history, the power of political leaders varies in relation to the structure of the society in which they govern. In the years immediately following the war, the centralized configuration of the U.S. political economy placed a handful of leaders in a uniquely advantageous position. The network of institutions that coalesced during the war now served as a means through which the power elite could more effectively attain their goals. He qualified this assertion with the point that, in spite of the rising influence of this select group, they could not direct political outcomes in an entirely predictable manner. Leaders in this position could take steps to work toward their broader agenda, but the results of their actions often failed to yield the consequences they hoped to achieve. In this sense, history did not unfold according to a planned scheme but evolved piecemeal and in relation to existing trends.[4]

To Mills, members of the power elite were not always united. Nor were they joined in a conspiratorial effort to reach a unified objective. Instead, they tended to coordinate their efforts and work collectively toward a mutually compatible set of ends. Because the economic, military, and political spheres had become interconnected, problems in one area could interfere with the functioning of the others. Leaders in each of the three domains responded to this development by working cooperatively with one another, thereby enhancing the stability of the whole.[5]

Mills argued that the political institutions typically seen as providing some degree of balance to decision making in liberal democratic societies had been relegated to middle levels of authority in this newer context. Members of the U.S. Congress and their associated lobbyists still retained a degree of influence in the ensuing hierarchy, but they had become largely ineffective as a countervailing force and could not significantly challenge the goals of the power elite. In Mills' view, this branch of government had been reduced to little more than a side show, preserving only the facade of participatory democracy. Yet in spite of this transition, liberal intellectuals continued to develop analyses on the basis of a presumed balance of power, often characterizing the workings of Congress as a valuable safeguard against the potential excesses of any single group.[6]

Members of the broader population were the least influential politically and were largely unable to draw the connections between their own private troubles and the social trends of their time. As a disjointed array of groups without sustained connections to one another, they had lost the interactive component of participation needed to operate in the form of viable publics with a strong and self-conscious hand in political affairs. They tended to embrace popular but simplified perspectives and lacked the ability to see the structure of power relations in the postwar period.

> The top of the American system of power is much more unified and much more powerful, the bottom is much more fragmented, and in truth, impotent, than is generally supposed by those who are distracted by the middling units of power which neither express such will as exists at the bottom nor determine the decisions at the top.[7]

Mills dismissed the idea that the masses could unite in an effort to seize control from the power elite, and he argued that in their anomic state they were not an independent political force of any sustained significance. They would on occasion come together in support of one cause or another, but only if sufficiently prompted by the persuasive appeals of a well-organized and well-endowed political group. In the absence of these appeals, they typically fell back into their own narrow worlds without a unified orientation or consistent sense of direction.[8]

Mills pointed out that members of the power elite did not operate in a solitary manner but were supported by a staff of consultants, spokesmen, and public opinion experts assisting them in the tasks of leadership and political administration. As the institutions of government and industry grew to be larger and more complex, they also became highly bureaucratic in nature. The newer bureaucracies were not of the sort seen earlier in human history as described by Weber, but were much more flexible and changing. Rather than consisting of a complex machinery interfering with the decisive implementation of policy, these newer organizations were structured in such a way as to respond quickly and effectively to the demands of leaders in the top rungs of power. This arrangement expanded the influence of elite authority and enhanced the ability of a few powerful individuals to influence the course of politics at the national and international levels.[9]

JOHN KENNETH GALBRAITH: THE PLANNING SYSTEM

Galbraith agreed that the institutions of government and business emerging in the postwar period had grown to be very influential in shaping the trends of Western society, but he did not accept the premise that they had fallen under the control of a small group of elite leaders. His experience in political matters gave him an insider's view of the dynamics of power at this level. Although his analysis differed from that of Mills, Galbraith did not embrace a traditional assessment of the postwar political economy. He argued that a series of connections between the workings of the modern corporation and the bureaucratic state had emerged following the war and that recent trends in political decision making could be best understood by looking at this relationship.[10]

Galbraith observed the rise of what he called the "mature corporation"— an institution that evolves over an extended period of time to develop a series of established ties to the public bureaucracy. He contrasted this with the "entrepreneurial corporation," which is comparatively new and limited in its connections to government. From Galbraith's perspective, any attempt to evaluate the conditions of political decision making in industrial societies must begin with an investigation into the inner workings of the mature corporation and its association with the state. He viewed the mature corporation as unique in that it failed to conform to the principles of traditional economic theory. It did not, for example, abide by the rule that the power of decision making in a corporation tends to lie with its owners or stockholders. A common assumption of the traditional perspective is that the stockholders' ability to provide or withdraw financial support enables them to collectively direct the policies of the corporation. Under this arrangement, employees are bound to conform to the wishes of their employers.[11]

Galbraith argued that as the problems of management in business and industry became more complex and technical in nature, resolving them required the services of professionals from a wide array of fields. Technicians, business consultants, engineers, public relations advisors, lawyers, and a host of other experts routinely come together to make the corporation's major decisions. He called this group the technostructure, claiming that it had developed into the standard apparatus for large-scale decision making in the newer order. Within this framework of organization, once a proposal is offered by a team of specialists, there is no single individual possessing the requisite knowledge to legitimately challenge it. Managers presented with such a proposal have a limited range of options available to them. They can simply reject it outright and send it back for further revision, or they can approve it and forward it to their superiors in its current form. Galbraith observed that attempts by managers to interfere with a recommendation of the technostructure typically resulted in a loss of profit, due to the managers' inability to adequately consider the myriad factors involved in forming the decision.[12]

From this vantage point, the stockholders of the corporation are even further removed than the administrators from the details of decision making and are able to develop only a very superficial image of the technical matters underlying corporate policy. Galbraith saw stockholders' meetings as designed to project an image of participation in the process while rarely facilitating any significant deviations from the suggestions of internal specialists. The result is that the members of the technostructure have a greater level

of authority in managing the affairs of the mature corporation. The specialized nature of the work they do requires that they play a central role in shaping each major decision while at the same time appeasing the concerns of
their superiors and the stockholders in a superficial manner.[13] "It will be evident that nearly all powers—initiation, character of development, rejection
or acceptance—are exercised deep in the company. It is not the managers
who decide. Effective power of decision is lodged deeply in the technical,
planning and other specialized staff."[14]

Galbraith argued that this set of conditions profoundly influenced trends
in the public sphere as well. He observed a number of mature corporations
working closely with the state to ensure that their private interests were well
served, and he called this network of interwoven institutions "the planning
system." The goals of public policy gradually shifted to accommodate the
collective priorities of this newer apparatus and marginalized the concerns
of groups outside this circle. The market still played a part in governing economic outcomes, but its influence was quickly becoming overshadowed by
the growing reach of the planning system.[15] This newer set of demands and
the resulting pressures on the modern corporation to join forces with the
state contributed to the bureaucratization of politics in this period. Members
of the technostructure now worked together with their counterparts in the
public bureaucracy to formulate policies attuned to their respective goals.
Galbraith attributed this development to the rise of technology and advances
in manufacturing, arguing that large-scale industrial projects required a high
level of coordination between government and industry. He concluded that
as societies move in the direction of expanding technology and industrial-
ization, they necessarily become bureaucratic in character and limited in
terms of their flexibility.[16]

From Galbraith's point of view, the interconnections of these agencies
meant that the power of political decision making in the industrialized
democracies did not lie in the hands of a select few. Under this system of organization, power is divided among a broad array of agents. Political leaders
are given a range of choices within which to act but cannot form policy in an
autonomous manner. They are required to yield at least in part to the recommendations of experts. Policy objectives in this context come to life
through the interplay of party leaders, public officials, and teams of specialists working collectively to address the many interrelated factors involved in
each decision.[17]

Galbraith argued that this trend could be seen occurring in other nations
in the West as well, where the collection of mature corporations and their
counterparts in national bureaucracies had been highly influential in re-
defining the course of Western society in this period. To him, this arrangement was inherently problematic in that issues falling outside the purview of
the planning system tended to decline in importance and were forced to take

a back seat to institutionally defined goals. He argued that while members of the planning system sought to project the impression that they were genuinely interested in addressing a wide range of social issues, this was simply standard public relations procedure at the institutional level.[18]

A consequence of this set of circumstances was that individual freedom had come under increasing scrutiny and control. The rise of secret intelligence agencies throughout the world and the persecution and ostracizing of dissidents during the Cold War signaled the advent of a new era of ideological management. Galbraith interpreted these trends as evidence that the goals of the planning system had risen to such a degree of prominence that they marginalized the value of civil rights and undermined the potential for democratic participation on a broad scale.[19]

Yet in the face of these observations, Galbraith did not adopt a pessimistic attitude with respect to the future of modern democratic society. He argued that the shift in responsibility for policy formation reconfigured the balance of power in the industrial establishment. In order to sustain its goals, the planning system needed the knowledge and guidance of the technostructure. He saw this as the Achilles' heel of the new industrial state and forged his analysis of the role of the intellectual in public affairs on the basis of this new institutional arrangement.[20]

SCIENCE AND THE PLANNING SYSTEM

Galbraith looked to the past to develop a broad sense of the contemporary interactions of knowledge, politics, and economy in the United States and found that in the early years of the twentieth century, this relationship had been a rocky one. During this time, differences in opinion and objective created an ongoing tension between business leaders, politicians, and the academic community. Within the university, scholars tended to be critical of commercial organizations and rarely offered their services to government institutions. Corporate magnates also scrutinized scholarly work, often questioning its utility and moral integrity. Business leaders of great wealth and prestige typically sat on university boards in the attempt to ensure that the ideas circulating in the halls of academia matched their own sensibilities. They attempted to use their financial position and political influence to keep academic research and analysis safely within the boundaries of what they considered to be acceptable discourse. Yet in spite of the pressure to conform to these expectations, many scholars continued to challenge contemporary business practices, sometimes at great risk to their own personal careers.[21]

Galbraith contrasted this scenario with the order he saw emerging in the postwar era. In this latter period, the institutional connections between government and business had grown to encompass the university, bringing an array of scholars into the fold of the planning system. The resulting growth of academia had transformed it into a much larger and politically significant body he called the "educational and scientific estate." As the responsibilities of the planning system had become more complex, it required the assistance of a greater range of intellectuals to meet its goals, and this meant maintaining a favorable relationship with the academic world. Scholars in the natural and social sciences had the potential to address these newer complexities and provide answers to some of the planning system's most pressing problems. Industrial and government officials had come to realize that cooperation with the university was essential to their continued success, and they strove to maintain the integrity of this relationship.[22]

Galbraith noted, above all, that the planning system had come to rely on intellectuals for the one aspect of their work that could not be replicated elsewhere: innovation. From this vantage point, the central value of intellectual knowledge lay in its ability to analyze current events and offer suggestions regarding the ways the planning system might respond to the ongoing changes taking place around the world. Leaders hoped to draw on the knowledge of academia to help ensure the continued stability of the planning system and its survival in the future. Thus, while the management of this machinery was something that past entrepreneurs thought of as beyond the realm of intellectuals, leaders in the new order had come to realize that it could not be done without them.[23]

Galbraith argued that this turn of events afforded members of the scientific community a degree of leverage in their relationship with the planning system. The innovative role of scientists meant that they were no longer bound to follow the path that had been established for them by industry and government. He noted that in the postwar era, business leaders sought university board membership not necessarily to control the directions of research, but to keep abreast of the most recent innovations emerging in this milieu. Corporate heads were now required to have a hand in the workings of the university to maintain an awareness of these changes. They wanted to stay in tune with the latest scholarly developments and remain on the cutting edge of scientific and technological discovery.[24]

Galbraith expressed his hopes that this newfound leverage would enable the educational and scientific estate to develop its own identity and form goals for society that extended beyond the objectives of the planning system. He argued that scientists could assert the importance of human-oriented concerns in the realm of policy rather than simply operating on the basis of a utilitarian or dispassionate point of view. Although he criticized the priority given to the goals of industry and government, he did not suggest that these be neglected altogether but that they be considered on a par with noneconomic interests and that scientists emphasize the importance of a wider range of issues facing humankind at this juncture in history, and in the future. He recognized the difficulties involved in the attempt to define such elusive ideals and did not expect them to be drawn in an absolute fashion, but hoped that they could be created on the basis of open discussion and include the interests of people from a variety of backgrounds and orientations.[25]

In his assessment of the educational and scientific estate, Galbraith observed that some researchers uncritically adopted the ideological leanings of the planning system, while others continued to operate independently of its influence. For instance, many of those who embraced the ideas of officialdom in the 1950s eagerly participated in war research, assisting in the efforts of the U.S. government to overcome the spread of Soviet Communism. This group included scientists who took on the task of calculating the number of lives that could be lost in a nuclear confrontation without diminishing the fighting power or economic viability of the United States after such a battle. Universities that had earlier focused their energies on the study of peace became, at that time, centers for military research, preoccupied with nearsighted questions of this nature.[26]

Galbraith understood the allure of research funding and the eagerness of scientists to identify with the goals of their clients, but he challenged the logic of this compliance. He found that scientific investigators would commonly claim that they were not responsible for the uses of their findings and that the principles of objective research demanded they refrain from allowing their own values to enter into their work. Galbraith responded with the comment that one might hear this chant being repeated by the last remaining scientist as nuclear warheads encircled the earth, bringing humanity to its fateful demise. He rejected the idea that scientists were obligated to be indifferent to the practical consequences of their findings and countered that these consequences should be factored into their research as among its central considerations.[27]

With the progression of the Cold War, members of the educational and scientific estate who had remained critical of institutional goals found the tide turning in their favor. As the dangers of the arms race grew increasingly evident, specialists in the area of war research gradually found themselves alienated from the rest of the academic community. The compliance that had earlier brought these researchers a degree of notoriety and prestige among their colleagues now became a detriment to their careers. Most researchers gradually came to see the mythology of the official claim that the differences between East and West were irreconcilable, and began to take a negative attitude toward the Cold War and the arms race. Galbraith pointed out that scientists were among the first to propose steps toward banning the development of nuclear weapons, and he argued that their intimate knowledge of these matters gave them a greater authority and responsibility to discuss these issues publicly.[28]

From his standpoint, while members of the technostructure experienced a great deal of pressure to conform to the expectations of the planning system, intellectuals in the educational and scientific estate were less restricted. The ties of the latter to scholarly institutions and peer associations obligated them to take a multifaceted approach to the issues they addressed. The enormous size of the educational and scientific estate facilitated a wide range of contrasting perspectives and opinions in discussing public affairs. It now included a substantial number of scientists with no direct ties to the planning system. Such a large and differentiated body of thinkers could not be expected to embrace a homogeneous outlook, and the availability of alternative critiques abounded in the newer order.[29]

> The educational and scientific estate and the associated intellectual community have—as repeatedly noted—grown to formidable proportions. And this growth has taken place, as also noted, at a time when there is a strong tendency to question established goals. In both foreign and domestic policy there is suspicion of what is believed, not inaccurately, to be the unexamined or automatic position of what has come to be called the Establishment. Such attitudes await the political lead here urged.[30]

Galbraith called on the members of this body to continue in the tradition of critical analysis and develop ideas that did not necessarily conform to the narrow goals of established bureaucracies. He accepted the point that many valuable innovations remained in the margins of public debate, but countered that while these may be controversial or ignored in the present, they have the potential to provide the foundation for new perceptions in the future. He concurred with Veblen's analysis that as the structure of society changes, lesser known interpretations can move into the domain of everyday knowledge. Ideas developed within the realm of critical scholarly thought can gain legitimacy over time, gradually rising in prominence to the level of accepted assumptions, influencing the ways members of society come to see the world, and setting the standards of value and concern in the future.[31]

MILLS: SOCIAL SCIENCE IN THE NEW ORDER

Mills' view of the power elite working cooperatively to control the vast bureaucracies of state capitalism led him to doubt the possibility that intellectuals on the whole could avoid the traps set for them. Yet he also expressed an underlying hope that a few particularly stubborn intellectuals might approach their work in an independent manner, and he offered his suggestions regarding the ways members of this group could pursue this ideal.[32]

Mills' assessment of intellectuals in the newer order also focused on the academic community, with an emphasis on the role of social scientists in this context. He saw their work as capable of having a profound impact on the course of human events in his time, and he examined the relationship between the institutional developments surrounding the war and the orientations and practices of social scientists in this setting.[33]

Mills saw that in the early years of the postwar era, the social sciences had undergone a shift from an orientation based on what he termed "liberal practicality" to a more conservative, managerial perspective. He understood the former of these two as growing out of the early modern belief in the ability of human beings to organize the world in a rational fashion. Liberal practicality emanated from the ideas of nineteenth-century industrialists who perceived human civilization to be advancing along a linear path of historical development, achieving progressively more complex forms of organization and higher modes of consciousness over time. In the social sciences, this outlook fostered a rationalized and mechanistic approach to the study of society. Its practitioners sought to emulate the style of research common in the natural sciences and to establish the social sciences as a positive form of inquiry that was well suited to address the questions of the modern order. In pursuit of this ideal, researchers typically divided their subject matter into small, isolated components that could be examined piece by piece, in the hope that these would eventually be reconnected to reveal an image of the larger whole.[34]

Mills maintained that the orientation of liberal practicality grew out of the provincial values of the early American small town, where the common beliefs and practices of the townsfolk seemed to them to represent the natural way to live. Researchers operating from this point of view tended to define social problems as the result of behavior that deviated from the middle-class, small-town way of life. They hoped to serve the community by working to understand the nature of this deviance and offering suggestions to effectively maintain the stability and integrity of this culture. Mills characterized the central assumptions of this viewpoint as narrow minded and as displaying a basic misunderstanding of the place of social science in the modern world.[35]

He argued that the managerial approach to inquiry differed from liberal practicality in a number of ways, but remnants of this earlier ethos carried forward into the assumptions and practices of social scientists following the war. Those emphasizing this newer perspective also sought to guide the inner workings of the social order, but in a more comprehensive manner than in the past. They came to believe that social science could ultimately serve as a grounding for a new systematic administration of society. From their standpoint, social science had not yet reached the stage where it could effectively accomplish such a task, but it was moving in the right

direction and would eventually attain this level of complexity. The underlying goal from this perspective was to engage in what Mills characterized
as social engineering, designed to resolve the major problems of mankind
on the basis of systematic observation and instrumental action.[36]

Mills argued that this failed to understand the dangers involved in attempting to control human beings in a functionally rational manner. He labeled the purveyors of this outlook the "technocratic philosophers," whose
limited vision of the world led them to see human beings as manipulable objects.[37] To Mills, this orientation and its associated practices constituted a
threat to the integrity and freedom of human social life, and he expressed
concern that a greater level of control might actually become a reality, given
the recent ascendancy of centralized authority in the West. This philosophy
of social science aligned itself with the logic of the growing bureaucracies,
operating on the basis of uniform and standardized methods of research and
engaging in inquiry that could be presented in a numerical format to give the
appearance of objectivity.

> Assuming the technocratic view, and as a social scientist trying to act upon it, is
> to act *as if* one were indeed a human engineer. It is within such a bureaucratic
> perspective that the public role of the social scientist is now frequently con-
> ceived. To act in this as-if-I-were-a-human-engineer manner might be merely
> amusing in a society in which human reason were widely and democratically in-
> stalled, but the United States is not such a society. Whatever else it is, surely this
> is evident: it is a society in which functionally rational bureaucracies are in-
> creasingly used in human affairs and in history-making decisions.[38]

The bureaucratic ethos of social science had, in this sense, evolved in response to changes in the structure of the university, adapting in terms of
both its methods and its goals to meet these newer demands. Mills agreed
with the position of Galbraith that the allure of research funding had facilitated a transition in the quality and style of academic work, but he was less
optimistic than his counterpart in this regard and emphasized instead the
ways researchers had chosen to conform to the pressures of institutional demands.[39]

Mills pointed out that the objective of institutional research is not to develop analyses of society that offer insight into the nature of power relations,
but to find ways to more effectively implement the agenda of the established
authorities. The primary task of social scientists from this perspective is not
to adjust policy in accordance with the predominant values and concerns in
their field or among members of the larger population, but to legitimate establishmentarian priorities. Their role becomes one of providing the ideological justification for the existing system of power, while maintaining the
appearance of objectivity.

Mills observed that a type of researcher emerged from this set of conditions who not only participated in the mundane tasks of a study but also supervised a large team of technicians working together on collective projects. He described these scholars as "intellectual administrators" and criticized their blind commitment to the logic of institutional research. While some in the first generation of this brand of social scientist possessed the passion for understanding needed to inform their work with a deeper sense of meaning, the more recent cohort operating on the basis of this framework lacked such a background or sense of conviction and tended to simply mimic the procedures of their predecessors. This newer set of social scientific "technicians" no longer carried with them an innate drive to form new insight into the nature of the social world, but primarily sought to achieve the expectations of their profession and enhance the future of their careers.[40]

In spite of this relatively bleak assessment, Mills also defended the potential of social science to provide the information and analyses needed on a broad level in the public arena. He suggested that in the postwar era, societal change was occurring at such a rapid rate that many people were unable to make sense of it in terms of traditional values. As their standard modes of understanding failed to provide the framework needed to comprehend these changes, they tended to retreat into the realm of narrow self-interest, focusing on their personal needs and neglecting those of the larger society. Once in this state, individuals seek to convince themselves that they are content with their situation, but they are continually plagued by the sense that there are aspects of the social world influencing their life that they do not understand and cannot control.[41]

Mills maintained the position that if done properly, the work of social science can help members of the larger population situate their own lives in the context of salient social trends and can enable people to better understand the ways these trends shape their personal experiences. The goal in this sense is to critically evaluate the nature of power relations in the societal order and offer these interpretations to the layman in straightforward terms. Mills raised the issue of alienation as an example and argued that it is the task of social inquiry to illustrate the structural foundations of this phenomenon and reveal the ways that large-scale changes such as the development of industry tend to exacerbate it. When social scientists approach their work in this fashion, they are not necessarily enabling institutions to accomplish their goals but are contributing to enlightened social thought and working toward a long-term vision of human civilization.[42]

> What I am suggesting is that by addressing ourselves to issues and to troubles,
> and formulating them as problems of social science, we stand the best chance,
> I believe the only chance, to make reason democratically relevant to human

affairs in a free society, and so realize the classic values that underlie the promise of our studies.[43]

Mills believed that social science could go beyond merely helping individuals to understand the world around them. He contended that its role extended to communicating key findings to leaders in positions of power, with the goal of broadening their perspectives and informing their decisions. Social science could not spell out the specific policies leaders should follow, but it could reveal to them the larger steps needed within the framework of a given historical period. In this sense, Mills created a middle ground between the ideas of Weber and Mannheim on this question. He went beyond the relatively reserved contention of Weber that social science should primarily provide information to political leaders, who must then make decisions on the basis of their own convictions and sense of responsibility; and he also distanced himself from the suggestion of Mannheim that research be used directly in the formation of public policy. Instead, Mills argued that social science has the potential to identify the larger trends in a given context, as well as the possible actions political leaders can take in response to these trends. The goal in this sense is to offer public officials a range of recommendations, thereby providing the starting foundation for a coherent policy platform. From Mills' vantage point, social science cannot supply all the answers, but it can help to clarify the changing conditions of a given period and locate the contemporary situation in its historical context, thus enabling leaders to develop a deeper understanding of the complex situations they are required to address.[44]

Mills went into great detail to show how researchers might go about accomplishing this task, and he referred to the approaches of the classical social scientists Durkheim, Marx, and Weber to illustrate the proper way to work toward this end. He implored contemporary social scientists to select topics that are relevant to the existing political, economic, and moral questions in their milieu and to avoid falling into the trap of defending the ideologies and goals of established institutions. Their task in this sense is to better understand the key social factors shaping their world and to share this insight with "kings" and "publics" to enable them to see the larger picture as well.[45]

PROPAGANDA AND PUBLIC OPINION

Both Mills and Galbraith recognized the attempts of government and industry to influence the perceptions of citizens in the postwar Western world. The institutional apparatus of official propaganda emerging during the war remained in place and served well in the effort to strengthen the legitimacy of the newly established order. Many of the social scientists in the United States who had helped develop the techniques of propaganda during the war retained their government positions and continued to work in this capacity in the years that followed.[46] Their expertise as innovators in the realm of ideas furthered the successes of these persuasive efforts.

Galbraith observed institutionally derived techniques of persuasion being applied to stabilize the purchasing habits of consumers and reduce the inherent risks of long-term investment. For instance, product advertising served to bring about a relatively consistent demand for goods and services and ensure a steady rate of economic growth. He saw this pattern emerging from the state apparatus as well, where support for institutional goals was carefully encouraged through subtle, but effective forms of political propaganda. The ideological influence of the planning system had reached such a level of complexity in the world of public opinion that it possessed the ability to manufacture the images and ideas needed in virtually any given situation. When leaders sought to justify investment in military weaponry, for example, they could foster the impression that the nation faced a great enemy. If the institutions of the planning system encountered unacceptable economic restrictions, they would then draw public attention to the threat to freedom posed by ever-increasing governmental regulation. The result of this new system of impression management in the West was that the goals of the planning system gradually became enmeshed within the logic of everyday thought and accepted even among groups with widely differing orientations. In this context, the citizens of industrial democracies developed beliefs they perceived to be self-defined, and relied on these beliefs in deciding how to act in their personal lives and in their connections to the larger institutional order. Galbraith contended that this phenomenon was so pervasive that individuals holding priorities other than those of the planning system seemed from the point of view of their mainstream peers to be somewhat strange and out of step with the cadence of contemporary progress.[47]

Mills added that the individualized nature of human social life in the United States enhanced the ability of the media and its opinion makers to manipulate ideas on a grand scale. To him, this practice had become a routine part of politics in the postwar era and a further threat to participatory democracy. He contended that while the many influences of mass media were difficult to measure in an absolute manner, one could conclude with a reasonable degree of certainty that this imagery contributed less to interactive public discussion than it did to the development of a unidirectional flow of information and ideas in a top-down fashion. Presented with messages in this way, an individual cannot respond to the source, but can only accept or reject the ideas as offered in their predigested form. Over an extended period of time, the persistence of these messages dampens one's resolve to maintain an independent stance relative to conventional beliefs, and most people eventually lose interest in questioning or revising them.[48]

Yet Mills also maintained that the sensationalized and exaggerated nature of these messages feeds the skepticism of even the most accepting of media audiences. In spite of their pervasiveness, the legitimacy of manufactured ideas quickly fades as members of the population become increasingly cynical and distrustful of the media in general. He pointed out that in response to this rising skepticism, opinion makers in the postwar era did not simply retreat from the attempt to influence mass sentiment altogether. They developed the newer strategy of studying the context of people's lives and working to gain a sense of the popular viewpoints among the groups whose support they needed most. They could then incorporate accepted frames of knowledge into future presentations to help create the images required by institutional authorities. This approach was far more subtle than the overt techniques of propaganda of the past, and it helped to strengthen the ideological influence of the power elite, while maintaining the illusion and formal structure of democracy.[49]

Mills' sense of the underhanded nature of these strategies led him to draw a distinction between legitimate authority and that obtained through ideological manipulation. Rather than attempting to govern on the basis of a concern for the broader public interest, political leaders more often relied on this newer form of propaganda, circumventing the essential requirements of democratic politics and forming policy in a unilateral and secretive manner.

> Such men as these are crackpot realists: in the name of realism they have constructed a paranoid reality all their own; in the name of practicality they have projected a utopian image of capitalism. They have replaced responsible interpretation of events with the disguise of events by a maze of public relations; respect for public debate with unshrewd notions of psychological warfare; intellectual ability with agility of the sound, mediocre judgment; the capacity to elaborate alternatives and gauge their consequences with the executive stance.[50]

Under the auspices of such a system, issues entered the political arena only as needed by the reigning authorities and in conjunction with their predetermined set of economic and political goals. To Mills, relying on propaganda and a top-down style of government further contributed to the massification of society in this period.[51]

Mills saw this variety of ideological persuasion as extending beyond the mass media and venturing into the realm of education as well. From his vantage point, schooling had become yet another means for powerful institutions to acclimate the younger members of the population to the established perspectives of the newer order. Universal compulsory education served to inculcate nationalist loyalties and manage the perceptions of students still in the process of developing their own worldview. Rather than teaching students to think critically, the focus of education in the postwar era had come to devote a great deal of attention to the task of encouraging a passive acceptance of an institutionally orchestrated way of life.[52]

Galbraith was not as easily convinced that education in its contemporary form routinely served the goals of the planning system. He agreed that the institutions of industry and government did influence the outlooks of the broader population and that this arrangement did have a dangerously monolithic character to it, but he also believed that such a level of control was not feasible in the modern order, given the scale and nature of educational systems in the West. He saw the conditions of schooling in this period as too diverse and independent to be co-opted in the manner Mills suggested. In this context, formal education could enlighten students regarding the benefits of critical thinking and teach them to question the messages and goals of the planning system. Galbraith was aware of the attempts to use education as a means to foster complicity with the ideas of the planning system, but he also recognized its emancipatory potential and its capacity to encourage pluralist thought.[53]

Both Galbraith and Mills challenged the position of the early Enlightenment thinkers that propaganda and education should serve as an avenue of ideological guidance in the modern world. They rejected the underlying belief that every social order requires a unifying orientation. Advanced industrial society was at its core pluralistic and differentiated, and this would not soon change. Although they subscribed to the fundamental principles of freedom and self-determination inherent in the liberal tradition, they dismissed the contention that these be systematically spread as a way to challenge more pernicious ideals. The task of the intellectual from this point of view is to maintain an open mind and a critical attitude toward a wide range of proposed ideas and forms of organization, and offer insightful alternatives to the dominant interpretations of the contemporary world. In the new industrial state, this means developing clear analyses of the power relationships of government and industry and working toward participatory democracy in the present and in the future.

THE ROLE OF INTELLECTUALS IN THE NEW INDUSTRIAL STATE

Mills and Galbraith observed that the bureaucracies of industry and government in the postwar world had become more tightly intertwined than in any previous time in human history. They saw that this arrangement restricted the options available to voters and narrowed the range of public debate on key political issues. In the industrialized nations, the demands of technically-sophisticated projects fostered an administrative perspective among public leaders, and created a strong incentive to manage political affairs in an imperious fashion. Democracy was now forced to compete with the overriding concerns of industry and long-term investment.

As newer media technologies broadened the influence of institutional authorities, the potential of citizens to coherently participate in politics further deteriorated. The routine use of propaganda in the new democratic order brought about a tenuous acceptance of large-scale institutional goals, but it also weakened the legitimacy of government leaders, and limited the political knowledge among members of the U.S. polity. Mills and Galbraith agreed that national populations had become a more potent force during the war, but they also observed the tendency of political administrations in the postwar era to undermine this influence through propaganda and secrecy. This newer leadership style involved developing policies behind closed doors, without the benefit of public deliberation or sustained intellectual dissent. As a result, the goals of the industrial state routinely took precedence over the concerns of less well-connected groups outside this circle of authority.

Yet, in spite of this negative assessment, Galbraith believed that this set of circumstances gave scientists a newfound opportunity to challenge the primacy of the planning system's objectives. The existing power structure had indeed eclipsed the potential for democratic participation, but it had also evolved to become more susceptible to collapse than earlier forms of government. Its inter-institutional connections and dependence on scientific knowledge increased its vulnerability, and afforded scientists the opportunity to assert human and civil concerns into the mix of policy objectives. He suggested that they use this leverage wisely and avoid the trappings of power that plagued their predecessors.

Mills was less optimistic that intellectuals could successfully counter the trends of the postwar world. His view of a highly-centralized and well-coordinated structure of power underscored his belief that the existing arrangement would likely continue in spite of concerted efforts to the contrary. He agreed that social scientific knowledge had become a crucial component of political decision making in this time, but he doubted that social scientists would collectively develop the political consciousness or will to stand up to traditional forms of administrative control. He observed their inclination to be easily drawn into the logic of bureaucratic authority, and join forces with established institutions in the effort to rationally manage the social order.

Together, Mills and Galbraith confirmed the expectations of Mannheim and Schumpeter that the interconnections of industry, government, and business would likely contribute to a tightly controlled and hegemonic form of political leadership in the industrialized democracies. In the tradition of these earlier authors, they recommended that intellectuals resist such tendencies in their own work, and focus instead on the ongoing needs of society as a whole. The irony they saw in this period was that, although intellectuals had become integral to the world of politics, they had largely relinquished the opportunity to draw on this newer position of influence to facilitate a broader understanding in the realm of public policy. While some scholars continued to develop independent analyses, most had adjusted their orientations to address the concerns of the current leadership. Mills and Galbraith appealed to the members of this group to think outside the domain of conventional thought, and utilize the power afforded them to act on the basis of the underlying values in their respective traditions. These two thinkers clearly understood the all-encompassing character of institutional authority in the industrialized world, but they also held firm to the belief that intellectuals had the potential to stand up to this authority, provided that they developed a greater degree of insight into the nature of their predicament, and the possibilities it presented to them.

NOTES

1. Rick Tilman (1984) offers a very interesting and thorough investigation into Mills' life and work, placing Mills in the American radical tradition. Tilman reviews Mills' intellectual roots and cites the influence of Marx, Mosca, Pareto, Weber, Veblen, Freud, and Mannheim on his ideas. He also discusses some of the ways Mills' work can be seen as having been influenced by Dewey and Mead. Tilman argues that Mills sought to carry forward the approaches and ideas of these authors and bring them into the realm of practice in contemporary scholarship. For more on Mills' intellectual background and his contribution to social thought, please see Rick Tilman, *C. Wright Mills: A Native Radical and His American Intellectual Roots* (University Park: Pennsylvania State University Press, 1984). Irving Horowitz (1983) also compiled a fairly extensive biography of Mills, reviewing his connections to Marx, Weber, and American pragmatism and outlining some of his major contributions to the field of sociology. Horowitz classifies Mills as an "American Utopian," characterizing him as one who was guided by a strong sense of moral purpose and driven to build the connections between an enlightened social science and the political dilemmas of the everyday world. For more on this view of Mills, please see Irving Louis Horowitz, *C. Wright Mills: An American Utopian* (New York: Free Press, 1983). John Alt (1985–1986) disagrees with the portrait of Mills as a radical or a utopian and instead situates him in the liberal tradition. Alt focuses on Mills' espousal of the values of individual freedom and democracy and his efforts to challenge elite control of public affairs. Please see John Alt, "Reclaiming C. Wright Mills," *Telos* 66, Winter, 1985–1986, pp. 6–43.

2. Richard Parker (2005) has written an extensive biography and assessment of Galbraith's work. In it, he provides a great deal of insight into the interactions of Galbraith during the Kennedy years and throughout his career. Parker also reviews and analyzes Galbraith's ideas on a range of issues. Please see Richard Parker, *John*

Kenneth Galbraith: His Life, His Politics, His Economics (New York: Farrar, Straus and Giroux, 2005).

3. For more on his interpretation of these trends, please see C. Wright Mills, "The Mass Society," in *The Power Elite* (New York: Oxford University Press, 1956), pp. 298–324.

4. Mills, *Power Elite*, p. 21.

5. Mills, *Power Elite*, pp. 7–8.

6. Mills, *Power Elite*, pp. 242–68, 360–61.

7. Mills, *Power Elite*, p. 29.

8. Mills, *Power Elite*, pp. 298–324.

9. Mills, *Power Elite*, pp. 43–44.

10. For instance, Galbraith rejected the neoclassical model and the idea that the free market, when left to its own volition, will necessarily produce favorable results for society as a whole. For more on his view on this, see John Kenneth Galbraith, *The Affluent Society* (Boston: Houghton Mifflin, 1998).

11. John Kenneth Galbraith, *The New Industrial State* (Boston: Houghton Mifflin, 1978), pp. 80–90.

12. Galbraith, *New Industrial State*, pp. 54–65.

13. Galbraith, *New Industrial State*, pp. 54–65, 129–51.

14. Galbraith, *New Industrial State*, p. 62.

15. Galbraith, *New Industrial State*, pp. 312–17.

16. Galbraith, *New Industrial State*, pp. 19–41.

17. Galbraith, *New Industrial State*, pp. 55–60, 364. Scott Gordon (1968) argues that while planning may take place at the level of the large corporation, the economic system as a whole is not coordinated by a central planning apparatus as Galbraith assumes. In Gordon's view, Galbraith jumps from this first proposition—that the corporation plans—to the conclusion that the economy is planned, without adequately demonstrating the connections between the two. Gordon further states that Galbraith's suggestion that the educational and scientific estate replace the technostructure is based on this initial faulty assumption and should therefore be called into question as well. For more on this assessment of Galbraith, please see Scott Gordon, "The Close of the Galbraithian System," *Journal of Political Economy* 76, no. 4, pt. 1, August, 1968, pp. 635–44. Charles Hession (1972) raises a similar point, arguing that while in *The Affluent Society* Galbraith saw aggressive competition on the part of corporations leading to a rampant consumption of material goods, *The New Industrial State* presents a view of corporations as coordinated institutions circumventing the competition of the market. Hession concludes that the extent of this coordination is overstated and misses the "interindustry" competition that continues to exist in the market. Please see Charles Hession, *John Kenneth Galbraith and His Critics* (New York: W. W. Norton, 1972).

18. Galbraith, *New Industrial State*, pp. 146–63, also pp. 312–17.

19. Galbraith, *New Industrial State*, pp. 267–68.

20. Galbraith, *New Industrial State*, pp. 257–69. Richard Parker (2004) argues that Galbraith's characterization of the nature of contemporary capitalism has endured criticism from a variety of perspectives over the years, but many of these alternatives have come up as failures when put into practice in various regions of the world. Parker argues that the validity of Galbraith's economic orientation is becoming ap-

parent, even to some of his former critics. For more on this evaluation of Galbraith, please see Richard Parker, "The Legacy of John Kenneth Galbraith," *Challenge* 47, no. 2, March–April, 2004, pp. 81–89. Arthur Schlesinger Jr. (1984) offers an insightful analysis of the political dimensions in Galbraith's work, including his refutation of neoclassical economics, his opposition to the Vietnam war, and his liberal social policies. Please see Arthur Schlesinger Jr., "The Political Galbraith," *Journal of Post Keynesian Economics* 7, no. 1, Fall, 1984, pp. 7–17.

21. Galbraith, *New Industrial State*, pp. 53, 257–69.

22. Galbraith, *New Industrial State*, pp. 263–65.

23. Galbraith, *New Industrial State*, pp. 267–69. Myron Sharpe (1973) contends that although Galbraith's image of the rise of an intellectual vanguard class sounds appealing, it is unrealistic and fails to acknowledge the overlapping associations typical of contemporary forms of social organization. Please see Myron Sharpe, *John Kenneth Galbraith and the Lower Economics* (White Plains, NY: International Arts and Sciences Press, 1973).

24. Galbraith, *New Industrial State*, pp. 265–69.

25. Galbraith, *New Industrial State*, pp. 267–69.

26. Galbraith, *New Industrial State*, pp. 295–310. Barry Smart (2003) characterized Galbraith as drawing on the classical approach to social analysis, taking a broad view, and factoring in economic, social, and cultural considerations. Smart distinguishes this approach from the more specialized forms of inquiry that are increasingly common in the social sciences today. For more on this assessment, please see Barry Smart, "An Economic Turn: Galbraith and Classical Sociology," *Journal of Classical Sociology* 3, no. 1, March, 2003, pp. 47–66.

27. Galbraith, *New Industrial State*, pp. 340–50.

28. Galbraith, *New Industrial State*, pp. 295–310. David Reisman (1980) challenged Galbraith's position on this issue, particularly his characterization of scholars as capable of acting independently of institutional pressures in a coordinated fashion. Reisman argued that this "Platonic" vision of Galbraith fails to acknowledge the power of ideas in shaping the course of history. For more on this evaluation of Galbraith, please see David A. Reisman, *Galbraith and Market Capitalism* (New York: New York University Press, 1980). Also see David A. Reisman, "Galbraith on Ideas and Events," *Journal of Economic Issues* 24, no. 3, September, 1990, pp. 733–60.

29. Galbraith, *New Industrial State*, pp. 257–69, 295–310.

30. Galbraith, *New Industrial State*, pp. 349, 350. James Stanfield (1996) provides a solid overview of a number of Galbraith's works, including his views on the relationship between knowledge and politics. Please see James Stanfield, *John Kenneth Galbraith* (New York: St. Martin's, 1996). Also see the collection of essays on John Kenneth Galbraith, compiled and edited by Michael Keaney, entitled *Economist With a Public Purpose: Essays in Honour of John Kenneth Galbraith* (London; New York: Routledge, 2001).

31. Galbraith, *New Industrial State*, pp. 336–42.

32. Guy Oakes and Arthur Vidich (1999) offer significant insight into the ways Mills' effort to boost his own career played a role in shaping the nature of his approach to social inquiry. Oakes and Vidich argue that Mills aspired to be a major player in the field and did so in many respects at the cost of his intellectual integrity. These two authors also delve into the issue of ethics in academic life generally, identifying and

challenging some of the common practices in the social sciences today. Please see Guy Oakes and Arthur J. Vidich, *Collaboration, Reputation, and Ethics in American Academic Life: Hans Gerth and C. Wright Mills* (Urbana, Chicago: University of Illinois Press, 1999).

33. The difficulty in assessing Mills' position on this question lies in his apparent tendency to straddle conflicting traditions. Some have argued, for example, that his call to inject an element of reason into politics seems to contradict his concern to prevent the rationalization of the social order. E. P. Thompson (1979) claims that this tension is resolved via the implicit distinction in Mills' work between the intellectual as "expert" and the intellectual as "craftsman." Thompson argues that rather than calling on intellectuals to use specialized knowledge in the scientific management of society, Mills suggested they challenge dominant institutions with the evidence and analysis of social inquiry. In Thompson's view, Mills had little hope in the ability of the working class to bring about the sort of changes he thought were needed and turned instead to intellectuals to play this revolutionary role. Mills maintained that too many young intellectuals were succumbing to the expectations of government and business, further bureaucratizing knowledge, and restricting the range of public debate on key issues. Thompson points out that writing during the Cold War led Mills to challenge the simplistic dichotomies of the period and implore intellectuals to develop analyses that directly confronted the problems of their time. For more on this assessment of Mills, please see E. P. Thompson, "C. Wright Mills: The Responsible Craftsman," *Radical America* 13, no. 4, July–August, 1979, pp. 61–73. Jim Miller (1986) also places the ideologies of the Cold War at the center of Mills' analysis of intellectuals, citing his contempt for those who simply echoed the positions of officialdom in both East and West. In Miller's view, Mills was obsessively concerned with the complacency and powerlessness of intellectuals and sought desperately to counteract their tendency to legitimate corrupt institutions and irresponsible leaders. Mills saw a strong connection between the independence of intellectual analysis and the existence of an autonomous and informed public, arguing that the latter was essential to the maintenance of effective government and responsible leadership. He saw the stereotypical visions of society promoted by the system of mass communications as cutting intellectuals off from potential publics, and appealed to intellectuals to expose the fallacy of these visions and offer more insightful and relevant assessments in their place. Please see Jim Miller, "Democracy and the Intellectual: C. Wright Mills Reconsidered," *Salmagundi*, nos. 70–71, Spring–Summer, 1986, pp. 82–101. Christopher Lasch (1986) argues that Mills places intellectuals in the position of Marx's proletariat, where the factory-like conditions under which they are expected to work, their alienation from the substance of their work, the demands for efficiency, and the prospect of large-scale unemployment all contribute to their disenchantment and tarnish their attitude toward the established order. Lasch sees Mills' attempt to stir the revolutionary potential of the intellectuals as dangerous because it appeals to their hopes to change the world and takes away from their role as interpreters of it. Please see Christopher Lasch, "A Typology of Intellectuals: II. The Example of C. Wright Mills," *Salmagundi*, nos. 70–71, Spring–Summer, 1986, pp. 102–7.

34. One can see the influence of Veblen on this aspect of Mills' writing. For further insight into his position on this question, see chapter 3, "Abstracted Empiricism," in

C. Wright Mills, *The Sociological Imagination* (New York: Oxford University Press, 1959).

35. Mills, *Sociological Imagination*, pp. 85–90.

36. Mills cites Paul Lazarsfeld's claim that "sociology is not yet in the stage where it can provide a safe basis for social engineering" as evidence of this belief. For more on this, see *Sociological Imagination*, p. 100.

37. Mills, *Sociological Imagination*, p. 114.

38. Mills, *Sociological Imagination*, p. 115.

39. For Mills' comments on the bureaucratic outlook in the social sciences, see "The Bureaucratic Ethos," in *Sociological Imagination*, pp. 100–118.

40. Mills, "Bureaucratic Ethos," p. 105.

41. Mills, *Sociological Imagination*, pp. 3–24.

42. Mills, *Sociological Imagination*, pp. 132–42, 165–94.

43. Mills, *Sociological Imagination*, p. 194.

44. Christopher Lasch (1987) argues that throughout his career, Mills demonstrated a consistent view of intellectuals as the voice of reason, conscience, and imagination in public life. Mills took it upon himself to live up to these expectations and abided by these standards in his own work. For more on this perspective, please see Christopher Lasch, "Conscience, Reason, and Imagination: C. Wright Mills and the Life of the Mind," *Social Science* 72, no. 1, Spring, 1987, pp. 81–85.

45. Mills, *Sociological Imagination*, pp. 177–94.

46. For a detailed account of this transition, see J. Michael Sproule, "Propaganda Studies in American Social Science: The Rise and Fall of the Critical Paradigm," *Quarterly Journal of Speech* 73, 1987, pp. 60–78, and "Progressive Propaganda Critics and the Magic Bullet Myth," *Critical Studies in Mass Communication* 6, no. 3, September, 1989, pp. 225–46.

47. John Kenneth Galbraith, *The Good Society: The Humane Agenda* (Boston: Houghton Mifflin, 1996). Also see *New Industrial State*, pp. 267, 268, 296–302.

48. In an unpublished manuscript entitled "The Cultural Apparatus," Mills addressed several key issues associated with public opinion, media, and social change. Kim Sawchuk reviews this manuscript and contends that Mills' analyses were one step ahead of what is now the field of cultural studies. Please see Kim Sawchuk, "The Cultural Apparatus: C. Wright Mills' Unfinished Work," *American Sociologist* 32, no. 1, Spring, 2001, pp. 27–49.

49. Mills, *Power Elite*, pp. 359–61.

50. Mills, *Power Elite*, p. 356.

51. Mills, *Power Elite*, pp. 343–61.

52. C. Wright Mills, *Power, Politics and People: The Collected Essays of C. Wright Mills*, ed. Irving Horowitz (New York: Oxford University Press, 1963; orig. pub. 1944).

53. Galbraith, *New Industrial State*, pp. 331–35.

6

Pierre Bourdieu:
Intellectuals, Symbolic Power,
and Social Change

The spread of state-centered capitalism following World War II continued into the 1980s and 1990s, facilitating the ongoing integration of the industrial nations and advancing the institutional consolidation observed by Mills and Galbraith. Transnational corporations became increasingly powerful in shaping the course of politics at the national level, and government bureaucracies continued to grow in response to their burgeoning administrative demands. Public officials focused their rhetoric on domestic issues but formed policy objectives in relation to these larger economic and political changes. Even the more powerful nations of the world yielded to this newer wave of structural pressures, confirming the presence of what had truly become a global political economy.

Pierre Bourdieu developed his analyses in the midst of this transformation, writing extensively on national and local cultures, the institutional hierarchies of academia, and the practices and ideas of intellectuals. His initial interests centered in the area of philosophy, and early in his career he addressed questions relating to epistemology, ethics, and aesthetics. He held a deep respect for the French philosophical tradition but also recognized some of its inherent limitations. Bourdieu understood, for instance, that the practice of self-examination and critique within this milieu served as a valuable way to broaden one's consciousness, but he also felt that the colloquialism of French academic life narrowed the scope of its basic assumptions and constrained the perspicacity of its insight.[1]

He turned to sociology and anthropology as a way to address these concerns and better understand the connections between ideas and the social conditions of their formation. He was particularly impressed with the work of Claude Lévi-Strauss and the emphasis of structuralism on the interplay

between habits of thought and patterns of behavior in constituting the social order in a given setting. He was also critical of the determinism of this
orientation and its tendency to view individual actors as puppets on a string,
destined to follow the paths set for them by larger natural and social forces.
He sought to balance this structural bias with the existentialism of Jean-Paul
Sartre, taking into consideration the ways actors create the social world
around them and looking more closely at the relationship between structure
and agency in the social world.[2]

Bourdieu applied this set of perspectives to the realm of politics, and he
developed a critique of the ways symbolic forces intersected with the structural conditions in French society to create the kinds of patterns he saw unfolding in his time. He observed that political decision making in France had
become closely tied to the organizational structure of its institutions, and that
this arrangement served to maintain the advantageous position of the dominant classes from one generation to the next. He embraced Weber's concept
of legitimacy and the notion that the state relies heavily on the management
of public perception to sustain itself, but he also argued that Weber failed to
sufficiently theorize the ways the state monopolizes the process of creating
and legitimating social forms.[3] Bourdieu focused on the routine practices
that enable the state to maintain what he called a "monopoly of the universal." He observed that in France in particular, the state had extended its ideological influence through education and the media, and this had had a profound impact on the development of everyday knowledge and on the
directions of public policy. Under the guise of disinterestedness and a loyalty to the common good, the state seeks to promote interpretations of the
social world that resonate with conventional beliefs while at the same time
advancing its own institutional goals, steadily weaving its interests and perspectives into the discourse of everyday life.[4] A consequence of this over
time is that the state comes to play a very powerful role in constructing the
classification schemes, starting assumptions, and ways of thinking that are
accepted among members of the wider population, and these in turn influence the course of politics at a fundamental level.[5]

> By stating with authority what a being (thing or person) is in truth (verdict) ac-
> cording to its socially legitimate definition, that is what he or she is authorized
> to be, what he has a right (and duty) to be, the social being that he may claim,
> the State wields a genuinely *creative*, quasi-divine, power. It suffices to think of
> the kind of immortality that it can grant through acts of consecration such as
> commemorations or scholarly canonization, to see how, twisting Hegel's fa-
> mous expression, we may say that: "the judgement of the state is the last judge-
> ment."[6]

Bourdieu argued that many people living within the confines of industrial
democracies fail to understand the subtle forms of domination inherent in

this milieu and routinely come to accept institutional perspectives as legitimate reflections of the undisputed truth. They do this, in part, because they are typically unaware of the arbitrary way these perspectives are formed and see them as grounded on the basis of solid fact. They are thus inclined to rely on established frames of knowledge to make sense of their surrounding environment and incorporate these perspectives into their own worldview.[7] This can happen even when the prevailing truths of a given social order do not bear much resemblance to economic and political realities. Bourdieu characterized this as the formation of a "collective unconscious," claiming that as institutional knowledge becomes increasingly widespread and embedded into mainstream culture, it is increasingly difficult to challenge, even though it may be fraught with internal contradictions and substantial weaknesses.[8]

Although some individuals reject the legitimacy of conventional belief, even the bearers of nonconformist positions are inclined to rely on the fundamentals of mainstream social thought in developing alternate points of view. Bourdieu maintained that critics who internalize institutionally derived perspectives and incorporate them into their own analyses are essentially strengthening the existing order. To the extent that this order is repressive, they are further contributing to their own subordination.[9]

He found a key example of this in the world of intellectuals, observing that while many French social thinkers present themselves as radical critics of the existing order, their assessments often indirectly support the goals of the dominant classes. They do this by developing formulations within the framework of the same starting assumptions and schemes of categorization inherent in the very ways of thinking they claimed to be attacking. To Bourdieu, this practice actually serves to enhance the credibility of traditional knowledge and undermine the efforts of thinkers attempting to develop qualitatively unique alternatives to the dominant worldview. "I believe that the blindness of intellectuals to the social forces which rule the intellectual field, and therefore their practices, is what explains that, collectively, often under very radical airs, the intelligentsia almost always contribute to the perpetuation of dominant forces."[10]

Intellectuals relying on the standard frames of knowledge in their field are also more likely to receive the institutional support they need to advance their career goals and solidify the legitimacy of their position from a professional standpoint.[11] Bourdieu observed that some intellectuals are able to successfully navigate these waters and align themselves with political and economic organizations, either in a research or advisory capacity. He added that those in this setting most often operate at a subordinate level, developing analyses and conclusions in relation to the concerns and goals of their more politically powerful superiors. Although their expertise in the symbolic arena renders their work an indispensable component of public policy formation, intellectuals have throughout history taken a backseat to political power. In light of this tendency, Bourdieu characterized intellectuals in general as "the dominated fraction of the dominant class." He claimed that while they had indeed come to play a significant role in the workings of the powerful, this did not provide them with any degree of independent authority in the political realm.[12]

Bourdieu observed a similar phenomenon occurring in the dynamics between intellectuals and members of the larger population. He saw that in France, the divisions between writings of an esoteric nature and those designed for a wider audience became blurred in the 1980s and 1990s as market pressures continued to push avant-garde ideas into the margins.[13] He was very critical of "the industrial literature," stating that while there was a place for this kind of writing in the contemporary world, the rising expectation that all published material fit into the rubric of market demand produced a growing abundance of low-level, popular analyses, which in turn tended to overshadow more subtle assessments. Relying on the forces of the market as a guide in determining the quality of intellectual work creates an environment where important but complex ideas have little opportunity to become salient in the public domain. This muffles the voices of intellectuals whose formulations could raise the level of political debate on a wide range of social issues. It shifts the focus of public attention to ideas that are more provocative or entertaining but less rigorous and less able to withstand substantial critique.[14]

Bourdieu claimed that the institutions of the mass media in France had become highly influential in accepting, promoting, and interpreting intellectual analyses, significantly shaping the character and focus of social thought at the public level. He did not take the position that media institutions in industrial democracies directly control public knowledge, but that their ability to select and frame social events and information gives them a great deal of power in deciding which messages reach broader segments of the population, and this in turn plays a large part in defining the perspectives of mainstream political consciousness. This pattern is nothing new, but from Bourdieu's vantage point, it had become much more pronounced in the second half of the twentieth century as television and other forms of electronic communication took center stage, and as the flow of information became increasingly unidirectional.[15]

Bourdieu's concern in this regard centered on the growing interconnections of government and media institutions in France. He saw that these organizations were so intertwined that they had come to resemble one another in terms of their logic and goals. Public policy experts forged ties with their cohorts in the media and promoted interpretations of social issues that resonated with their collective concerns. Technocrats, journalists, marketing

advisors, and opinion-polling experts gradually took on the tasks traditionally reserved for intellectuals, creating new forms of institutional knowledge
and connecting it to the matrix of everyday understanding. The ideas of this
new media-centered network moved public debate in a direction consonant
with official ideas and objectives. Bourdieu labeled the members of this
group the "mediatic" intellectuals, arguing that they tend to project an image
of being independent and critical, while actually developing analyses in relation to institutional forms of knowledge and ongoing trends in popular belief.[16] This shifts the framework of public discussion to accommodate the interests of industry and business, and frames political issues in very simple
terms, as though they were merely technical questions to be addressed by
experts. Bourdieu called this "the technocracy of communication" and argued that the combined efforts of these institutional voices helps to create
the newer boundaries of legitimate public discourse.

> One of the characteristics of journalistic judgment is that, for want of the neces-
> sary capacities of discernment, journalists systematically mix in their judgments
> the most autonomous and the most heteronomous producers—the latter being
> "essays," true doxosophers in the sense of Plato, whose mastery of the art of ap-
> pearances, like that of advertising agents, pollsters, journalists, etc., allows them
> to create the appearance of science.[17]

Media influence from Bourdieu's point of view is not purely propaganda or
organized deception, but an ongoing "babble" filling up and overcrowding
the space where meaningful, insightful, and informed discussion could take
place.[18]

This situation leaves competent intellectuals with a difficult choice. They
can attempt to communicate through the media and take the chance of
having their ideas be distorted, misunderstood, or exploited, or they can
remain silent and refrain from participating in public discussions to avoid
this risk. When faced with this dilemma, many choose the latter option and
stay out of public life as much as possible, lowering the caliber of political
debate and further undermining the potential for informed democratic participation.[19]

Bourdieu conceded that there are some intellectuals who do strive to
achieve high standards in their work and possess a sincere desire to form incisive and relevant conclusions of the contemporary social world. He acknowledged that members of this group tend to be interested in sharing their
ideas with others and influencing the directions of political decision making.
But he held that the institutional orders within which intellectuals develop
and disseminate their views are fraught with hidden obstacles, and these often shape the content of intellectual knowledge and the ideas that become
prominent in the domain of public discussion in the long run.[20]

POLITICAL KNOWLEDGE AND
THE WORLD OF SOCIAL SCIENCE

Bourdieu observed that French intellectuals had steadily made their way into the realm of academia throughout the latter decades of the twentieth century, and he studied the relationship of this trend to the changes in social thought in this period. He maintained that intellectuals operating within the confines of the university are less able to form independent perspectives and typically find themselves in the position of having to abide by the norms, traditions, and worldviews that are dominant within their particular academic field. He focused primarily on social science, arguing that its ongoing relevance placed it at the center of the connections between knowledge and politics. Since the subject matter of social science is inherently tied to important political questions, its fields often become battlegrounds for competing factions seeking to legitimate predetermined political agendas. These struggles can result in overt ideological conflict, but they can also manifest themselves in more subtle ways, at the level of everyday interpersonal interaction. Bourdieu maintained that conflict is evident even in areas of research that seem on the surface to be neutral or meritocratic, and can significantly influence the directions of social thought in the field over time.[21]

The system of hierarchy, for instance, is crucial in shaping the kinds of ideas that become salient in a given field. The high level of competition in the social sciences creates a strong incentive for beginning researchers to conscientiously abide by the norms and traditions in their discipline. As newcomers strive to establish themselves professionally, they are inclined to adjust the focus and tenor of their work to follow in the footsteps of their predecessors. Those who perform well within the confines of these limitations—both in terms of their personal interactions and in their research—are likely to gain the admiration and support of their more experienced colleagues. As they make their way up the hierarchical ladder, they tend to adhere to the strategies that brought them earlier success, further solidifying the legitimacy of the standard practices and predominant systems of thought in their field. Rather than acting as free thinkers developing new assessments of the world, social scientists in this environment tend to become the purveyors of conventional modes of investigation and the supporters of accepted belief.[22]

Bourdieu also observed the inclination of social scientists to uncritically accept and emulate the work of scholars who have reached the higher levels of prestige in their field. He saw that in France in particular, the more influential figures in the social sciences tended to garner praise, even when their ideas were not very insightful or profound. Having achieved this status, he argued, they are then in a position to create very mundane or even contradictory conclusions about the social world and face little in the way of substantial criticism. This further narrows the range of thought within each

discipline and lessens the possibility that new ideas can emerge from the social sciences on a regular basis.[23]

OBJECTIVISM VERSUS SUBJECTIVISM

Bourdieu characterized social scientific knowledge as directly related to the
starting orientations of scholars involved in research. He argued that the underlying theoretical assumptions in a given field can play a crucial role in shaping the ways an investigation is conducted and alter the nature of its conclusions. These prevailing assumptions are typically unstated, but they are widely
understood and routinely employed by the researchers in each discipline.[24]
One of his principal observations in this regard centered on the notion of objectivity and the belief among social scientists that their task is to develop findings of a purely objective nature. He was particularly critical of American researchers and their claim to be operating on the basis of a disinterested
attitude. To Bourdieu, social scientists are perhaps the most skilled of any
group in weaving their own personal biases into analyses that appear on the
surface to be objective. They are typically very reluctant to reveal their own social location and starting assumptions when engaging in research, and seek instead to paint an image of themselves as impartial observers, primarily interested in discovering objective facts about the social world. Bourdieu drew on
Weber in challenging this assertion, arguing that while the goal of research is
to work toward clarity of understanding, social science is an inherently interpretive endeavor, grounded in the norms and cultural orientations of its practitioners. He maintained that social scientists have an obligation to limit the extent to which values play a role in their research, but he did not conclude from
this assertion that any investigation could ever be completely value free.[25]

Bourdieu argued that the belief in absolute objectivity became more common in American social science as investigators increasingly relied on standard methodologies and formal theoretical models in their studies. The underlying assumption of this approach is that formalizing investigative
procedures lessens the extent to which personal bias can enter into the equation. Bourdieu argued that while this practice may give social scientists the
sense that they are transcending interpretation, it does not reduce the extent
to which they are involved in constructing their subject matter, sometimes on
the basis of their own orientations, but most often in relation to the prevailing perspectives in their field. In this sense, social scientists operating within
the objectivist framework often fail to realize that they are relying on subjective definitions and socially defined systems of classification in drawing up
the frameworks of their studies, and that these set the foundation for their
conclusions. Rather than facilitating absolute objectivity, the practice of following standard procedures ensures that researchers are operating within

the perspectival boundaries of their field, which in turn helps to strengthen the legitimacy of their findings. To Bourdieu, the tendency of social scientists to uncritically rely on conventional thought locks them into ways of knowing that ironically interfere with their ability to form new insight into the social world and challenge the common myths circulating in society at a broader level.[26]

> In short, studies that simply confirm the constructions of common sense and ordinary discourse by transcribing everyday assumptions into scientific definitions have every chance of being approved by the scholarly community and its audiences, especially if they comply strictly with the more superficial rules of scientific discipline, whereas research that breaks with the false obviousness and the apparent neutrality of the constructions of common sense—including scholarly common sense (*sens commun savant*)—is always in danger of appearing to be the result of an act of arbitrary imposition, if not of ideological bias, and of being denounced as deliberately producing the data fit to validate them (which all scientific constructions do).[27]

Bourdieu saw the pursuit of objectivity as a normative tendency tied to the ongoing struggles for power within the larger social order. He characterized this orientation as part of the upper-class effort to distance itself from the vulgarity of middle- and lower-class groups and from the working-class focus on material needs. Operating from the standpoint of the objectivist position is seen in this sense as a task that requires a refined level of insight and is therefore of a higher order than the more common forms of understanding of everyday life. This reinforces the idea of a heightened sensitivity among the upper classes with regard to the realities of the social order, and provides an incentive for social climbers to aspire to this view.[28]

While he criticized the tendency of the positivists to neglect the socially constructed nature of the categories they employ, Bourdieu also challenged many of the underlying assumptions of the subjectivist position and refuted some of the central proclamations of the postmodernists. He acknowledged the normative nature of social science but also argued that building assessments of the world on the basis of relativism was contradictory and politically irresponsible. One of its main contradictions, from Bourdieu's point of view, is that it involves the presentation of unstated or hidden assertions—such as the idea that truth is relative—while at the same time claiming the impossibility of a grounding for such assertions. He pointed out that when postmodernists do this, they are actually putting forth truth claims of their own in spite of their effort to present an image of themselves as having escaped that trap.[29]

> There is today, for example, a neo-nihilist current called postmodernism, which originated in France and which now also spreads in the United States. It is a sort

of campus radicalism which depends on challenging the kinds of questions that I have formulated so as to deny the possibility of a social science. It is said, for example, "All science is text, and what the anthropologists bring back with them from the field are texts; there are only ever texts on texts, metatexts: reality does not exist." This means that young French ethnologists can produce "brilliant" work without ever going through the considerable ordeal of actual field work. What is the point of field work if it is only going to result in a text? This is a French perversion.[30]

Bourdieu saw this approach as irresponsible in that it emphasizes the notion that no single conclusion is inherently superior to any other, and that one can only make such a determination using subjective criteria. This implies a comparable level of adequacy in all interpretations of the social world and negates the possibility of assessing the validity of any social analyses. He argued that the attempt to deny the legitimacy of evaluating criteria places simplistic and speculative positions on a par with those formed on the basis of rigorous empirical investigation. He was particularly critical of the deconstructionists and their unwillingness to take a firm stand on political issues, arguing that this served to further obscure the nature of domination in the social order and enable power holders to escape criticism. Thus, in spite of his critique of the objectivist orientation, Bourdieu maintained the view that the primary aim of social research is to develop a deeper understanding of the social world, and that an awareness of its interpretive dimension does not relieve researchers of their responsibility to work toward this goal.[31]

In rejecting the polar extremes of relativism and positivism, Bourdieu developed an intermediary position that acknowledged the subjective aspects of social science, while at the same time emphasizing its potential to reveal new knowledge about the social world.[32] He directed and participated in a number of studies using both qualitative and quantitative data, and argued that social research—when done properly and with a full view of its strengths and limitations—can be of a higher order than less systematic forms of inquiry. Much of his own work involved gathering empirical data, but he did not attempt to put these findings together solely on the basis of the standard systems of classification in sociology. Instead, he relied on a broader conceptual framework, taking into consideration the formulations of philosophy, economics, and politics, as well as his own theoretical constructs.[33] He understood that engaging in social analysis involves observing and deciphering aspects of the world in ways that do not simply mimic the fundamental precepts of one's colleagues. Researchers are inevitably involved in making some form of judgment about their subject matter, but this fact alone does not necessarily lower the caliber of their work. It is very possible, Bourdieu argued, to be cognizant of one's own subjectivity while at the same time developing insightful and relevant conclusions about the social world.[34]

In his attempt to strike a balance between these two extremes, Bourdieu stated that the emphasis on empirical observation characteristic of American social science served as a valuable counterweight to the tendency in France to develop conclusions in relation to philosophical considerations. He also suggested that the insights of French scholars into epistemological and theoretical questions provided the understanding needed to temper the positivist inclinations of the American tradition.[35] The strengths in each of these two approaches, when put together in a self-conscious manner, could yield much more interesting and revealing interpretations of the social world than either one could do on its own. Bourdieu's overriding conclusion in this regard was that researchers have a responsibility to rely on systematically derived data in their work and to interpret this data with an informed perspective and a willingness to consider new modes of understanding each step of the way.[36]

THE GOALS OF SOCIAL RESEARCH

In outlining the characteristics of what he considered to be an enlightened form of social inquiry, Bourdieu devoted much of his attention to the notion of reflexivity. He maintained that scholars often proceed in their investigations with only a vague awareness of the ways their own background and social position may be shaping the directions, framing, and conclusions of their research. He suggested they focus on these factors in order to address some of the ways their own research might be skewed as a result. To Bourdieu, recognizing such influences can be liberating in that it has the potential to reveal some of the ingrained but unconscious habits of thought that researchers routinely rely on in their work. Being aware of and acknowledging one's own predispositions and the conventional perspectives of one's field can, in this sense, be a way to move beyond them.[37]

> By turning the instruments of social science back upon himself, in the very movement whereby he constructs his objects, the social scientist opens up the possibility of escaping yet another fateful, and apparently insuperable, antinomy: that between historicism and rationalism. A genuinely reflexive social science, then, gives its practitioners appropriate motives and appropriate weapons for grasping and fighting the social and historical determinants of scientific practice.[38]

The goal of reflexivity is thus to broaden the scope of social inquiry and build a more self-conscious and influential discipline. What it can do is help social scientists free themselves from their illusions, "and first of all from the illusion that they do not have any."[39] In particular, he hoped it would enable them to better understand the ways their work has historically served to maintain the legitimacy of the dominant classes, and perhaps lessen the extent to which they do this in the future.[40]

In addition to emphasizing the importance of reflexivity, Bourdieu also encouraged social scientists to recognize the inherently critical dimensions of their work. He argued that even though some scholars may not realize this, the basic statements they make are forms of criticism or condemnation and have a political dimension to them. He focused on sociology in particular when making this assertion, arguing that it is, at its core, a form of investigation that challenges the fundamental assumptions of everyday social life. For instance, the simple act of studying and analyzing the class structure of a given society can serve as the foundation for a harsh critique of its underlying system of organization. It can expose the myth of equality in regions where opinion leaders seek to promote the notion of a level playing field for all members. To Bourdieu, the process of examining the social world with the goal of genuinely trying to understand it and then conveying that understanding to others is itself a radical endeavor. It is a means through which to challenge the symbolic monopoly traditionally held by society's dominant political and economic institutions, and it opens the door to alternative perspectives.[41]

Bourdieu argued that the social sciences can be reflexive and critical only when they are not controlled by powerful institutions and when scholars are able to maintain some level of independence in their work. He pointed out that the struggle for autonomy has been a central concern of social scientists throughout modern history. One of the main issues they have had to deal with is the question of who has the power to select and define the problems considered to be worthy of investigation. He observed that in France in particular, the state had come to take on much of this role, using its influence to push research in directions best serving its larger objectives.[42] This leaves social scientists in the position of having to design their investigations in relation to prevailing institutional goals, fitting their own perceptions and concerns into a predetermined starting framework. Catering to state pressures in this way diminishes the political influence of social science and undermines its potential to independently form the foundations of knowledge, not only in academia but in the broader society as well. Bourdieu argued that without this level of autonomy, social research ceases to be scientific and reflects instead the vested interests of its supporters.[43]

In spite of these concerns, Bourdieu was not completely pessimistic about the prospect of expanding the autonomy of social science, and he cited examples in which social science maintained a degree of independence as it evolved throughout modern history. He stated that one of the most important assets of social scientists is their ability to critically evaluate each other's work on the basis of the collective standards of judgment in their respective fields. Although in some contexts these standards have been compromised by administrative and financial pressures, this practice continues to stand as a fundamental component of social research that has protected the field against unsubstantiated claims and poorly formed interpretations and conclusions.[44] Bourdieu argued that it is crucial for social scientists to recognize the significance of this tradition and take the steps necessary to preserve and enhance it. The goal of doing this is not to help one's colleagues retreat into the safety and security of the ivory tower, but to assist them in building the organizational structure they need to stay connected to the activities of the outside world, while at the same time maintaining at least some degree of control over the focus and character of their work. To the extent that they strengthen peer-based forms of evaluation, social scientists are broadening the intellectual autonomy in their field.[45]

Bourdieu was aware of the many ways social research has been compromised, but he maintained that it has the potential to reveal new insight into a host of important issues. Rather than merely pointing to the faults of social scientists, he appealed to them to look at themselves critically and approach their work in a more self-conscious and deliberate manner. His hope was that they would move beyond the habit of engaging in research on the basis of unconscious, ritualistic traditions and take the steps necessary to raise the caliber of their analyses in the future.[46]

INTELLECTUAL AUTONOMY AND POLITICAL PARTICIPATION

Bourdieu characterized the issue of intellectual autonomy as part of a broader pattern of conflict between intellectuals and the organizational pressures they encounter on a regular basis. This tension typically emerges in relation to the efforts of powerful political groups seeking to rein in the ideas of intellectuals and keep them within a circumscribed set of boundaries. In addition to setting up barriers to the formation of iconoclastic ideas, established institutions provide the incentives intellectuals need to work cooperatively with them and create the symbolic justification for their objectives. In France, the state had become the largest employer of intellectuals and was very influential in determining the conditions of their employment. As an impersonal, bureaucratic organization, it projected an image of neutrality while at the same time preventing intellectuals from stepping too far outside the limitations considered appropriate by the dominant classes. Bourdieu knew this trend would be difficult to challenge, but he hoped intellectuals would eventually see beyond their own narrow worlds to acknowledge the common underpinnings of their efforts and realize the extent to which this conflict is a fundamental component of the work they do.[47]

To Bourdieu, the ongoing effort to broaden intellectual autonomy is at its core a political task that involves operating at the level of very practical,

everyday problems. He argued that intellectuals have historically been ambivalent about their involvement in politics and tend to be unsure of how to
intervene, even at times when circumstances demand that they do so. Their
habit of advocating a separation between pure thought and engagement
leads them to view participation in politics as likely to undermine the credibility of their conclusions. Bourdieu saw some merit to this argument and
agreed that when intellectuals do maintain a degree of distance from power,
they are better able to critically evaluate it.[48] But he also argued that intellectuals have a series of collective interests, and that the ethic of avoiding political involvement completely has historically interfered with their potential
to address these broader concerns in a direct and self-conscious manner.[49]

Rather than asserting their own interests, intellectuals tend to enter the political realm as "fellow travelers," associating their work with the causes of
other groups.[50] They are inclined to latch on to what they perceive to be the
goals of one oppressed segment of society or another, indirectly playing a
part in political affairs while at the same time trying to maintain an image of
themselves as unattached and impartial observers. Bourdieu argued that this
approach fails to acknowledge the basic fact that in order to effectively defend the interests of others, an effort must first be made to strengthen the position of the defenders themselves.[51] Without at least a minimal level of autonomy, intellectuals cannot have the power to bring about the kinds of
social change they claim to be advocating.

He observed that successful campaigns to foster intellectual independence
in the past have been inherently social. He cited the Dreyfus affair as a classic example of this, pointing out that it was not until the intellectuals involved found themselves backed into a corner that they came out of the
ivory tower and acted collectively to defend their own goals. When operating as individuals, he argued, intellectuals are far less powerful than they believe themselves to be, but when working together, they have much more
power than they realize.[52]

> This is something that intellectuals very seldom recognize, who are typically in-
> clined to think in singular fashion and who expect salvation from individual lib-
> eration, in the logic of wisdom and initiatory conquest. Intellectuals too often
> forget that there is a politics of intellectual freedom. On the basis of everything
> I have said, one can clearly see that an emancipatory science is possible only if
> the social and political conditions that make it possible are gathered.[53]

Bourdieu drew attention to the fact that in Europe, the technocrats, bankers,
and business leaders managed to garner a significant degree of influence in the
world of politics, but intellectuals on the whole continued to be largely powerless in this domain. He proposed that intellectuals work together to
strengthen their position and more effectively achieve their goals in the public
arena. To this end, he advocated the formation of an international collective of

intellectuals, committed to addressing matters of autonomy as well as a broader range of social and political issues throughout the world. This collective would be organized in a self-conscious and deliberate manner, with an emphasis on political involvement. It would enable intellectuals to retain individuality in their own work, but would also provide them with a means through which to communicate and interact with one another across local, regional, and national boundaries. He did not envision it as a centralized monolithic institution with a fixed hierarchical framework, but as a loosely structured, informal network with no concentrated center. It would be capable of accommodating diverse perspectives and goals and would place a high level of importance on intellectual freedom.[54]

> This is a difficult state to achieve. It is a task to which I have devoted myself for a long time. I am trying to organize intellectuals in such a way that they can intervene collectively using their specific competences. For example, we have just organized a committee with the aim of supporting Algerian intellectuals. And we are in a very complex situation. The fact that we are a group of competent intellectuals is very important because the individual political biases that anyone may have are corrected by his/her membership in the group, through discussions and so on. In particular, specific competences can be accumulated, and in accumulating our competences we produce complex (multidimensional) judgments which are absolutely different from what could be achieved by the universal intellectual in the Sartrean sense, or the specific intellectual in Foucault's conception, not to mention Gramsci's organic intellectual, who is pure mythology.[55]

Bourdieu knew that there would be major obstacles to the formation of such a collective and that his ideal in this regard would be subject to harsh critique in many circles. He understood that this goal ran counter to the sensibilities of independent thinkers and that some would see it as an attempt to pressure intellectuals to form a unified perspective or to accept positions that did not resonate with their own views. He was well aware of the contradictions involved in trying to coordinate the actions of a group whose members prided themselves on individuality, but argued that intellectual autonomy was something that could be maintained and broadened only through a collective effort. From his standpoint, unless intellectuals realized this fundamental fact and acted together to defend their interests, they would likely see their independence diminish over time.[56] And without working together, politics at the national and transnational levels would continue to drift in its current direction, with little possibility of positive change in the future. Bourdieu did not expect intellectuals to be able to dramatically alter the course of human history in a sudden or revolutionary way, but saw them as integrated social actors, capable of playing an ongoing role in changing society in a gradual fashion. He felt that a network of this sort would strengthen their influence among political leaders and give them a more powerful voice in the realm of public affairs.[57]

In a style reminiscent of Veblen, Bourdieu first established the basics of his ideal and then reverted to the position that it was largely untenable in the present context. He argued that although an international collective would certainly elevate the political influence of intellectuals, on the whole they were not quite ready for it yet. He listed a range of practical obstacles to their working together on a global scale and did not see it as something that would likely come to fruition in the near future.[58]

One of the more significant obstacles he observed in this regard was the widespread misunderstanding common in the international exchange of ideas. He pointed out that while intellectuals tend to see themselves as cosmopolitan thinkers capable of transcending provincial attitudes, most find it difficult to communicate with one another across national boundaries. Intellectuals are often interested in the work of colleagues outside their immediate milieu, but are prone to interpret foreign conclusions on the basis of their own circumscribed orientations, and in relation to the set of conditions with which they are most familiar. Doing this leads them to draw their international colleague's assessment away from its initial application and transform it into something other than what he or she intended. As this knowledge passes from one group of intellectuals to the next, the potential for misunderstanding grows, and the essence of the initial meaning is often lost.[59] Bourdieu called this a "double historicization," arguing that the conditions and perceptions in place at either end of a given exchange can influence it very strongly and ultimately create something entirely at odds with the fundamental claims of the original author.[60] Ideas that are particularly open or elastic can be appropriated, revised, and exploited by intellectuals wishing to enhance the legitimacy of their own position, taking advantage of the lack of clarity in this regard and treating context-specific tenets as though they were universal in nature. When intellectual formulations do manage to survive in this way, they can go through many changes and perhaps even serve as the ideological justification for political action considered reprehensible by the thinker who initially created them.[61]

In an attempt to address these issues, Bourdieu focused on the differences in the modes of understanding that intellectuals employ in their work. He argued that while contemporary intellectuals often see their own analyses as very complex and subtle, even the highest levels of thought rely on very basic schemes of classification. These patterns underscore one's orientation at a fundamental level, which, Bourdieu maintained, is part of the reason why it is so difficult to be conscious of them. Intellectuals characteristically build their own assessments on the frames of knowledge passed down to them from previous generations of thinkers via education, and this pushes their analyses in a predetermined direction. While uneducated thinkers may lack the background to develop formulations of this sort, those who have had this degree of schooling tend to be locked into the habits of thought of their predecessors.[62] Relying on these starting foundations in their work may enable intellectuals to approach their subject matter in a coherent and well-thought-out manner, but it also limits their ability to make sense of the knowledge of those operating outside this schema.

> Therefore, we are constantly threatened by this intellectual ethnocentrism which consists in allowing categories of historically constituted thought, which are often related to the education we have received, to think in our place. The educational system is a great producer of taxonomies. This is why I like to say, to irritate my colleagues, that the worst obstacle to the development of scientific thought is the teaching of the professors, who, when they should be teaching things openly, in a supple, elastic and multiple way, spend their time making dichotomies and classifications.[63]

Bourdieu argued that intellectuals need to work toward providing some means of guarding against these ongoing misunderstandings. The first step to achieving this goal, he suggested, would be to develop a scientific assessment of the transmission process itself. This could take place through a study of the educational systems in various nations, including an examination of the dominant perspectives of different groups of intellectuals within each locale.[64] Such an investigation would entail, for instance, evaluating the routine practices of editors and publishers involved in making decisions about the exchange of scholarly material across international boundaries. The focus would be on the criteria used in selecting the ideas to be passed along, and those to be rejected, seeing how ideas are characterized as they are transmitted from one culture to the next and how they are interpreted by intellectuals on the receiving end. Bourdieu argued that no matter how altruistic scholars are in this regard, they typically have some underlying motive for doing things one way and not another. Researchers might ask, who is doing the selection? What criteria are they using in evaluating this work? What are their interests and goals? Bourdieu maintained that while material factors shape these decisions, they are also influenced by culturally specific norms and standards. An editor may select a particular essay because it is appealing or because it resonates with what he or she feels is important. Bourdieu did not condemn this side of it, but simply stated that it is something to acknowledge and understand. From his vantage point, studying this scientifically would help to reveal the nature of the conditions involved and expose some of the mitigating factors behind this exchange. It might provide a deeper assessment of the fundamental categories underlying the views of intellectuals in one's own milieu, as well as those of thinkers from different parts of the world, which could in turn serve as a means through which to diminish this misunderstanding in the future.[65]

Bourdieu had the opportunity to observe the international transfer of ideas first hand, both as director of the Center for European Sociology and as the senior editor of the journal *Actes*.[66] He also created the journal *Liber* later in his career with the express goal of fostering intellectual communication across national lines. Through these experiences, he came to see the difficulties involved in attempting to manage the exchange of ideas in ways that did not succumb to personal or regional bias. Differences in language, he observed, are not simply resolved via translation. Subtle variations in the ways ideas are put together continually surface as one moves from one language to the next. He concluded that in order for communication across national boundaries to be effective, there must be an awareness of the strategies used both in the development of ideas and in their interpretation. Without this knowledge, he argued, the common confusions interfering with the work of intellectuals throughout history will likely continue into the future. He recognized the many challenges involved in the attempt to better understand the dynamics of international exchange, but felt that this was a crucial first step in overcoming the divisions that have plagued intellectuals for so long.[67]

TRANSFORMING THE CONDITIONS OF INTELLECTUAL LIFE

Bourdieu's experiences in late-twentieth-century France led him to develop a very different image of the relationship between intellectuals and politics than his American counterparts. He observed the challenges brought about by the growing involvement of business in the political realm, but also became keenly aware of the problems associated with the influence of the state in academia. He could see that large-scale economic and political institutions had become increasingly powerful in underwriting the activities of the university, and that the ideas of intellectuals in this environment shifted accordingly. Social scientists in France were for the most part supported financially by the state, and this limited their ability to venture outside the boundaries of accepted critique. Their knowledge had in this sense drifted in the direction of accommodating the powerful institutional forces surrounding it.[68]

Yet Bourdieu's emphasis on culture and the independence of the symbolic in the constitution of society prevented him from adopting a purely structuralist framework. He did not characterize the knowledge of social scientists as simply determined by the conditions of their surroundings, but argued that their ongoing traditions and practices had also come to play a key role in shaping the kinds of analyses they developed. Normative systems of hierarchy, ingrained procedures of acceptance and exclusion, and the passing down of preset modes of understanding from one generation to the next all contributed to the tendency of social scientists to conform to the established ideas in their respective fields. Bourdieu's main point in this regard is that while the obstacles to intellectual freedom are indeed formidable, they are not as all-encompassing and controlling as they seem. From his perspective, social scientists are not required to be as complicit in their work as they have become in recent years. They are operating within a system of organization they themselves have created, and as its principal architects, they possess the ability to reconstruct it on the basis of new modes of understanding and alternative forms of organization. He saw the limitations of social science, but maintained the position that underneath its bureaucratic and specialized exterior, it has the potential to serve as a source of enlightenment on an array of important political issues.[69]

Bourdieu recognized the habit of scholars to uncritically follow the standard practices in their field and often lose touch with the very subject matter they claimed to be investigating, but he sought to provide the theoretical tools they need to become more aware of these practices and improve the quality of their work. He hoped to raise the caliber of social research to the point where it could serve as a valid source of knowledge in the public sphere and act as a guide to political decision making in the future. He was well aware of the Machiavellian dimensions of modern politics and did not assume its many foibles could be easily remedied by infusing it with the allegedly higher knowledge of social science. But he believed that the absurdities of contemporary society should be addressed by a more enlightened form of inquiry than in the past, and he criticized the determinist tendency to disregard the role of agency in shaping human history.

Bourdieu's suggestion to form a transnational collective, therefore, should not be interpreted as a Comtean attempt to place intellectuals in a position of political power. His goal was to find a way to balance the shortsighted character of contemporary politics with the deeper knowledge of independent and free-thinking intellectuals. His main concern was that without an alternative base of support to the state apparatus, intellectuals would not be able to challenge its authority or effectively critique its perspectives and goals. Working collectively in this way would provide the starting framework through which to move out from under the heavy hand of the state, assert their independence, and expose its various forms of domination.

Bourdieu's proposal in this regard may be somewhat unorthodox, but it nevertheless provides a relevant alternative to conventional social thought on this topic. He understood that the course of modern history could have evolved in a number of directions, and he encouraged social scientists to acknowledge the fact that the future of human civilization is similarly unclear. Although they may be operating within the confines of what appear to be powerful limitations, they actually have much more flexibility than they realize and can move beyond the common frames of understanding that have become so prevalent in their time. To Bourdieu, if they were to take the steps necessary to assert their own independence, the impact on the kinds of knowledge emerging in their respective fields and in the public arena would be significant and, in his view, ultimately favorable. He rejected Mannheim's recommendation that social scientists become directly involved in the management of politics, but he did agree that they could go a long way toward addressing some of its more egregious absurdities by approaching their work in a reflexive and rigorous way, and by interpreting their findings in terms of creative analyses, rather than simply echoing those of convention.

Bourdieu's goal was not to further rationalize the social order, but to draw on the informed insight of social science as a way to broaden the range of perspective in the public realm and possibly redirect the course of political and economic trends in the future. He knew that this ideal was controversial and would be difficult to achieve, but he was willing to go against the norms in his field to suggest a constructive way to bring together social science and politics in this tumultuous era. His incisive analyses of the central dilemmas of modern society continue to elevate contemporary social thought and provide scholars with a view of the world that highlights not only their involvement in it, but also their potential to play an important role in its ongoing transformation.

NOTES

1. For more on Bourdieu's philosophical origins, see the introduction to Richard Shusterman, ed., *Bourdieu: A Critical Reader* (Oxford: Blackwell, 1999). Jeremy Lane (2000) also considers the influence of key social thinkers on Bourdieu's ideas, including Durkheim, Marx, and Weber as well as Barthes, Touraine, Sartre, and Fanon. Lane also examines Bourdieu's work on the media, on higher education, and on politics in contemporary society. Please see Jeremy F. Lane, *Pierre Bourdieu: A Critical Introduction* (London; Sterling, VA: Pluto Press, 2000).

2. Regarding Bourdieu's interest in structuralism and existentialism, see George Ritzer and Douglas J. Goodman, *Modern Sociological Theory*, sixth edition (New York: McGraw-Hill, 2004), pp. 387–98.

3. Please see Pierre Bourdieu, "Rethinking the State: Genesis and Structure of the Bureaucratic Field," trans. Loïc Wacquant and Samar Farage, *Sociological Theory* 12, no. 1, March, 1994, pp. 1–18.

4. On the state and its monopoly of the universal, please see Pierre Bourdieu, "The Corporatism of the Universal," *Telos* 81, Fall, 1989, pp. 99–110.

5. Mary S. Pileggi and Cindy Patton (2003) discuss the importance of Bourdieu's work in the realm of cultural studies, arguing that there continues to be some misunderstanding about Bourdieu's ideas on this topic. This paper is an introduction to a special issue in the journal *Cultural Studies* devoted to Bourdieu and his contributions to the social sciences. Please see Mary S. Pileggi and Cindy Patton, "Introduction: Bourdieu and Cultural Studies," *Cultural Studies* 17, nos. 3–4, May–July, 2003, pp. 313–25.

6. Bourdieu, "Rethinking the State," p. 12.

7. Pierre Bourdieu, "Intellectuals and the Internationalization of Ideas: An Interview with M'Hammed Sabour," *International Journal of Contemporary Sociology* 33, no. 2, October, 1996, pp. 237–53.

8. Bourdieu, "Intellectuals and the Internationalization of Ideas."

9. On Bourdieu's position regarding the tendency of individuals to play a role in their own subordination, see Pierre Bourdieu, Alain Darbel, et al., *The Love of Art: European Art Museums and Their Public*, trans. Caroline Beattie and Nick Merriman (Stanford, CA: Stanford University Press, 1990). Also see Pierre Bourdieu, "Rethinking the State," p. 13.

10. Loïc Wacquant, "For a Socio-Analysis of Intellectuals: On Homo Academicus," *Berkeley Journal of Sociology* 34, 1989, p. 18.

11. Wacquant, "For a Socio-Analysis of Intellectuals," pp. 1–29. Loïc Wacquant (1996) also reviews Bourdieu's work on a range of topics and provides a solid overview of many of his concepts. Please see Loïc Wacquant, "Reading Bourdieu's Capital," *International Journal of Contemporary Sociology* 33, no. 2, October, 1996, pp. 151–70.

12. Pierre Bourdieu, *Distinction: A Social Critique of the Judgement of Taste*, trans. Richard Nice (Cambridge, MA: Harvard University Press, 1984).

13. Bourdieu, "Corporatism of the Universal."

14. Bourdieu, "Corporatism of the Universal."

15. Bourdieu, "Corporatism of the Universal." Bourdieu characterized the deliberate manipulation of ideas as "symbolic violence." This theme runs through much of his work and underscores his analysis of intellectuals. For further clarification of his position on this, please see Pierre Bourdieu, "Symbolic Power," in *Identity and Structure: Issues in the Sociology of Education*, ed. Dennis Gleason (Dimiffield, England: Nefferton, 1977), pp. 112–19.

16. Bourdieu, "Symbolic Power," p. 108. On Bourdieu's analysis of mediatic intellectuals, please see his "Intellectuals and the Internationalization of Ideas," p. 246.

17. Bourdieu, "Corporatism of the Universal," p. 107.

18. Bourdieu, "Intellectuals and the Internationalization of Ideas." Jacques Coenen-Huther (1998) discusses Bourdieu's position on the issue of the relationship of the media and intellectuals, arguing that while Bourdieu did see media institutions as debilitating to the integrity of intellectual work, these organizations also have the potential to serve in a positive way, as a means for intellectuals, and in particular social scientists, to communicate their ideas to a broader spectrum of the population. Please see Jacques Coenen-Huther, "The Paths of Recognition: Boudon, Bourdieu and the 'Second Market' of Intellectuals," *International Journal of Contemporary Sociology* 35, no. 2, October, 1998, pp. 208–16.

19. Bourdieu, "Intellectuals and the Internationalization of Ideas," p. 246.

20. Bourdieu outlines his position regarding the influence of institutions on intellectual knowledge in Pierre Bourdieu, *Language and Symbolic Power*, ed. John B. Thompson, trans. Gino Raymond and Matthew Adamson (Cambridge, MA: Harvard University Press, 1991).

21. For more on Bourdieu's view on the subtle cultural dynamics in the social sciences and their influence on social thought, please see Pierre Bourdieu, *Homo Academicus*, trans. Peter Collier (Stanford, CA: Stanford University Press, 1988).

22. Pierre Bourdieu, "The Peculiar History of Scientific Reason," *Sociological Forum* 6, no. 1, 1991, pp. 3–25.

23. Bourdieu, "Peculiar History."

24. Pierre Bourdieu, "The Scholastic Point of View," *Cultural Anthropology* 5, no. 4, November, 1990, pp. 380–91.

25. On Bourdieu's position regarding the values of social inquiry, see Pierre Bourdieu, "Vive la Crise! For Heterodoxy in Social Science," *Theory and Society* 17, 1988, pp. 773–87. Charles Lemert (2000) assesses Bourdieu's claim that it is important for social scientists to be aware of the significance of social location as a factor in shaping one's orientation. Lemert argues that while there may be some validity to this assertion, it nevertheless leaves us with the question of how to weave this insight into social scientific work. Please see Charles Lemert, "The Clothes Have No Emperor: Bourdieu on American Imperialism," *Theory, Culture, & Society* 17, no. 1, February, 2000, pp. 97–106.

26. On systems of classification and their influence on social thought, see Pierre Bourdieu, "Thinking About Limits," *Theory, Culture, & Society* 9, 1992, pp. 37–49.

27. Bourdieu, "Vive la Crise!" p. 777.

28. For more on Bourdieu's position regarding objectivity as a means of separation from the lower classes, see Bourdieu, *Distinction*. Also see Bourdieu, "Scholastic Point of View."

29. On the contradictions of postmodernism from Bourdieu's point of view, see Bourdieu, "Thinking About Limits."

30. Bourdieu, "Thinking About Limits," pp. 46–47.

31. For more on Bourdieu's position regarding the irresponsible nature of postmodern claims, see Pierre Bourdieu, "Passport to Duke," *Metaphilosophy* 28, no. 4, October, 1997, pp. 449–55.

32. Bourdieu characterized his position as "constructivist structuralism or structuralist constructivism." See Pierre Bourdieu, "Social Space and Symbolic Power," *Sociological Theory* 7, 1989, pp. 14–25.

33. Bourdieu developed a series of conceptual tools in an effort to reframe the orientation of contemporary social thought. In some instances, he drew on existing terms that were not well known (e.g., habitus), and in others he would formulate new concepts as a way to present his alternative perspective (e.g., hysteresis). For more on the creative dimensions of Bourdieu's theoretical framework, please see Bourdieu, "Social Space and Symbolic Power." David Swartz (1997) provides an in-depth overview and explication of Bourdieu's work, from the concepts of habitus and field to his ideas on intellectuals and politics. Swartz also reviews some of the major critiques of Bourdieu's analyses and develops his own assessment of them as well. Please see David L. Swartz, *Culture and Power: The Sociology of Pierre Bourdieu* (Chicago: University of Chicago Press, 1997). Bridget Fowler (1997) identifies some of the classical thinkers influencing Bourdieu's conceptual framework and clarifies Bourdieu's understanding of culture, focusing on concepts such as cultural and symbolic capital. Please see Bridget Fowler, *Pierre Bourdieu and Cultural Theory: Critical Investigations* (London; Thousand Oaks, CA: Sage, 1997).

34. Bourdieu, "Scholastic Point of View." Rogers Brubaker (1985) reviews Bourdieu's notion of class, as well as several other concepts, and suggests that while Bourdieu's ideas are enlightening in many respects, there is still a degree of tension in his

work due to the attempt to find universals while also paying careful attention to contextual specifics. Please see Rogers Brubaker, "Rethinking Classical Theory: The Sociological Vision of Pierre Bourdieu," *Theory and Society* 14, 1985, pp. 745–75.

35. Pierre Bourdieu and Jean-Claude Passeron, *The Inheritors: French Students and Their Relation to Culture*, trans. Richard Nice (Chicago: University of Chicago Press, 1979).

36. Bourdieu, "Vive la Crise!" Nedim Karakayali (2004) provides an interesting appraisal of the ideas of both Bourdieu and Adorno on this topic. Karakayali argues that while Adorno's critique of scientism challenges the misguided belief that rigorous scientific investigation will enable us to cut through some of the limitations we face as social scientists, Bourdieu's critique of theoreticism emphasizes the importance of developing analyses within the context of empirical investigation in order to better understand social reality. For more on this discussion, please see Nedim Karakayali, "Reading Bourdieu with Adorno: The Limits of Critical Theory and Reflexive Sociology," *Sociology* 38, no. 2, April, 2004, pp. 351–68.

37. Louis Pinto (2000) examines Bourdieu's suggestions regarding the ways intellectuals can find a balance between their scientific and political roles and argues that this is possible within the framework of reflexivity. The goal in this sense is to draw on the intellectuals' ability to understand and interpret the social world, and to bring this insight into the public domain. Please see Louis Pinto, "A Militant Sociology: The Political Commitment of Pierre Bourdieu," in *Reading Bourdieu on Society and Culture*, ed. Bridget Fowler (Oxford: Blackwell, 2000), pp. 88–104.

38. Bourdieu, "Vive la Crise!" p. 784.

39. Wacquant, "For a Socio-Analysis of Intellectuals," p. 23. Also on reflexivity, please see Pierre Bourdieu, *In Other Words: Essays Towards a Reflexive Sociology*, trans. Matthew Adamson (Stanford, CA: Stanford University Press, 1990).

40. Derek Robbins (2002) considers the influence of a range of thinkers on Bourdieu's thought and focuses on the ways reflexivity became a more prominent feature of his social analysis. Please see Derek Robbins, "Sociology and Philosophy in the Work of Pierre Bourdieu, 1965–75," *Journal of Classical Sociology* 2, no. 3, November 2002, pp. 299–328. Jane Kenway and Julie McLeod (2004) also examine Bourdieu's notion of reflexivity and compare his approach to those of feminist theory. Kenway and McLeod argue that Bourdieu advocated the idea of looking at social issues from a range of theoretical perspectives while at the same time avoiding the trap of relativism. Please see Jane Kenway and Julie McLeod, "Bourdieu's Reflexive Sociology and 'Spaces of Points of View': Whose Reflexivity, Which Perspective?" *British Journal of Sociology of Education* 25, no. 4, September, 2004, pp. 525–44.

41. Bourdieu, "Intellectuals and the Internationalization of Ideas."

42. Bourdieu, "Intellectuals and the Internationalization of Ideas."

43. Bourdieu states in an interview with Loïc Wacquant that "autonomy is the condition of scientificity" (Wacquant, "For a Socio-Analysis of Intellectuals," p. 16), but he also states that the issue is more complicated than can be fit into a single statement. For more on Bourdieu's position on this question, please see Wacquant, "For a Socio-Analysis of Intellectuals."

44. Much of Bourdieu's critique can be read as an attempt to enhance the quality and integrity of social inquiry, but one of the more explicit examples of his concern in this regard can be found in Pierre Bourdieu and Loïc Wacquant, *An Invitation to*

Reflexive Sociology (Chicago: University of Chicago Press, 1992). Franck Poupeau and Thierry Discepolo (2004) review Bourdieu's political activism, discussing the ways he managed to bring his scientific and scholarly derived knowledge into the realm of public affairs. Poupeau and Discepolo reflect on many of the issues Bourdieu addressed publicly, and they argue that his approach served as a powerful example for social scientists in public affairs in the present. Please see Franck Poupeau and Thierry Discepolo, "Scholarship with Commitment: On the Political Engagements of Pierre Bourdieu," *Constellations* 11, no. 1, March, 2004, pp. 76–96.

45. Bourdieu and Wacquant, *An Invitation to Reflexive Sociology.*

46. David Swartz (2003) examines Bourdieu's shift from being a relatively peripheral sociologist to being a public intellectual and considers some of the changes in society and in the field that precipitated this transformation. Swartz argues that in spite of these changes in approach, Bourdieu demonstrated a consistency in his effort to maintain and enhance the autonomy of intellectuals. For more on this assessment, please see David L. Swartz, "From Critical Sociology to Public Intellectual: Pierre Bourdieu and Politics," *Theory and Society* 32, nos. 5–6, December, 2003, pp. 791–823.

47. Please see the interview of Bourdieu by Loïc Wacquant, "For a Socio-Analysis of Intellectuals."

48. Bourdieu, "Intellectuals and the Internationalization of Ideas." Dick Pels (1995) critically reviews Bourdieu's notion of intellectual autonomy in relation to the practical constraints facing scholars in the sciences. Pels points out that there are influential constraints to intellectual freedom in the present, and these pose a series of contradictions for scholars. He nevertheless suggests that it is a worthwhile endeavor for intellectuals to continue to work toward autonomy, as this is essential to the development of new forms of knowledge. Please see Dick Pels, "Knowledge Politics and Anti-Politics: Toward a Critical Appraisal of Bourdieu's Concept of Intellectual Autonomy," *Theory and Society* 24, no. 1, February, 1995, pp. 79–104.

49. For more on Bourdieu's position regarding the interests of intellectuals, please see Bourdieu, *Distinction*; also see Bourdieu, *In Other Words*. Loïc Wacquant (2004) points out that Bourdieu's work was based on a view of social science as potentially able to strengthen democracy and help bring about social justice. He outlines some of Bourdieu's major contributions in this regard and considers the relevance of his work to contemporary political developments. Please see Loïc Wacquant, "Pointers on Pierre Bourdieu and Democratic Politics," *Constellations* 11, no. 1, March, 2004, pp. 3–15.

50. Bourdieu actually qualified this claim, stating that intellectuals tend to serve as the fellow travelers of second-rate intellectuals who align themselves with what they perceive to be the causes of the subordinate classes. See Bourdieu, "Corporatism of the Universal," p. 103.

51. Bourdieu, "Corporatism of the Universal," p. 103.

52. Bourdieu, "Intellectuals and the Internationalization of Ideas," pp. 246–47.

53. Pierre Bourdieu quoted in Wacquant, "For a Socio-Analysis of Intellectuals," p. 16.

54. On Bourdieu's idea of a collective of intellectuals, see Pierre Bourdieu and Loïc Wacquant, "From Ruling Class to Field of Power: An Interview with Pierre Bourdieu on *La noblesse d'Etat*," *Theory, Culture, & Society* 10, 1993, pp. 19–44.

55. Bourdieu, "Intellectuals and the Internationalization of Ideas," p. 246.

56. Wacquant, "For a Socio-Analysis of Intellectuals."

57. Bourdieu clarifies his position on the idea of developing a network of intellectuals in the interview with Loïc Wacquant in Bourdieu and Wacquant, "From Ruling Class to Field of Power."

58. Bourdieu and Wacquant, "From Ruling Class to Field of Power," pp. 38–39.

59. Pierre Bourdieu, "The Social Conditions of the International Circulation of Ideas," in Shusterman, ed., *Bourdieu: A Critical Reader*, pp. 220–28. Bourdieu was particularly concerned about his own ideas in this regard and took great care to reduce the possibility that this would happen to his work. One of the steps he took to avoid this was to conduct interviews and publish essays where he would review the main formulations of his earlier writings and address some of the criticisms and misunderstandings of these by other authors. An example of this can be found in Bourdieu, "Social Space and Symbolic Power."

60. Bourdieu, "Thinking About Limits," p. 38.

61. Andrew Miller (2003) assesses Bourdieu's ideas on the problem of misunderstanding of ideas as they travel from one contextual sphere to another and the ways this phenomenon influences the work of intellectuals attempting to communicate across national boundaries. Please see Andrew John Miller, "Pierre Bourdieu and the Perils of Allodoxia: Nationalism, Globalism and the Geopolitics of Intellectual Exchange," *Cultural Studies* 17, nos. 3–4, May–July, 2003, pp. 553–71.

62. Bourdieu, "Thinking About Limits," pp. 38–40.

63. Bourdieu, "Thinking About Limits," p. 40.

64. On Bourdieu's suggestion to study the international exchange of ideas scientifically, see Bourdieu, "Social Conditions."

65. Bourdieu, "Social Conditions."

66. The full title of this journal is: *Actes de la Recherche en Science Sociales*.

67. Bourdieu outlines his position on the importance of understanding international exchange in Bourdieu, "Intellectuals and the Internationalization of Ideas," and in Bourdieu, "Social Conditions."

68. Bourdieu, "Thinking About Limits."

69. Bourdieu, "Thinking About Limits."

7

The Social Scientist as Public Intellectual

The early Enlightenment thinkers Auguste Comte and Henri de Saint-Simon assumed they had answered the question of the proper role of the intellectual in public affairs. They believed the savants should be given the responsibility of political leadership in the new society to transcend the narrow conceptions of local viewpoints and systematize the process of policy formation. Once in this position of power, they would then govern on the basis of faultless conclusions, solving the problems that had plagued previous generations and establishing superior forms of social organization in the future.

The naïveté of Comte and Saint-Simon in this regard stemmed from their unwavering faith in the infallible nature of social scientific knowledge and their limited vision regarding the future trajectory of modernity. They could see that the material and ideological foundations of the feudal system had collapsed, but they could only speculate regarding the possible directions of the new order. Their hope that the savants would be placed in a position of authority grew out of their underlying assumption that human consciousness was moving from a metaphysical to a positive state and that in this newer context, only this elite group of experts would be capable of operating at the level of complexity needed to manage the practical realities of modern politics.

Subsequent thinkers focusing on this topic had the advantage of being able to observe the consequences of Western rationalization with their own eyes. Max Weber and Thorstein Veblen could see that the structure of modern society had in fact changed, but not in ways the early theorists imagined. Rather than being organized on the basis of scientific assessments of the social world, public policy continued to unfold in relation to very unscientific concerns. Political and economic institutions became increasingly intertwined with one another, fostering a type of leadership where decisions were made not on the basis of experience and reason, but in relation to the goals of vested interests and the requirements of rapidly expanding bureaucracies. Emotions, religious beliefs, and a range of newer cultural traditions in the West also influenced the directions of politics in illogical and unpredictable ways and undermined the potential for the rational management of society.

Weber and Veblen observed that social science had not developed into a mode of understanding that transcended cultural values, but continued to be essentially normative in its orientation. This type of inquiry held the potential to offer new insights into the phenomena of the social world, but its interpretive nature limited the extent to which it could act as a direct guide in the realm of policy. Political decision making in this context had come to be heavily influenced by the conflict between groups with varying goals and was not fully reducible to scientific calculation. Modern society had indeed become more rational in a number of respects, but this did not bring about the advance of civilization. Instead, it fostered new forms of political oppression, where premodern habits of thought remained prevalent. Many of the superstitions of the feudal era continued to thrive, and these shaped political trends throughout the modern world.

Weber and Veblen addressed the question of the social scientist's public role from the point of view of the ways their colleagues had chosen to react to this set of circumstances, as well as how one might respond to similar trends in the future. They were not optimistic that intellectuals on the whole would be capable of deviating from the paths set for them by institutional pressures, but nevertheless outlined what they considered to be the appropriate steps to take in this environment. Weber's distinction between the ethics of science and politics established a new set of standards for scholars concerned about maintaining the integrity of their work in the face of conflicting pressures. Veblen added to this assessment by showing how economic interests permeated the realm of government and shifted the character of scientific inquiry. Their writings provided the starting foundation for twentieth-century debate on this topic and influenced the analyses of subsequent thinkers who also focused on the increasingly mechanized and controlling nature of politics in this period.

In the years leading up to World War II, Karl Mannheim and Joseph Schumpeter developed these insights further, but did so within the context of modern-day military conflict. They saw that even as political and economic institutions became more functionally rational, a growing irrationality spread throughout the social world. Nationalism, ethnic strife, and war had persisted and, in some cases, escalated throughout the course of the twentieth century. These trends seemed from their vantage point to directly contradict the modernist expectation that civilization would automatically progress over time. Mannheim addressed this issue by attempting to revive the notion of applying social scientific knowledge to the increasingly complicated sphere of political administration. He understood that this was a drastic step to take, but he believed that under the circumstances, it was necessary as a way to preserve the traditions of free speech and open debate that had become such an integral part of liberal democracy. Schumpeter rejected this solution, arguing that the confused and shortsighted orientations of intellectuals led them to formulate naive and ill-conceived policy proposals. He saw intellectuals as inclined to unwittingly speed up the process of rationalization that had become characteristic of this era and doubted that they could provide the guidance needed to address the many complex dimensions of the global political economy. These two authors disagreed with each other regarding the public role of the social scientist, but they uniformly recognized the newer dilemmas of political administration in the modern order. They observed that public opinion had become a very significant factor in twentieth-century politics, and they raised the question of whether social scientists should get involved in the effort to consciously manage popular sentiment. While Mannheim claimed it was the only option available to contemporary political leaders, Schumpeter countered that such deliberate action would be dangerous and likely lead to a greater degree of authoritarianism in the long run. When read in juxtaposition to one another, the contrasting perspectives of these authors draw attention to the growing influence of propaganda in the modern world and the central role of intellectuals in this newer environment.

Following the war, C. Wright Mills and John Kenneth Galbraith expanded these analyses to evaluate the influence of the postwar bureaucracies on the character and directions of policymaking in the industrialized nations. They saw that political and economic decisions more closely reflected the objectives of established institutions than in the past, and that Western society had become increasingly administered as opposed to governed. They also observed the rationalizing tendencies of bureaucratic administration and the newer types of repression that followed. Decisions were now largely based on pecuniary and technical demands, raising the perceived importance of institutional priorities and placing basic human concerns in a secondary position. Propaganda and emotional appeals continued to influence popular viewpoints and undermine the potential for reasoned political debate. Informed democratic participation in the public realm had been overtaken by more subtle modes of administrative control, and the newer techniques of persuasion served as a way to bring mass sentiment in line with establishmentarian policy objectives and the goals of management-oriented political leaders. Mills and Galbraith argued that social scientists on the whole had acquiesced to these changes and tended to frame their work to accommodate the goals of their institutional supporters. They urged their colleagues to acknowledge the ways traditional scientific work served to strengthen these newer forms of domination, and to take the steps necessary to assert their own independence in the field.

Pierre Bourdieu carried this call for autonomy a step further and proposed the formation of a global collective of intellectuals, organized with the intention of building the connections needed to become a more significant force in the world of politics. He argued that intellectuals faced tremendous pressure to conform to institutional expectations, and that only by establishing an alternative base of support could they free themselves of this form of control. He characterized the work of social scientists as particularly important in politics due to their involvement in the arena of symbolic production. The members of this stratum, in his view, played a key role in interpreting the ongoing changes in the everyday world and in providing the foundations of social thought that eventually became salient throughout society. He observed their inclination to frame analyses in ways that legitimated the authority of the dominant classes, and he argued that this interfered with the development of alternative perspectives and diminished the potential for genuine social reform. Bourdieu did not see intellectuals as detached observers, capable of transcending the practical realities of the everyday world, but as integrated social actors, with predispositions, interests, and convictions, and he suggested that they acknowledge this in their own investigations. He did not propose that they abandon the effort to forge rigorous and revealing assessments of the social world, but suggested that they approach the task of inquiry with an awareness of their own underlying idiosyncrasies and potential biases to raise the caliber of their work in the long run.

Although writing in different periods and regions, these thinkers collectively observed the trend toward bureaucratic leadership and institutional domination unfolding in the West throughout the twentieth century. They characterized this trend not only as the product of technological and industrial development, but also as evolving in relation to the particular cultural norms and traditions in their respective milieus. They did not expect changes in the outlooks and practices of intellectuals to immediately bring about the reforms they envisioned, but they emphasized the unpredictable quality of human history and argued that seemingly inconsequential steps taken in the present could have a significant impact on the course of public affairs in the future. Their belief in the potential of ideas to shape the directions of society motivated them to develop analyses of the public role of the social scientist in a reserved but prescriptive manner. They provided both explicit and implicit images of their ideals, with the hope that this would inform intellectuals of their responsibilities in the years to come.

These authors were critical of the early Enlightenment views on this topic but did not disregard the potential value of strengthening the connections between social science and politics. The increasingly bureaucratic character of political decision making in the modern order and the consequences of this in terms of freedom and reason motivated them to address this issue with the objective of resisting such trends and bringing an element of wisdom to public affairs. They did not recommend that intellectuals be placed in positions of authority or that their ideas serve as a direct guide to policy making, but expressed the view that a broad knowledge of the social world could inform a range of political actors regarding the complex issues at hand. Rather than seeking a narrow, technical mode of leadership, they outlined the ways social science could enhance the available interpretations of political questions within a framework of respect for individual autonomy and democratic participation.

The writings of these authors, when taken together, reveal the larger point that there is not a single, unified public role to be played by social scientists, but many different ways they can approach their craft, depending on the circumstances in which they are operating and the goals they are striving to meet. Social scientists engaged in research and teaching have a very different set of responsibilities than those assisting in public administration, and these responsibilities also differ from the tasks of scholars operating in the arena of public opinion. The goals in each of these spheres vary considerably and have a bearing on not only the orientations of the social scientists involved but also the ethics they abide by in determining how to proceed on a day-to-day basis. Their ideals at times contradict one another, but they are also complementary in many respects and provide an important starting foundation for contemporary scholars seeking to better understand the public dimensions of their work.

THE SOCIAL SCIENTIST AS RESEARCHER

Among social scientists at the university level, the principle of limiting the influence of personal values in one's research continues to be very strong today. This is more prevalent in the United States, but it is also integral to the attitudes of scholars in Europe and other regions of the world. Underlying this principle is the idea that value neutrality can help investigators better understand their subject matter and gain a closer view of the realities they are studying. This is clearly a worthwhile goal, and the effort to minimize values in this context is appropriate. However, as Mills pointed out long ago, it is not possible to eliminate the influence of values in social research altogether. The endeavor of scientific inquiry is not simply a matter of objectively gathering information and then letting the data do the talking. It involves constructing categories, developing systems of classification, and drawing on existing analyses to frame the material being studied. Even the relatively fundamental goal of seeking to expand one's knowledge is grounded in the normative assumption that such an end is important and worth pursuing. In this sense, every social scientific investigation begins with an initial constellation of ideas that researchers use when forming their project and carrying it out, and this ultimately has a bearing on its findings.[1]

Although social science is inherently interpretive, it is nevertheless very able to serve as a means of developing new forms of knowledge about the social world. As a precursor to analysis, social research cannot lead to complete objectivity, but it can go a long way toward debunking some of the prevailing myths people carry around with them in their everyday lives. It can, for instance, shed new light on unfamiliar cultural practices and help diminish the misunderstanding that comes from a lack of exposure to regions outside one's immediate surroundings. It can also, as Mills suggested, reveal the connections between small-scale personal situations and larger societal trends, and inform political actors about the options they have available to them. Social science is, in this sense, a valuable way to learn about aspects of the social world that are not readily apparent to the casual observer.

One of the strengths of social science relative to other forms of inquiry is its emphasis on empirical investigation. The requirement that researchers tie their assessments to systematic observation helps lessen the extent to which their work is speculative or centered in the realm of personal opinion. Although social scientists develop their analyses in an interpretive manner, the fact that their findings are grounded in empirical study places them at an advantage relative to less rigorous forms of knowing. When looking, for instance, at the issue of social stratification, the common practice of sociologists to group members of society on the basis of class position is a clear example of relying on socially constructed categories. The process of drawing these dividing lines is undeniably a subjective endeavor, but taking such an initial step can expose the dynamics of a given social order and reveal some of the factors influencing the lives of individuals in this setting. Researchers can then clarify the differences in experience and opportunity that exist between the wealthy and the poor, and show how other social issues relate to this underlying framework. Their conclusions do not transcend interpretation, but have the potential to be enlightening and provide the foundations for newer perspectives in the future. When social scientists engage in empirical research, they are involved in the task of drawing attention to the dimensions of society they consider to be important and presenting these in ways that help others to make sense of them as well.

In addition to this fundamental tradition, the practice of relying on peer review also acts as a powerful buffer against the proliferation of poorly formed and contradictory analyses. When social scientists critically evaluate each other's work, they are able to ferret out inconsistencies, invalid assertions, and unsubstantiated claims and ultimately raise the caliber of their assessments. There are, of course, instances where this may actually inhibit the spread of unconventional perspectives—as for example when new ideas fail to conform to the prevailing beliefs of the reviewers—but this form of constraint is not all-encompassing, and the diversity of orientation within the social sciences provides a range of venues where even iconoclastic thinkers can find a receptive audience for their conclusions.[2] The practice of relying on peer-based forms of critique, when approached in a fair and open-minded manner, serves the important function of exposing the shortcomings of a study while it is still in formation and raises the standards of social analyses reaching a wider spectrum of the population. Peer review cannot bring social science into the realm of pure objectivity, but it can ensure that a researcher's ideas are well thought out and not easily torn down by unforeseen criticisms.

A third important asset of social science is the expectation that investigators provide an original contribution to the existing knowledge in their field. This convention creates a strong incentive for scholars to look beyond the topics of research that have been studied in the past and shift their gaze toward new areas of inquiry. It encourages them to break through the boundaries of the dominant perspectives in their discipline and develop fresh and innovative ways to understand the issues they are addressing.

As is the case with peer review, however, this tradition also has its shortcomings. It has the potential to lead to the development of an abundance of novel claims that on the surface may appear to be solid but at their core are unable to withstand the challenges of critical scrutiny. Pushing social scientists to perpetually come up with new discoveries can be beneficial as a catalyst for the formation of new knowledge, but it can also lead to the promotion of faddish ideas that come and go in very brief periods of time. Under these circumstances, peer critique becomes more valuable as a form of protection against low-level work. It can limit the influx of superficially appealing but misguided analyses and act as a balance to the ongoing pressure to develop new material. Thus, the requirement that each study offer a new contribution to its field can elevate the quality of social scientific knowledge on the whole, provided that this requirement is coupled with empirical research and critical peer review.

These traditions do not, of their own accord, ensure the validity of all social scientific conclusions, but they have provided the foundation for the development of new insight throughout the course of modernity. One need only consider the many empirically oriented assessments of the authors examined in this text to see the extent to which social science has served as an important source of enlightenment in the twentieth century. When scholars approach the task of inquiry with an awareness of its underlying values and practices, they can elevate the caliber of their analyses and help build the foundations of knowledge needed in the public realm.

DILEMMAS OF CONTEMPORARY SOCIAL RESEARCH

While many researchers identify with these traditions and abide by them in their work, there continue to be significant obstacles to achieving higher levels of scholarship in the present. One of the more influential of these is the growing emphasis on careerism in the field. In the United States in particular, there is a strong expectation that scholars adopt a rationalized approach to managing their careers. This requirement seems on the surface to be relatively harmless, but in practical terms it means operating in ways that resonate with one's own professional goals as a social scientist. This can lead scholars to engage in research in terms of the impressions it will foster among their colleagues rather than on the basis of a genuine concern to expand the knowledge of their discipline. It can elevate the work of those who choose topics in relation to what is salient in their field in the present and self-consciously interpret new data within the framework of prevailing or "cutting-edge" perspectives. It also encourages younger scholars to refrain from critiquing the work of their more senior colleagues, particularly if the latter might be able to assist them in achieving future career goals. One can see the influence of this phenomenon in the personal interactions taking place at the various association meetings held in each field on a regular basis. Whether it is the pedantic style of presentation used by scholars to convey their findings or the ritual exchange of preprinted business cards, the evidence of this trend is readily apparent in the social sciences today.[3]

The significance of this in terms of the quality of research is that it can shift the focus of each field away from broadly addressing contemporary realities and toward the narrow language and ideas of a select group. It creates an other-directedness that can perpetuate enticing but simplistic modes of thought, while also inhibiting the development of unestablished interpretations.[4] A given perspective can remain dominant under this set of conditions for an extended period of time, in spite of its shortcomings. Certainly the pressure to impress one's colleagues and successfully meet their expectations can also have an entrepreneurial influence on scholars and lead them to improve the quality of their work. However, it can also encourage conformity in terms of both the underlying ideas of one's research and the mode of its presentation. Career opportunism, in this sense, can foster a situation not unlike the story of the emperor wearing no clothes, where regality, hubris, and self-doubt contribute to an environment of collusion and obsequiousness, even when the evidence of the situation plainly suggests that misunderstanding is afoot.[5]

Another trend that has been particularly influential in shaping the directions of social scientific knowledge is the growing tendency toward specialization in each field. Researchers are increasingly expected to narrow the scope of their inquiry to deepen their level of insight into their subject matter and better understand its more subtle complexities. This can serve as an effective way to sharpen their focus on a given topic, but it can also limit the breadth of their knowledge in other areas. As Bourdieu observed, specialization creates a situation in which social scientists are less informed about the activities of their colleagues on the other side of the fence. It exacerbates the divisions in a given discipline and leads members in each camp to be suspicious or critical of the work taking place outside their immediate milieu, thus creating undue misunderstanding and dissension among divergent groups.[6] The drift toward specialization also means that there are fewer social scientists with the ability to bring together the pieces of information in each specialty and synthesize them into a broader framework. Under these circumstances, social science moves in the direction of becoming a collection of individual experts able to answer specific questions about their subject area but not very adept when stepping outside this domain.[7]

This presents somewhat of a dilemma for social scientists in the sense that it reveals the need to develop both specialized knowledge and perspectives of a broader variety. The work of specialists is crucial as a way to gather detailed information on a particular issue, just as the analyses of the comprehensive scholar can be important in bringing this material together in terms of the larger picture. It may seem reasonable in this context to recommend that social scientists simply select one approach on the basis of their interests, either focusing on the specifics of a topic or working toward the development of wide-ranging perspectives. However, while the conditions in social science are generally conducive to specialization, they are not very user friendly to those seeking to form more comprehensive analyses. Scholars attempting to venture outside their area of specialization must familiarize themselves with the vast array of newer data and associated literature continually emerging in the distinct subareas they are pursuing. This may be manageable when their study is relatively limited, but when an effort is made to broadly assess the findings on a range of areas within a given discipline, it quickly becomes a task that is beyond the pale of any single scholar.

One approach that has been used to bridge this gap is to form teams of researchers from different areas, working collectively to develop a more expansive understanding on a topic of study. For example, there are currently scholars in the United States studying ecological issues from the standpoint of social, political, and economic dimensions. Their work includes the study of migration patterns, climate change, cultural dynamics, and a host of other related factors. They are seeking in this context to integrate analyses from each of these various domains to address some of the larger questions associated with the interconnections between them.[8] What they are discovering, however, is that the perspectives in each of these areas are qualitatively different from one another, and that trying to combine them is much like putting together pieces of different puzzles, each with its own twists and turns and unique formations. Scholars taking this approach have been able to amass a collection of varying insights that are related to one another, but have also found it extraordinarily difficult to form a comprehensive picture of their subject. Thus, while there are indeed efforts underway to address the trend toward specialization in the social sciences, these are encountering a range of obstacles, both in terms of the organizational structure of the profession and in the orientations of its practitioners.

A third factor influencing the directions of social scientific knowledge in the present is the growing expectation that investigators actively seek out and secure external funding to support their research. Most social scientists in the United States are familiar with this routine and have grown accustomed to submitting proposals to various funding organizations as a part of their ongoing research program. Under the auspices of this arrangement, they typically seek ways to match their scholarly interests with the criteria of the institutions to which they are applying. The resulting changes in the framework of a single investigation may be relatively minor on a case-by-case basis, but when seen broadly, this practice shifts the focus of inquiry to accommodate prevailing institutional objectives and lessens the extent to which social scientists on the whole are able to approach their work independently.[9] Decisions about what to study and how to study it, while still technically in the hands of researchers, tend to be increasingly made by the representatives of various funding organizations underwriting their work. Of course, some individual scholars have been able to buck this trend and find support for research they consider interesting and worthwhile, but among those operating collectively and seeking to engage in large-scale projects, there is little opportunity to escape the obligation that they frame their inquiry to meet the requirements of potential funders.[10]

While there will always be practical factors involved in shaping the directions of social research, investigators can nevertheless make an effort to minimize the extent to which these play a role in undermining their larger objectives. In today's institutionally dominated environment, it is relatively easy to allow external pressures to weave their way into the domain of scholarly inquiry. When social scientists are aware of this ongoing phenomenon and take steps to retain a degree of independence in their own work, they can elevate the integrity of their findings and enhance the caliber of social scientific knowledge as a whole.[11]

THE SOCIAL SCIENTIST AS EDUCATOR

One can see the significance of these factors in the classroom as well. Weber observed the tendency of university professors to bring their own political leanings to the podium, often cloaking personal convictions in the language and methods of social science. He strongly objected to the habit of his colleagues to frame ideologically charged agendas as though they were grounded in objectivity and to claim they were simply passing on neutral information to their students.[12] The value of Weber's observations in the present can be found in the fundamental idea that, while it may be important for social scientists to participate in politics, the classroom is not the place for soapbox speeches, no matter how neatly they are packaged. Underlying this theme is the point that the public role of the social scientist, when in the position of educator, is to broaden the horizons of one's students. This means providing them with the range of information they need to make informed judgments about the social world. It also means at times passing along findings that may run counter to the professor's own political perspective, even though doing so could lead some students to develop alternative conclusions on the issues being discussed.

At the same time, the interpretive nature of social scientific analysis suggests that it is not possible for professors to present material in a completely value-free manner. One might conclude from this apparent contradiction that there is no way for them to fully escape the habit of passing their own biases along to students. This argument fails to acknowledge the basic point that some interpretations of social phenomena are of a higher caliber than others. Yes, social scientists must rely on a normative set of criteria to make such distinctions and evaluate the validity of various claims, but these norms are grounded in an effort to broaden human understanding. The pursuit of reason, freedom, and truth as suggested by Mills may be specific to the habits of thought in Western cultural traditions, but it has nevertheless opened the doors to new insight in a variety of domains and continues to provide a solid foundation for the development and communication of new and multifaceted ways of contemplating the social world.[13] Social scientists drawing on these fundamental principles are indeed operating on the basis of values, but these values are associated with the quest for enlightened understanding. This is very different from the goal of trying to convince students to accept the merits of a partisan political view.

It is customary for social scientists in the classroom to see their task as one of sharing with students the abundance of information gathered in their field through empirical research. This is an important aspect of teaching in the social sciences and is essential as a way to challenge some of the unsubstantiated myths circulating throughout society. However, the role of the educator is not only to introduce this new information, but also to encourage students to think independently about the topics being discussed. It involves nurturing their capacity to develop ideas in ways that do not necessarily conform to the perspectives presented to them. In this sense, the tradition of critique that is such an inherent part of social inquiry is a crucial dimension of learning as well. Rather than simply telling students what to think, the task of the social scientist in this context is to provide the starting foundations for new knowledge, while at the same time allowing a space for students to question prevailing assumptions and consider new ways to make sense of the world around them.

Even when acting in a reserved and scholarly fashion, social scientists in the classroom are taking on a public role. They are providing students with the information, analyses, and tools of interpretation needed to understand social issues in an informed and critical manner. When students realize that a professor is genuinely interested in helping them broaden their knowledge, they tend to be more accepting of unfamiliar ideas, even if these contradict their own preconceived beliefs. An educator using restraint in terms of personal values can ironically be much more powerful in expanding the horizons of students than one who is determined to impose his or her biases on them.

Whether involved in research or teaching, social scientists have the ability to significantly influence the course of public affairs, but in a subtle and indirect way. Their work seems in many respects to be detached from the events of the everyday world, but it does have a political dimension. When approached in an open-minded and balanced fashion, it can provide the information needed to address difficult political questions and can give rise to new forms of social thought. It can build a diverse base of knowledge that clarifies for political actors things they would not be able to see otherwise, and it can inform members of the larger population about the less apparent changes taking place in their own environment. When social scientists are aware of the importance of this task and consciously take the steps needed to fulfill its expectations, they are acting as public intellectuals.

THE SOCIAL SCIENTIST AS POLITICAL ACTOR

This leads to the question of the role of social scientists who are more directly involved in politics. Weber pointed out that the realm of public affairs is not one in which decisions are made solely in terms of moral concerns. It is a harsh and deceptive milieu, where cunning, strategy, and an intuitive sense of the proper action to take in difficult circumstances must serve as a guide. The scholar entering this world with a pious or rationalistic attitude toward policymaking will likely be brushed aside as the more experienced and shrewd political actors follow the course of their usual routine.[14] Galbraith affirmed this view, arguing that political matters are often poorly understood by social scientists and that this leads them to offer policy suggestions that are naively idealistic and lacking in applicability.[15]

Yet these authors did not suggest that social scientists refrain from engaging in political work altogether. They presented their critiques to better draw the connections between the worlds of academia and public policy, albeit in a tempered fashion. Researchers at the university level play an important role in expanding social scientific knowledge, but their ability to carry that knowledge into the public arena and translate it into political action is limited. This is the task of scholars who are familiar with the information and analyses of social science but also skilled in navigating the uncertain and often treacherous waters of modern politics. Intellectuals of this sort can serve as a liaison between these two worlds, informing political actors on the basis of scientific findings and challenging academics to connect their work to ongoing trends.

One way social scientists have done this is through their involvement in funded research organizations, or think tanks. Scholars in this environment are also participating in the quest for new knowledge, but their work differs from that of their university-based colleagues in the sense that it is usually organized around a specific set of political goals.[16] Their primary objective in this context involves broadening the knowledge of others, but it also includes developing findings that address the circumscribed concerns of the organization with which they are affiliated. The information they produce in this sense falls under the rubric of what Mannheim called political knowledge. It may be gathered scientifically but is inherently directed toward a practical political agenda.

The analyses emerging from these organizations can be relatively one-sided, but they nevertheless fulfill an important need in that they are inclined to push the envelope of knowledge in directions that may not have been considered from the standpoint of traditional academic research. Scholars working from within the environment of a think tank often come up with assessments that shed new light on existing issues and expose weaknesses in the orientations of their political opponents. This can stir up conventional forms of thought and infuse new life into older and taken-for-granted assumptions about the social world.

These organizations can also, however, contribute to misunderstanding as a result of their effort to demonstrate the validity of what are, at times, very narrow or ideologically charged points of view. Researchers in this setting tend to look for evidence that supports their predetermined conclusions, disregarding information that negates their ideals and taking data out of context to build a more favorable foundation for their preferred perspective.[17] When scholars approach their work with this sort of tunnel vision, they are actually obscuring more than they reveal.

One could argue that there is little to prevent social scientists in this environment from unabashedly pursuing the path laid out for them by their institutional supporters, and this may be the case. However, conclusions of this nature cannot be sustained indefinitely and tend to fall apart when subject to substantive critical scrutiny. The task of social scientists in this regard is to take the steps necessary to challenge the validity of deliberately misleading positions and contrast these positions with ideas that are more solidly grounded in empirical reality. Public intellectuals have a responsibility in this sense to focus their criticisms on obscurantist claims and do what they can to expose the myths these claims can perpetuate. This may not always be a feasible goal in the unethical and often corrupt world of politics, but it is one of the more important actions they can take when encountering this kind of deception.[18]

In their role as liaison between the worlds of academia and public affairs, scholars throughout history have had the opportunity to be more directly involved in the activities of government, and at times have been asked to participate as political advisors.[19] In this capacity, they are faced with the question of whether to try to infuse their own worldview into the formation of policy or to assume a relatively reserved stance and simply offer analyses to political leaders, who can then make decisions on the basis of their own convictions and sense of responsibility. Social scientists may be particularly knowledgeable about the topics in their field, but this does not guarantee their familiarity with the wide range of factors involved in political decision making. They cannot dogmatically follow the leanings of scientific conclusions, but must take into consideration the practical dimensions of the issues they face. When dealing with questions of international relations, for instance, politicians must factor in traditional practices, the varied concerns of national leaders, and potential repercussions among domestic constituents. This requires a great deal of experience and political savvy, as well as a range of information from a number of different sources. The role of the political advisor in this regard is less one of creating policy single-handedly than one of providing leaders with well-informed analyses of the issues and events they address. Their task is to situate specific developments in terms of larger societal trends and suggest possible steps that might be taken from the standpoint of a broader perspective.

Political advisors are not expected to adopt a leading role in this setting, but they have a responsibility to avoid being overly accepting of the ideology and goals of the administration with which they are affiliated. They are not required to passively accept the decisions of their superiors regardless of lax ethical standards or strategic flaws, but their task is to critique these in a constructive manner and seek to offer workable alternatives. The degree to which political administrations allow dissent in their inner circle is a factor that advisors must contend with, but their range of tolerance for poorly formed policies should also be tightly circumscribed. Advisors are expected to be team players and accept a measure of deviation from their ideals, but they can do so only to the extent that this cooperation does not limit their long-term ability to influence decision making in a manner that is consistent with their own values and goals. The task of scholars in this capacity is to maintain an open perspective relative to proposed policy suggestions, but to also weigh these against their personal standards and the ethics of their profession.

The involvement of social scientists in the halls of government has the potential to broadly inform the actions of political leaders; however, the practical realities of contemporary industrial democracies have significantly limited this opportunity. The tendency in the United States, for example, is to rely on social scientists to help facilitate the predetermined goals of a political administration and provide the technical support needed to carry out institutional objectives. Mills and Galbraith observed that although decision making in the postwar order required the involvement of intellectuals with the ability to see the larger picture, their colleagues continued to become more specialized and narrow, disavowing this important aspect of their role. They expressed concern that the endeavor of policy formation would fall into the hands of bureaucratically oriented managers with little sense of the relationship between the specifics of their work and the broader historical trends with which they were intertwined.[20] While it may be true that in the present context, business and governmental bureaucracies in the United States continue to rely on the technical skills of social scientists to more effectively manage public policy, one can also see that the need for broad-minded analyses has not diminished. The issues facing political leaders in the present are more complex than they were in the past and demand a greater degree of interdisciplinarity to evaluate them in a workable fashion. The broad-minded intellectual thus continues to be an indispensable player in the formation of policy today.

A crucial dimension of the social scientist's work in this capacity entails developing an understanding of the range of options available to an administration in a given historical setting. Political advisors cannot assume that the world around them is made up of objects to be manipulated at will. Fulfilling this task wisely requires an awareness of the interpersonal and relational circumstances involved, as well as insight into the ways people's lives will be changed by the actions being proposed. This means avoiding the trap of romanticizing a final set of goals to the point of disregarding the harm that may befall individuals as society bends to meet these glorified expectations. Advisors must develop a sense of the larger picture they are seeking to address, and not lose sight of the human dimensions of their work. Their role is not one that can be approached instrumentally, with the ends assumed to be given, but involves an acceptance of the principles of democratic participation and a willingness to yield to public concerns, even when these may stray somewhat from one's personal vision of society's future.

The task of social scientists in this sense is to develop an understanding of the various viewpoints circulating among members of the broader population and incorporate these viewpoints into their policy recommendations.

The standard outlooks of social science do not routinely inform the orientations of individuals outside of this realm. Advisors deeply embedded in the
logic of scientific research run the risk of projecting a rationalistic mind-set
onto others and creating proposals that fail to consider the meanings these
suggestions may have for those who do not conform to such ways of seeing
the world. Social scientists in this position can raise the standards of their
work by offering policy suggestions that account for the unscientific dimensions of contemporary culture, and by recognizing the limitations of scholarly frames of knowledge.[21]

Adopting a rationalistic stance in relation to policy is also problematic in
that it can lead one to assume that the evolution of society is something that
can be predicted in a positive manner. Advisors are obligated to consider the
likely consequences of their suggestions, but they cannot ignore the fact that
future developments are largely subject to unexpected change. The logic of
planning may be appealing from the point of view of rationally oriented
thinkers seeking to apply their knowledge to the progress of society, but the
unpredictable nature of the social order limits the efficacy of this approach
when attempting to forecast events over an extended period of time. Public
policy, therefore, cannot be fashioned in ways that rely too heavily on a narrow range of expectations. Social scientists offering advice to political leaders can refer to the larger trends of the past to formulate a sense of where
current circumstances will likely lead, provided that they do so with an
awareness of the possibility that this pattern may change without warning in
the future.

The attempt of an administration to organize the social order within the
framework of a given vision of the future typically means establishing an apparatus to bring that vision to life. However, doing so involves building institutional structures on the basis of existing conditions and can therefore
limit the potential of a society to alter its course as unexpected developments
unfold. The primary task of advisors in this regard is to resist the tendencies
of political administrations to adopt a managerial attitude toward public affairs. Scholars in this situation can ground their suggestions in an awareness
of the nebulous nature of the social order and thereby avoid falling into the
trap of developing narrow-minded attempts to systematically direct civilization toward a utopian ideal.

Social scientists involved in politics can thus play a key role in the formation of public policy. They can bring to the political arena an element of So-
cratic irony and point to the fragile nature of the existing order, while raising
alternatives to technically minded policy proposals. Their task in this setting
is to draw on the assessments of their academic colleagues to find ways to
creatively incorporate the best of this work into their own policy suggestions. This does not necessarily entail providing a rational foundation for the
sphere of political decision making as Comte and Saint-Simon suggested, but

factoring in the less tangible dimensions of everyday life and resisting the institutional pressure to contribute to the bureaucratization of political leadership.[22]

THE SOCIAL SCIENTIST AS OPINION LEADER

In addition to informing public policy, social scientific work can also involve stepping into the arena of public opinion. This raises the question of the place of social scientific knowledge in relation to the perspectives of members of the broader population in democratically organized societies. Is the goal of social inquiry in this setting to influence the directions of popular sentiment, or is it to provide assessments of the social world that are limited in their persuasive appeal but enlightening to those who may seek them out on their own? The expertise of social scientists in the realm of the symbolic gives them the potential to be effective contributors to the formation of institutional propaganda. They might, as Mannheim asserted, participate in this activity to encourage a broad acceptance of a multiplicity of perspectives, and work against a rising cultural uniformity. Within the framework of this logic, their talents in the techniques of persuasion can best be used to expand the outlook of citizens and preserve the principles of liberalism that are crucial to informed participation, such as reasoned social thought and a respect for individual freedom.[23]

This argument may seem appealing when taken at face value, but Mills, Galbraith, and Bourdieu raised the point that the centralized and bureaucratic administrations of the type emerging after the war were inclined to exploit these newer techniques of propaganda to build support for their own goals. While social scientists working in an official capacity might aspire to Mannheim's ideals, the dynamics of administrative leadership typically demand that they apply their innovative skills toward forming persuasive appeals to strengthen institutional authority. Under these conditions, official propaganda rarely serves to broaden popular perspectives but more often nurtures a complacency with respect to officially sanctioned norms and objectives.

Rather than act as an aide in creating institutional propaganda, the goal of social scientists in this regard is to share independently derived information and analyses about the social world with a wider segment of society. This includes ideas that may run counter to the preferred assessments of institutional authorities or have an initially disruptive influence on public opinion. Scholars can, for instance, expose the ways contemporary political regimes use techniques of propaganda to further their own goals. Their primary objective in this sense is to provide "publics" with viable alternatives to the established outlooks of reigning authorities and limit the extent to which dominant institutions are able to secure a hegemonic hold on the directions of popular sentiment. Schumpeter pointed out that even though the state had become much more involved in systematically managing public opinion during World War II, there remained a window of opportunity for critical viewpoints in the period that followed. This minimal level of autonomy continues to be a necessary feature of industrial-technological society. Leaders in this context can restrict challenges to their authority only by jeopardizing the freedoms of their clients in business and industry.[24]

Social scientists involved in public debate can seize this opportunity to critically evaluate the actions and orientations of established institutions and, if needed, promote alternative views. The goal of the social scientist in the public realm is not to steer the consciousness of members of the larger population toward a uniform set of beliefs, but to provide independent alternatives to state-generated perspectives. The trend toward the massification of industrial society may have restricted the ability of people to participate effectively in public affairs, but this does not necessarily imply that sound policy formation requires the management of public opinion on a grand scale. Social scientists confronting this trend can offer interpretations of the contemporary world that enhance the potential of individuals to participate in matters of politics in an informed manner. To the extent that participatory democracy is able to survive in a bureaucratically organized society, the goals of social scientists in this setting are to challenge conventional ideas and nurture the development of independent thought.[25]

This leaves us with the question of whether or not it is the proper role of social scientists to provide moral guidance in the newer order. Comte and Saint-Simon eagerly asserted the view that it was among the foremost tasks of the intellectual in the modern world to strengthen the moral fiber of the masses and to ground the morality of modernity in the findings of systematically derived truths. From this vantage point, every society requires a common set of moral standards upon which to base its organization, and the failure of intellectuals to develop and teach these to the masses can result in a disjointed and chaotic social order.[26]

Yet the inability of intellectuals to develop infallible conclusions about the social world calls the logic of this assertion into question. The notion that social scientists are obligated to bring the less educated into the circle of their own morality is based on the belief that their vision of the world is inherently superior to that of others. It also assumes that they themselves are capable of developing a uniform worldview. An awareness of the interpretive foundations of knowledge about the social world suggests that the task of intellectuals is not to seek a universal set of moral standards to be applied in all instances, but to engage in debate on moral questions that takes into consideration this variation. They might examine the different morals of a given culture, assess them, and critically evaluate them, but the inherent limitations of social inquiry reduce the extent to which scholars can conclusively assert the superiority of one collection of morals over another.[27]

Although social scientists are not able to construct a universal morality based purely on research and analysis, the fact that their work is grounded in a set of values suggests that it does have a moral component. The expectation, for instance, that they approach research in a way that is mindful of its potential consequences in the larger society clearly stems from a set of moral concerns. When one considers the potential influence of social scientific findings on the ideas and actions of political leaders and members of the larger population, its underlying moral dimensions become clear.[28] Scholars in the political arena may be required to compromise their own standards temporarily when working toward a larger future goal, and those in the classroom might need to exercise restraint when discussing political issues, but the work of the social scientist is, at its core, a moral endeavor.

This begs the question of how to reconcile these moral imperatives with the expectation that social scientists refrain from promoting a universal morality to others. One can find the solution to this seemingly paradoxical challenge by focusing on the value of individual freedom and the negative consequences involved in the effort to rationalize the social order. From this standpoint, social scientists can see the importance in drawing a distinction between their own set of standards and those to which they hold other members of society. A key component of their work is to strive toward a given set of ideals, but their efforts must also be tempered by a sense of the dangers involved in seeking to control the morality of others.

As actors in the arena of public opinion, social scientists invariably confront the often absurd and unpredictable dynamics of mass media. They quickly learn that ideas do not weave their way into public consciousness simply on the basis of merit, but are more often connected to a host of practical factors. Institutional authorities typically exert a great deal of effort to promote images and interpretations that connect with their larger objectives. In the United States, for example, media and governmental organizations prioritize their own interests when determining how to characterize events and social issues. These often coincide with one another, but can also vary significantly depending on the particular circumstances and issues involved.[29] Organizational factors strongly influence the character of media presentations in the United States, but their underlying frames also have much to do with financial concerns and a corporate interest in maintaining a strong public following to ensure continued economic viability. When public opinion strays significantly from the preferred assessments of government officials, media organizations tend to seek out a balance between the two, characterizing issues in ways that avoid straying too far beyond the boundaries of acceptable discourse, while at the same time striving to preserve the loyalty of their regular audiences. In this sense, writers and producers in the media must continually look for ways to fit their messages into the rubric of popular sentiment, satisfying both the institutional and ideological demands of their trade.[30]

This phenomenon is more pronounced in the televised media, due in part to its extraordinarily enticing and seductive imagery but also to its suitability as a form of entertainment for viewers. Most Americans rely on television as their primary source of news and information, and this further narrows the opportunity for scholars seeking to bring detailed or complex ideas into the public domain.[31] There are, of course, exceptions to this, and one can find examples of televised presentations that do indeed shed new light on important political issues. However, the vast majority of programming in this medium is designed to captivate its audiences rather than inform them. This creates, as Bourdieu asserted, an abundance of babble that takes up much of the space where meaningful and enlightened discussion could occur.[32] Scholars attempting to operate in this environment are invariably required to reduce their analyses to very brief and concise statements or find ways to fit them into the dynamics of entertainment. This limits the extent to which they can convey the substance of their ideas or inspire the development of new interpretations of the social world.[33]

The challenge of social scientists in the face of these obstacles is to seek out ways to communicate with a greater number of people, without compromising the integrity of their work. It is certainly worthwhile to try to engage in public discussions from within the domain of the televised media; however, doing so means running the risk of becoming a "mediatic intellectual" and lowering the level of one's analysis to accommodate the dynamics of this medium. Television has been very powerful in shaping the directions of public opinion, but there are other means of communication that intellectuals have successfully used to reach broader segments of the population. Newspapers, books, radio, film, and the Internet offer viable avenues for them to share their views in more detailed and comprehensive ways. There are limitations to these forms of media as well, and some are subject to the same influences as television, but such constraints are not all-encompassing, and social scientists operating in this environment can often find the space they need to present their ideas in a more enlightening form. The Internet, for example, has provided a valuable way to circumvent some of the restrictions of the mainstream media, in part due to its interactive nature, but also as a function of the fact that its sources of information are not centralized or limited by region, enabling users to participate in discussions with others outside their immediate milieu. These opportunities suggest that intellectuals have the potential to extend their analyses into the public realm, provided that they are persistent, creative, and willing to work within an environment that is less than ideal.[34]

THE PLACE OF SOCIAL SCIENCE IN PUBLIC AFFAIRS

The structure of Western civilization continues to shift from a liberal democratic order grounded in the principles of the free market to a global political economy in which government and business have a much greater degree of influence over the course of social life. The dominant institutions of contemporary society are much more bureaucratic and all-encompassing in terms of their organizational structure than in the past, and this has significantly altered the nature of politics in our time. This set of conditions has produced political leaders who are more closely attuned to institutional goals and less willing to focus on the social consequences of their actions. It has deteriorated the quality of public debate and has undermined the potential for enlightened democratic participation.

Social scientists in this environment have found it increasingly difficult to approach their work independently and share their findings with others. They have encountered a growing array of material and cultural pressures designed to push them down a preset path and organize their investigations in ways that best serve establishmentarian ends. From the burgeoning demand that they garner external sources of funding to support their research to the expectation that they subscribe to the relatively narrow cultural norms and practices in their field, the constraints placed on scholars in this context are many.

In spite of these pressures, social scientists continue to possess the ability to approach their work as public intellectuals. Their connections to empirical reality and their skills in the symbolic domain render them uniquely able to frame information in ways that help others make sense of the world. Social scientists cannot guide humanity to new levels of consciousness, but they can clarify some of the underlying dynamics of the ongoing transformations taking place in the present.[35]

A key dimension of their work involves adopting a critical stance relative to institutionally derived perspectives and goals. This means thinking beyond routine interpretations of social phenomena and becoming more actively involved in critically evaluating conventional assumptions. There may be elements of standardized knowledge that can serve the function of guiding the management of practical affairs on a case-by-case basis, but this form of knowing cannot of its own accord provide the insight needed to approach political questions from a broader standpoint. The task of social scientists in this regard is to avoid the habit of unconsciously providing the symbolic justification for official claims and instead to construct new and relevant ways to understand the contemporary social world.

The public role of social scientists is thus to approach their work in a manner that considers both the immediate and future consequences of their analyses, conclusions, and policy suggestions. The allure of research funding and career opportunity may lead some to subscribe to the dominant orientations in their field, but there is an inherent value associated with engaging in social inquiry from an independent point of view. Scholarly analyses that do not fall in line with the norms of conventional social thought have the potential to inform future perspectives and eventually weave their way into the mainstream of everyday belief as the character of society changes over time.

An awareness of the threat to individual freedom posed by the rationalization of the social order should not lead intellectuals to reject the philosophical discourse of modernity entirely, but should inspire them to consider the importance of critique and innovation. Their collective goal in this sense is to develop ideas within the framework of an informed but skeptical attitude that relies not only on the traditions of past knowledge but also on their own insight into the events of the present.

Although social scientists are expected to engage in research in an analytical and systematic manner, their conclusions are not based solely on utilitarian considerations. The structure of modern society is grounded in the meanings individuals bring to their everyday experience, and these are at least as important as the practical concerns of the established order. To the extent that social scientists are able to incorporate the human dimension into their work, they can provide a valuable contribution to the ongoing reformation of traditional knowledge and to the future directions of modern civilization.

NOTES

1. Soma Hewa (1993) addresses the question of value neutrality as it relates to public policy, pointing out that value-free social science does not necessarily imply a disregard for the consequences and implications of one's research. Please see Soma Hewa, "Sociology and Public Policy: The Debate on Value-Free Social Science," *International Journal of Sociology and Social Policy* 13, nos. 1–2, 1993, pp. 64–82.

2. The potential of researchers to find a receptive group of colleagues will certainly vary from one setting to the next, but given the changes in electronic communication in recent years, the potential to step outside of one's immediate milieu is much greater today than it has been in the past.

3. For more on the issue of career opportunism in the social sciences, please see Guy Oakes and Arthur J. Vidich, *Collaboration, Reputation, and Ethics in American Academic Life: Hans H. Gerth and C. Wright Mills* (Urbana; Chicago: University of Illinois Press, 1999).

4. Ben Agger (2000) addresses the tendency of mainstream social scientists to uncritically conform to the practices in their field. He identifies some of the main weaknesses that stem from the efforts of sociologists to fit the interpretive dimensions of social inquiry into the positivist framework characteristic of the natural sciences. He also argues that sociology could be much improved if its practitioners were willing to

acknowledge some of the ways their own ritualistic adherence to the standard methodologies and theoretical assumptions of their discipline influences their work. For more on this analysis, please see Ben Agger, *Public Sociology: From Social Facts to Literary Acts* (Lanham, MD: Rowman & Littlefield, 2000).

5. For more on the ways academic institutions can have a constraining influence on the ideas and actions of intellectuals, please see Russell Jacoby, *The Last Intellectuals: American Culture in the Age of Academe* (New York: Basic Books, 1987). Jacoby provides an interesting and provocative analysis of the ways in which left intellectuals of the 1960s gradually made their way into the realm of academia, sanitizing their critiques and drifting away from their former connections in the public sphere. John Michael (2000) also discusses some of the principal tensions in the work of intellectuals in academia and discusses a range of authors who have written on this topic, from Todd Gitlin to Allan Bloom. Please see John Michael, *Anxious Intellects: Academic Professionals, Public Intellectuals, and Enlightenment Values* (Durham, NC: Duke University Press, 2000).

6. Pierre Bourdieu, "The Corporatism of the Universal: The Role of Intellectuals in the Modern World," *Telos* 81, Fall, 1989, p. 109.

7. Gaile Cannella and Yvonna Lincoln (2004) focus on the increasingly insular nature of contemporary academic discourses, arguing that this trend is problematic in the sense that it further removes the insight of social scientific conclusions from the realm of public affairs. Please see Gaile S. Cannella and Yvonna S. Lincoln, "Epilogue: Claiming a Critical Public Social Science—Reconceptualizing and Redeploying Research," *Qualitative Inquiry* 10, no. 2, April, 2004, pp. 298–309.

8. For further discussion on the effort to transcend disciplinary boundaries, see Stephen G. Perz and D. A. Alves, "Fashioning an Interdisciplinary Environmental Science for the 21st Century: Key Issues and the Contributions of IAI Research and Training Initiatives," *Inter-American Institute for Global Change Research, Annual Report 2003–2004.* Also see R. R. Rindfuss and P. C. Stern, "Linking Remote Sensing and Social Science: The Need and the Challenges," in *People and Pixels: Linking Remote Sensing and Social Science*, ed. D. Liverman, E. F. Moran, R. R. Rindfuss, and P. C. Stern (Washington, DC: National Academy Press, 1998), pp. 1–27.

9. Leroy Pelton (2000) argues that many of the current practices within the social sciences tend to disregard the concerns of individuals who are not in some way connected to the larger institutions of society. Pelton also argues that a growing reliance on aggregate data tends to perpetuate misunderstanding on a range of social issues. Please see Leroy H. Pelton, "Misinforming Public Policy: The Illiberal Uses of Social Science," *Society* 37, no. 5, July–August, 2000, pp. 61–69.

10. Susan McDaniel (1995) outlines the constraints placed on social scientists as public budgets continue to shrink and as the forces of the private sector more effectively weave their way into the realm of academia. McDaniel argues that sociology can serve as a powerful means for debunking conventional mythologies and providing insightful and relevant knowledge in the public sphere, but she also asserts that scholars face a great many obstacles in their effort to meet this potential. Please see Susan A. McDaniel, "Reflections of a Very Public Sociologist," *Society/Société* 19, no. 2, May, 1995, pp. 3–5.

11. Thomas Bender (1997) provides a lucid and insightful account of some of the past ways academic intellectuals have managed to step out of the ivory tower and

become engaged in public affairs without compromising the integrity of their work. Bender recognizes the obstacles involved in the effort to make the connections between intellectual and public discourses but shows, through the examples of Dewey and others, that these challenges are not insurmountable. Please see Thomas Bender, *Intellect and Public Life: Essays on the Social History of Academic Intellectuals in the United States* (Baltimore: Johns Hopkins University Press, 1997).

12. Max Weber, "Science as a Vocation," in *From Max Weber: Essays in Sociology*, trans. Hans Gerth and C. Wright Mills (New York: Oxford University Press, 1958; orig. pub. 1919), pp. 129–56.

13. Richard Bernstein (1992) offers a very in-depth and insightful analysis of this issue in his book *The New Constellation: The Ethical-Political Horizons of Modernity/Postmodernity* (Cambridge, MA: MIT Press, 1992).

14. Max Weber, "Politics as a Vocation," in *From Max Weber*, pp. 77–128.

15. John Kenneth Galbraith, *The New Industrial State* (Boston: Houghton Mifflin, 1978), p. 292.

16. Of course, many university-based scholars also engage in research to support their own political views as well, but social scientists in this position are more closely tied to the norms, conventions, and habits of thought in their respective fields than are researchers outside this milieu. This can have a constraining influence on the former and reduce the extent to which they can organize their research around a specific political agenda.

17. There have been quite a few studies in recent years documenting the ways special-interest groups play a role in shifting the findings of social science to accommodate their preconceived objectives. See, for example, Andrew Austin, "Advancing Accumulation and Managing Its Discontents: The U.S. Antienvironmental Countermovement," *Sociological Spectrum* 22, no. 1, January–March, 2002, pp. 71–105.

18. An example of this type of skewed analysis can be found in the book by Richard Hernstein and Charles Murray entitled *The Bell Curve* (New York: Free Press, 1994). For information about the ways private-interest groups funded this project and assisted in its promotion upon completion, please see Charles Lane, "The Tainted Sources of *The Bell Curve*," *New York Times Review of Books* 41, no. 20, December, 1994, pp. 14–19.

19. In England, for example, sociologist Anthony Giddens served for many years as an advisor to Prime Minister Tony Blair. He also served as an advisor to the Clinton administration. For more on his experiences in this capacity, please see Anthony Giddens, *Where Now for New Labour?* (Cambridge: Polity Press, 2002).

20. For more on their positions on this matter, see C. Wright Mills, *The Sociological Imagination* (New York: Oxford University Press, 1959), and Galbraith, *New Industrial State*.

21. Harold L. Wilensky (1997) outlines some of the characteristics of public policy research, arguing that one of its primary goals should be to focus on persistent social problems. Wilensky does not see social research as able to directly influence the course of public policy, but he does see it as having a long-term impact through its tendency to shape perceptions of social issues. For more on this assessment, please see Harold L. Wilensky, "Social Science and the Public Agenda: Reflections of the Relation of Knowledge to Policy in the United States and Abroad," *Journal of Health Politics, Policy and Law* 22, no. 5, October, 1997, pp. 1241–65.

22. William Julius Wilson (1993) maintains that social science has not been living up to its potential as a valuable and important contributor to the underlying knowledge of public policy. Wilson argues that social scientists have a responsibility to bring their work into the public realm and make a more concerted effort to shape the public agenda. Please see William Julius Wilson, *Sociology and the Public Agenda* (Thousand Oaks, CA: Sage, 1993).

23. Karl Mannheim, *Freedom, Power, and Democratic Planning*, ed. E. K. Bramstedt and Hans Gerth (London: Routledge & Kegan Paul, 1951), pp. 35, 138–40.

24. Joseph Schumpeter, *Capitalism, Socialism, and Democracy* (New York: Harper & Row, 1962; orig. pub. 1942).

25. Joel Best (2004) focuses on the distance between the knowledge and ideas of sociology and those in the public sphere, and he considers possible reasons for this gap. He also suggests possible ways social scientists might be able to more effectively communicate their ideas to a broader public. Please see Joel Best, "Why Don't They Listen to Us? Fashion Notes on the Imperial Wardrobe," *Social Problems* 51, no. 1, February, 2004, pp. 154–60.

26. Auguste Comte, "Plan of the Scientific Operations Necessary for Reorganizing Society," in *On Intellectuals: Theoretical Studies, Case Studies*, ed. Phillip Rieff (Garden City, NY: Anchor Books, 1970), and Saint-Simon, *Le Politique*, sections of which can be found in *The Political Thought of Saint-Simon*, ed. Ghita Ionescu (London: Oxford University Press, 1976).

27. Helen Small (2002) brought together the work of several key authors writing on the subject of the public intellectual, including Edward Said and Rita Copeland. These authors gathered together for a conference entitled "The Public Role of Writers and Intellectuals" at Oxford University in September 2000. These essays examine a range of issues on this topic, from music and art to philosophy and politics. Please see Helen Small, ed., *The Public Intellectual* (Oxford: Blackwell, 2002).

28. Robert Bellah (1985) argues in favor of rekindling the connections between sociology and philosophy, with the goal of better understanding the inherent moral dimensions of social inquiry. Bellah argues that social science is never value free, and that it is crucial for scholars to recognize the extent to which their work is relevant to the ongoing transformations taking place in the social world. Please see Robert N. Bellah, "Creating a New Framework for New Realities: Social Science as Public Philosophy," *Change* 17, no. 2, March–April, 1985, pp. 35–39.

29. For example, during the United States' occupation of Iraq beginning in 2003, most of the mainstream media organizations sought to stay within the boundaries of institutionally defined discourses; however, even these institutions were unable to completely ignore the insurgent bomb attacks occurring throughout the country, in spite of the attempts of U.S. government officials to convey the impression that the military conflicts of this war had subsided. For more on this issue, please see Douglas Kellner, "Media Propaganda and Spectacle in the War on Iraq: A Critique of U.S. Broadcasting Networks," *Cultural Studies Critical Methodologies* 4, no. 3, August, 2004, pp. 329–38.

30. Kellner, "Media Propaganda and Spectacle."

31. For more on the use of television as a source of information in the United States, please see S. Robert Lichter, *Prime Time: How TV Portrays American Culture* (Washington, DC: Regnery, 1995).

32. Pierre Bourdieu, "Intellectuals and the Internationalization of Ideas: An Interview with M'Hammed Sabour," *International Journal of Contemporary Sociology* 33, no. 2, October, 1996, pp. 237–53.

33. Richard Posner (2002) argues that the rise of the media and the tendency toward academic specialization has contributed to a decline in the quality of work of public intellectuals. Posner maintains that the abundance of oversimplified and uninformed public discussions contributes to a lack of understanding both at the level of everyday discourse and in public policy. Please see Richard Posner, *Public Intellectuals: A Study of Decline* (Cambridge, MA: Harvard University Press, 2002). Bruce Robbins (1993) challenges the notion of a decline of the public intellectual, arguing that the spirit of critique that has been an inherent component of intellectual life is still alive today. Robbins discusses examples of scholars, such as Raymond Williams and Edward Said, who managed to maintain a critical orientation with respect to the established order, showing how they successfully navigated the obstacles present both within and outside of academia. Please see Bruce Robbins, *Secular Vocations: Intellectuals, Professionalism, Culture* (London; New York: Verso, 1993).

34. Jeffrey Goldfarb (1998) argues that intellectuals have a responsibility to facilitate intelligent and informed discussion about political issues in ways that challenge existing beliefs while offering realistic alternatives to conventional mythologies. Please see Jeffrey Goldfarb, *Civility and Subversion: The Intellectual in Democratic Society* (Cambridge; New York: Cambridge University Press, 1998).

35. In his presidential address to members of the American Sociological Association in 2004, Michael Burawoy (2005) strongly argued in favor of a public sociology. Burawoy maintained that this approach to social science could provide a way to elevate public debate, enhance the long-term vision of public policy, and strengthen civil society against the institutional pressures of the market and of the state. Please see Michael Burawoy, "For Public Sociology," *American Sociological Review* 70, February, 2005, pp. 4–28. Also see Michael Burawoy, "Public Sociologies: Contradictions, Dilemmas, and Possibilities," *Social Forces* 82, no. 4, June, 2004, pp. 1603–18.

Bibliography

Agger, Ben, *Public Sociology: From Social Facts to Literary Acts* (Lanham, MD: Rowman & Littlefield, 2000).

Aldcroft, Derek H., *From Versailles to Wall Street, 1919–1929* (Berkeley: University of California Press, 1977).

Allen, Robert Loring, *Opening Doors: The Life and Work of Joseph Schumpeter* (New Brunswick, NJ: Transaction, 1991).

Alt, John, "Reclaiming C. Wright Mills," *Telos* 66, Winter, 1985–1986, 6–43.

Beetham, David, *Max Weber and the Theory of Modern Politics* (London: Allen & Unwin, 1974).

Bell, Daniel, "Veblen and the Technocrats: On the Engineers and the Price System," in *The Winding Passage: Essays and Sociological Journeys 1960–1980* (Cambridge, MA: Harvard University Press, 1980), 69–90.

Bellah, Robert N., "Creating a New Framework for New Realities: Social Science as Public Philosophy," *Change* 17, no. 2, March–April, 1985, 35–39.

Bender, Thomas, *Intellect and Public Life: Essays on the Social History of Academic Intellectuals in the United States* (Baltimore: Johns Hopkins University Press, 1997).

Bernstein, Richard J., *The New Constellation: The Ethical-Political Horizons of Modernity/Postmodernity* (Cambridge, MA: MIT Press, 1992).

Best, Joel, "Why Don't They Listen to Us? Fashion Notes on the Imperial Wardrobe," *Social Problems* 51, no. 1, February, 2004, 154–60.

Bourdieu, Pierre, *Bourdieu: A Critical Reader*, edited by Richard Shusterman (Oxford: Blackwell, 1999), 220–28.

Bourdieu, Pierre, "The Corporatism of the Universal," *Telos* 81, Fall, 1989, 99–110.

Bourdieu, Pierre, *Distinction: A Social Critique of the Judgement of Taste*, translated by Richard Nice (Cambridge, MA: Harvard University Press, 1984).

Bourdieu, Pierre, *Homo Academicus*, translated by Peter Collier (Stanford, CA: Stanford University Press, 1988).

Bourdieu, Pierre, *In Other Words: Essays Towards a Reflexive Sociology*, translated by Matthew Adamson (Stanford, CA: Stanford University Press, 1990).

Bourdieu, Pierre, "Intellectuals and the Internationalization of Ideas: An Interview with M'Hammed Sabour," *International Journal of Contemporary Sociology* 33, no. 2, October, 1996, 237–53.

Bourdieu, Pierre, *Language and Symbolic Power*, edited by John B. Thompson, translated by Gino Raymond and Matthew Adamson (Cambridge, MA: Harvard University Press, 1991).

Bourdieu, Pierre, *The Logic of Practice* (Stanford, CA: Stanford University Press, 1990).

Bourdieu, Pierre, *L'Ontologie Politique de Martin Heidegger* (Paris: Minuit, 1988).

Bourdieu, Pierre, "On the Cunning of Imperialist Reason," *Theory, Culture, & Society* 16, no. 1, 1999, 41–58.

Bourdieu, Pierre, *Pascalian Meditations* (Stanford, CA: Stanford University Press, 2000).

Bourdieu, Pierre, "Passport to Duke," *Metaphilosophy* 28, no. 4, October, 1997, 449–55.

Bourdieu, Pierre, "The Peculiar History of Scientific Reason," *Sociological Forum* 6, no. 1, 1991, 3–25.

Bourdieu, Pierre, *Practical Reason: On the Theory of Action* (Stanford, CA: Stanford University Press, 1998).

Bourdieu, Pierre, "Rethinking the State: Genesis and Structure of the Bureaucratic Field," translated by Loïc Wacquant and Samar Farage, *Sociological Theory* 12, no. 1, March, 1994, 1–18.

Bourdieu, Pierre, "The Scholastic Point of View," *Cultural Anthropology* 5, no. 4, November, 1990, 380–91.

Bourdieu, Pierre, *Science of Science and Reflexivity* (Chicago: University of Chicago Press, 2004).

Bourdieu, Pierre, "Social Space and Symbolic Power," *Sociological Theory* 7, 1989, 14–25.

Bourdieu, Pierre, *Sociology in Question* (London: Sage, 1993).

Bourdieu, Pierre, *The State Nobility: Elite Schools in the Field of Power* (Stanford, CA: Stanford University Press, 1996).

Bourdieu, Pierre, "Symbolic Power," in Dennis Gleason, editor, *Identity and Structure: Issues in the Sociology of Education* (Dimiffield, England: Nefferton, 1977), 112–19.

Bourdieu, Pierre, "Thinking About Limits," *Theory, Culture, & Society* 9, 1992, 37–49.

Bourdieu, Pierre, "Understanding," *Theory, Culture, & Society* 13, no. 2, 1996, 17–37.

Bourdieu, Pierre, "Vive la Crise! For Heterodoxy in Social Science," *Theory and Society* 17, 1988, 773–87.

Bourdieu, Pierre, Jean-Claude Chamboredon, and Jean-Claude Passeron, *The Craft of Sociology: Epistemological Preliminaries*, edited by Beate Krais, translated by Richard Nice (Berlin; New York: Walter de Gruyter, 1991). (Originally *Métier de Sociologue*, 1968.)

Bourdieu, Pierre, A. Darbel, et al., *The Love of Art: European Art Museums and Their Public*, translated by Caroline Beattie and Nick Merriman (Stanford, CA: Stanford University Press, 1990).

Bourdieu, Pierre, and H. Haacke, *Free Exchange* (Stanford, CA: Stanford University Press, 1995).

Bourdieu, Pierre, and Jean-Claude Passeron, *The Inheritors: French Students and Their Relation to Culture*, translated by Richard Nice (Chicago: University of Chicago Press, 1979).

Bourdieu, Pierre, and Jean-Claude Passeron, *Reproduction in Education, Society, and Culture*, second edition (London: Sage, 1990).

Bourdieu, Pierre, Jean-Claude Passeron, and M. de Saint Martin, *Academic Discourse: Linguistic Misunderstanding and Professional Power* (Stanford, CA: Stanford University Press, 1994).

Bourdieu, Pierre, and Loïc Wacquant, "From Ruling Class to Field of Power: An Interview with Pierre Bourdieu on *La noblesse d'Etat*," *Theory, Culture, & Society* 10, 1993, 19–44.

Bourdieu, Pierre, and Loïc Wacquant, *An Invitation to Reflexive Sociology* (Chicago: University of Chicago Press, 1992).

Bourdieu, Pierre, and Jean-Claude Passeron, *The Students and Their Studies* (Paris: Mouton, 1964).

Breiner, Peter, *Max Weber and Democratic Politics* (Ithaca, NY: Cornell University Press, 1996).

Brubaker, Rogers, *The Limits of Rationality: An Essay on the Social and Moral Thought of Max Weber* (London; Boston: Allen and Unwin, 1984).

Brubaker, Rogers, "Rethinking Classical Theory: The Sociological Vision of Pierre Bourdieu," *Theory and Society* 14, 1985, 745–75.

Burawoy, Michael, "For Public Sociology," *American Sociological Review* 70, February, 2005, 4–28.

Burawoy, Michael, "Public Sociologies: Contradictions, Dilemmas, and Possibilities," *Social Forces* 82, no. 4, June, 2004, 1603–18.

Burawoy, Michael, Charles Derber, Milliam Gamson, Stephen Pfohl, Charlotte Ryan, Juliet Schor, and Diane Vaughan, "Public Sociologies: A Symposium from Boston College," *Social Problems* 51, no. 1, February, 2004, 103–30.

Calhoun, Craig, Edward LiPuma, and Moishe Postone, editors, *Bourdieu: Critical Perspectives* (Chicago: University of Chicago Press, 1993).

Cannella, Gaile S., and Yvonna S. Lincoln, "Epilogue: Claiming a Critical Public Social Science—Reconceptualizing and Redeploying Research," *Qualitative Inquiry* 10, no. 2, April, 2004, 298–309.

Carsten, Francis L., *The Rise of Fascism* (Berkeley: University of California Press, 1980).

Ciaffa, J. A., *Max Weber and the Problems of Value-Free Social Science* (London: Associated University Presses, 1998).

Coenen-Huther, Jacques, "The Paths of Recognition: Boudon, Bourdieu and the 'Second Market' of Intellectuals," *International Journal of Contemporary Sociology* 35, no. 2, October, 1998, 208–16.

Collins, Randall, "Weber and Schumpeter: Toward a General Sociology of Capitalism," in *Weberian Sociological Theory* (Cambridge: Cambridge University Press, 1986), 117–44.

Comte, Auguste (1822), "Plan of the Scientific Operations Necessary for Reorganizing Society," in *System of Positive Polity*, reprinted in Philip Rieff, editor, *On Intellectuals: Theoretical Studies, Case Studies* (Garden City, NY: Anchor Books, 1970), 248–51.

Comte, Auguste (1830), "The Positive Philosophy," reprinted in *Man and the Universe: The Philosophers of Science* (New York: Random House, 1947), 217–37.

Comte, Auguste, *The Positive Philosophy of Auguste Comte*, condensed and translated by Harriet Martineau (London: George Bell & Sons, 1896).

Comte, Auguste, *System of Positive Polity* (London: Longmans, Green, and Co., 1875).

Congi, Gaetano, "Sociology and the Social Question in Auguste Comte," *Sociologia e Ricerca Sociale* 18, no. 52, 1997, 24–64.

Coser, Lewis A., *Masters of Sociological Thought: Ideas in Historical and Social Context*, second edition (New York: Harcourt Brace Jovanovich, 1977).

Dahms, Harry F., "From Creative Action to the Social Rationalization of the Economy: Joseph Schumpeter's Social Theory," *Sociological Theory* 13, no. 1, March, 1995, 1–13.

Dewey, John, *The Public and Its Problems* (Chicago: Swallow, 1954).

Diggins, John Patrick, *The Bard of Savagery: Thorstein Veblen and Modern Social Theory* (New York: Seabury, 1978).

Diggins, John Patrick, "Thorstein Veblen and the Literature of the Theory Class," *The International Journal of Politics, Culture, and Society* 6, 1993, 481–89.

Edgell, Stephen, *Veblen in Perspective: His Life and Thought* (London: M. E. Sharpe, 2001).

Elliott, Philip, "Intellectuals, the 'Information Society' and the Disappearance of the Public Sphere," in Richard Collins et al., editors, *Media, Culture, and Society: A Critical Reader* (London: Sage, 1986), 105–15.

Emge, Richard Martinus, "Saint-Simon and the Sociology of Knowledge and Science," *Kolner Zeitschrift fur Soziologie und Sozialpsychologie* Supplement 22, 1980, 317–34.

Foster, John Bellamy, "The Political Economy of Joseph Schumpeter: A Theory of Capitalist Development and Decline," *Studies in Political Economy* 15, Fall, 1984, 5–42.

Fowler, Bridget, *Pierre Bourdieu and Cultural Theory: Critical Investigations* (London; Thousand Oaks, CA: Sage, 1997).

Freund, Julien, "La Politique d'Auguste Comte," *Revue Philosophique de la France et de l'Etranger* 110, no. 4, October–December, 1985, 461–87.

Frick, Jean-Paul, "The Question of Power in Auguste Comte's Theory and the Significance of His Political Philosophy," *Revue Philosophique de la France et de l'Etranger* 113, no. 3, July–September, 1988, 273–301.

Galbraith, John Kenneth, *The Affluent Society* (Boston: Houghton Mifflin, 1998).

Galbraith, John Kenneth, *The Anatomy of Power* (Boston: Houghton Mifflin, 1983).

Galbraith, John Kenneth, *Economics and the Public Purpose* (Boston: Houghton Mifflin, 1973).

Galbraith, John Kenneth, *The Good Society: The Humane Agenda* (Boston: Houghton Mifflin, 1996).

Galbraith, John Kenneth, *Interviews with John Kenneth Galbraith*, James Stanfield and Jacqueline Bloom Stanfield, eds., Conversations with Public Intellectuals Series (Jackson: University Press of Mississippi, 2004).

Galbraith, John Kenneth, *The New Industrial State* (Boston: Houghton Mifflin, 1978).

Galbraith, John Kenneth, *The Voice of the Poor: Essays in Economic and Political Persuasion* (Cambridge, MA: Harvard University Press, 1983).

Giddens, Anthony, *Politics and Sociology in the Thought of Max Weber* (London: Macmillan, 1972).

Goldfarb, Jeffrey, *Civility and Subversion: The Intellectual in Democratic Society* (Cambridge; New York: Cambridge University Press, 1998).

Gordon, Scott, "The Close of the Galbraithian System," *Journal of Political Economy* 76, no. 44, pt. 1, August, 1968, 635–44.

Gouhier, Henri Gaston, *La Jeunesse d'Auguste Comte et la Formation du Positivisme* (Paris: J. Vrin, 1933–1941).

Gouldner, Alvin W., *The Future of Intellectuals and the Rise of the New Class: A Frame of Reference, Theses, Conjectures, Arguments, and an Historical Perspective on the Role of Intellectuals and Intelligentsia in the International Class Contest of the Modern Era* (New York: Seabury, 1979).

Grange, Juliette, *La Philosophie d'Auguste Comte: Science, Politique, Religion* (Paris: Presses Universitaires de France, 1996).

Habermas, Jürgen, "Discussion on Value-Freedom and Objectivity," in Otto Stammer, editor, *Max Weber and Sociology Today*, translated by Kathleen Morris (New York: Harper and Row, 1971), 59–66.

Habermas, Jürgen, *On the Logic of the Social Sciences*, translated by Shierry Weber Nicholsen and Jerry A. Stark (Cambridge, MA: MIT Press, 1988).

Habermas, Jürgen, *The Philosophical Discourse of Modernity: Twelve Lectures*, translated by Frederick G. Lawrence (Cambridge, MA: MIT Press, 1987).

Hekman, Susan, "Max Weber and Post-Positivist Social Theory," in Asher Horowitz and Terry Maley, editors, *The Barbarism of Reason: Max Weber and the Twilight of Enlightenment* (Toronto: University of Toronto Press, 1994), 267–86.

Hession, Charles, *John Kenneth Galbraith and His Critics* (New York: W. W. Norton, 1972).

Hewa, Soma, "Sociology and Public Policy: The Debate on Value-Free Social Science," *International Journal of Sociology and Social Policy* 13, nos. 1–2, 1993, 64–82.

Hodder, H. J., "Political Ideas of Thorstein Veblen," *Canadian Journal of Economics and Political Science* 22, August, 1956, 347–57.

Horkheimer, Max, and Theodor W. Adorno, *Dialectic of Enlightenment*, translated by John Cumming (New York: Continuum, 1993).

Horowitz, Irving Louis, *C. Wright Mills: An American Utopian* (New York: Free Press, 1983).

Hughey, Michael W., and Arthur Vidich, "Veblen, Weber and Marx on Political Economy," *International Journal of Politics, Culture, and Society* 6, 1993, 491–505.

Ionescu, Ghita, "Saint-Simon and the Politics of Industrial Societies," *Government and Opposition* 8, no. 1, 1973, 24–47.

Jacoby, Russell, *The Last Intellectuals: American Culture in the Age of Academe* (New York: Basic Books, 1987).

Jennings, Jeremy, and Anthony Kemp-Welch, editors, *Intellectuals in Politics: From the Dreyfus Affair to Salman Rushdie* (London: Routledge, 1997).

Karakayali, Nedim, "Reading Bourdieu with Adorno: The Limits of Critical Theory and Reflexive Sociology," *Sociology* 38, no. 2, April, 2004, 351–68.

Keaney, Michael, editor, *Economist With a Public Purpose: Essays in Honour of John Kenneth Galbraith* (London; New York: Routledge, 2001).

Kellner, Douglas, "Media Propaganda and Spectacle in the War on Iraq: A Critique of U.S. Broadcasting Networks," *Cultural Studies Critical Methodologies* 4, no. 3, August, 2004, 329–38.

Kenway, Jane, and Julie McLeod, "Bourdieu's Reflexive Sociology and 'Spaces of Points of View': Whose Reflexivity, Which Perspective?" *British Journal of Sociology of Education* 25, no. 4, September, 2004, 525–44.

Kettler, David, "Political Education for a Polity of Dissensus: Karl Mannheim and the Legacy of Max Weber," *European Journal of Political Theory* 1, no. 1, July, 2002, 31–51.

Kettler, David, and Volker Meja, *Karl Mannheim and the Crisis of Liberalism: The Secret of These New Times* (New Brunswick, NJ: Transaction, 1995).

Kettler, David, Volker Meja, and Nico Stehr, *Karl Mannheim* (London: Tavistock, 1984).

Kettler, David, Volker Meja, and Nico Stehr, "Rationalizing the Irrational: Karl Mannheim and the Besetting Sin of German Intellectuals," *American Journal of Sociology* 95, no. 6, May, 1990, 1441–73.

Kettler, David, Nico Stehr, and Volker Meja, "Is a Science of Politics Possible? The View From Mannheim," *Society* 24, no. 3, March–April, 1987, 76–82.

Konrád, Gyorgy, and Ivan Szelenyi, *The Intellectuals on the Road to Class Power*, translated by Andrew Arato and Richard E. Allen (New York: Harcourt Brace Jovanovich, 1979).

Lane, Jeremy F., *Pierre Bourdieu: A Critical Introduction* (London; Sterling, VA: Pluto Press, 2000).

Lasch, Christopher, "Conscience, Reason, and Imagination: C. Wright Mills and the Life of the Mind," *Social Science* 72, no. 1, Spring, 1987, 81–85.

Lasch, Christopher, "A Typology of Intellectuals: II. The Example of C. Wright Mills," *Salmagundi*, nos. 70–71, Spring–Summer, 1986, 102–7.

Lefebvre, Georges, *The Coming of the French Revolution* (Princeton, NJ: Princeton University Press, 1988).

Lemert, Charles, "The Clothes Have No Emperor: Bourdieu on American Imperialism," *Theory, Culture, & Society* 17, no. 1, February, 2000, 97–106.

Littré, Emile, *Auguste Comte et la Philosophie Positive*, third edition (Paris: Aux Bureaux de la Philosophie Positive, 1877).

Loader, Colin, "Free Floating: The Intelligentsia in the Work of Alfred Weber and Karl Mannheim," *German Studies Review* 20, no. 2, May, 1997, 217–34.

Loader, Colin, *The Intellectual Development of Karl Mannheim* (Cambridge: Cambridge University Press, 1985).

Loader, Colin, and Rick Tilman, "Thorstein Veblen's Analysis of German Intellectualism: Institutionalism as a Forecasting Method," *American Journal of Economics and Sociology* 54, no. 3, July, 1995, 339–55.

Mannheim, Karl (1943), *Diagnosis of Our Time* (New York: Oxford University Press, 1944).

Mannheim, Karl, *Freedom, Power, and Democratic Planning*, edited by E. K. Bramstedt and Hans Gerth (London: Routledge & Kegan Paul, 1951).

Mannheim, Karl (1936), *Ideology and Utopia: An Introduction to the Sociology of Knowledge* (New York: Harcourt, Brace & World, 1968).

Mannheim, Karl, *Man and Society in an Age of Reconstruction* (New York: Harcourt, Brace & World, 1940).

Mannheim, Karl (1932), "The Sociology of Intellectuals," *Theory, Culture & Society* 10, 1993, 69–80.

Manuel, Frank E., *The New World of Henri Saint-Simon* (Cambridge, MA: Harvard University Press, 1956).

März, Eduard, *Joseph Schumpeter: Scholar, Teacher, and Politician* (New Haven, CT: Yale University Press, 1991).

McDaniel, Susan A., "Reflections of a Very Public Sociologist," *Society/Société* 19, no. 2, May, 1995, 3–5.

Medearis, John, *Joseph Schumpeter's Two Theories of Democracy* (Cambridge, MA: Harvard University Press, 2001).

Michael, John, *Anxious Intellects: Academic Professionals, Public Intellectuals, and Enlightenment Values* (Durham, NC: Duke University Press, 2000).

Miller, Andrew John, "Pierre Bourdieu and the Perils of Allodoxia: Nationalism, Globalism and the Geopolitics of Intellectual Exchange," *Cultural Studies* 17, nos. 3–4, May–July, 2003, 553–71.

Miller, Jim, "Democracy and the Intellectual: C. Wright Mills Reconsidered," *Salmagundi*, nos. 70–71, Spring–Summer, 1986, 82–101.

Mills, C. Wright (1944), *Power, Politics and People: The Collected Essays of C. Wright Mills*, edited by Irving Horowitz (New York: Oxford University Press, 1963).

Mills, C. Wright, *The Power Elite* (New York: Oxford University Press, 1956).

Mills, C. Wright, *The Sociological Imagination* (New York: Oxford University Press, 1959).

Mills, C. Wright, *White Collar: The American Middle Classes* (New York: Oxford University Press, 1956).

Oakes, Guy, and Arthur J. Vidich, *Collaboration, Reputation, and Ethics in American Academic Life: Hans Gerth and C. Wright Mills* (Urbana; Chicago: University of Illinois Press, 1999).

Oestereicher, Emil, "Politics, Class and the Socially Unattached Intellectual: A Re-Examination of Mannheim's Thesis," *State, Culture and Society* 1, no. 3, Spring, 1985, 209–24.

Osterhammel, Jürgen, "Varieties of Social Economics: Joseph Schumpeter and Max Weber," in *Max Weber and His Contemporaries*, edited by Wolfgang J. Mommsen and Jürgen Osterhammel (London: Allen & Unwin, 1987).

Parker, Richard, *John Kenneth Galbraith: His Life, His Politics, His Economics* (New York: Farrar, Straus and Giroux, 2005).

Parker, Richard, "The Legacy of John Kenneth Galbraith," *Challenge* 47, no. 2, March–April, 2004, 81–89.

Pels, Dick, "Knowledge Politics and Anti-Politics: Toward a Critical Appraisal of Bourdieu's Concept of Intellectual Autonomy," *Theory and Society* 24, no. 1, February, 1995, 79–104.

Pelton, Leroy H., "Misinforming Public Policy: The Illiberal Uses of Social Science," *Society* 37, no. 5, July–August, 2000, 61–69.

Pileggi, Mary S., and Cindy Patton, "Introduction: Bourdieu and Cultural Studies," *Cultural Studies* 17, no. 3–4, May–July, 2003, 313–25.

Pinto, Louis, "A Militant Sociology: The Political Commitment of Pierre Bourdieu," in Bridget Fowler, ed., *Reading Bourdieu on Society and Culture* (Oxford: Blackwell, 2000), 88–104.

Posner, Richard, *Public Intellectuals: A Study of Decline* (Cambridge, MA: Harvard University Press, 2002).

Poupeau, Franck, and Thierry Discepolo, "Scholarship with Commitment: On the Political Engagements of Pierre Bourdieu," *Constellations* 11, no. 1, March, 2004, 76–96.

Reisman, David A., *Galbraith and Market Capitalism* (New York: New York University Press, 1980).

Reisman, David A., "Galbraith on Ideas and Events," *Journal of Economic Issues* 24, no. 3, September, 1990, 733–60.

Riesman, David, "The Social and Psychological Setting of Veblen's Economic Theory," *Journal of Economic History* 13, no. 4, Fall, 1953, 449–61.

Ritzer, George, and Douglas J. Goodman, *Modern Sociological Theory*, sixth edition (New York: McGraw-Hill, 2004).

Robbins, Bruce, *Secular Vocations: Intellectuals, Professionalism, Culture* (London; New York: Verso, 1993).

Robbins, Derek, "Sociology and Philosophy in the Work of Pierre Bourdieu, 1965–75," *Journal of Classical Sociology* 2, no. 3, November, 2002, 299–328.

Roels, Jean, "Saint-Simon and the Technocratic Representation of Interests," *Res Publica* 15, no. 4, 1973, 745–56.

Rosenberg, Bernard, "A Clarification of Some Veblenian Concepts," *American Journal of Economics and Sociology* 12, no. 2, January, 1953, 179–87.

Roth, Guenther, and Wolfgang Schluchter, *Max Weber's Vision of History: Ethics and Methods* (Berkeley: University of California Press, 1979).

Rutherford, Malcolm, "Thorstein Veblen and the Problem of the Engineers," *International Review of Sociology*, new series, 2, no. 3, 1992, 125–50.

Sadri, Ahmad, *Max Weber's Sociology of Intellectuals* (New York: Oxford University Press, 1994).

Sadri, Ahmad, "Max Weber's Sociology of Religion as a Sociology of Intellectuals," *State, Culture, and Society* 1, 1985, 85–106.

Said, Edward W., *Representations of the Intellectual* (New York: Pantheon, 1994).

Saint-Simon, Claude-Henri (1825), *Henri Saint-Simon (1760–1825)*, translated and edited by Keith Taylor (London: Croom Helm, 1975).

Saint-Simon, Claude-Henri (1822), *The Political Thought of Saint-Simon*, edited by Ghita Ionescu (London: Oxford University Press, 1976).

Sawchuk, Kim, "The Cultural Apparatus: C. Wright Mills' Unfinished Work," *American Sociologist* 32, no. 1, Spring, 2001, 27–49.

Schlesinger, Arthur, "The Political Galbraith," *Journal of Post Keynesian Economics* 7, no. 1, Fall, 1984, 7–17.

Schumpeter, Joseph A., *Business Cycles, A Theoretical, Historical, and Statistical Analysis of the Capitalist Process* (New York: McGraw-Hill, 1939).

Schumpeter, Joseph A. (1942), *Capitalism, Socialism, and Democracy* (New York: Harper & Row, 1962).

Schumpeter, Joseph A., "Capitalism in the Post-War World," in *Essays of Joseph A. Schumpeter*, edited by Richard V. Clemence (Cambridge, MA: Addison-Wesley, 1951), 170–83.

Schumpeter, Joseph A. (1940), *The Economics and Sociology of Capitalism*, edited by R. Swedberg (Princeton, NJ: Princeton University Press, 1991).

Schumpeter, Joseph A., *History of Economic Analysis*, edited by Elizabeth Bookdy Schumpeter (New York: Oxford University Press, 1954).

Schumpeter, Joseph A., *Imperialism and Social Classes*, edited by Paul M. Sweezy, translated by Heinz Norden (New York: Augustus Kelly, 1951).

Schumpeter, Joseph A., "Science and Ideology," *American Economic Review* 39, no. 2, March, 1949, 345–59.

Schumpeter, Joseph A., *The Theory of Economic Development*, translated by Redvers Opie (New York: Oxford University Press, 1961).

Scott, Alan, "Between Autonomy and Responsibility: Max Weber on Scholars, Academics and Intellectuals," in Jeremy Jennings and Anthony Kemp-Welch, editors, *Intellectuals in Politics: From the Dreyfus Affair to Salman Rushdie* (London: Routledge, 1997), 45–64.

Scott, Alan, "Politics and Method in Mannheim's 'Ideology and Utopia,'" *Sociology* 21, no. 1, February, 1987, 41–54.

Shannon, Christopher, *Conspicuous Criticism: Tradition, the Individual, and Culture in American Social Thought, from Veblen to Mills* (Baltimore: Johns Hopkins University Press, 1996).

Sharpe, Myron, *John Kenneth Galbraith and the Lower Economics* (White Plains, NY: International Arts and Sciences Press, 1973).

Shionoya, Yuichi, and Mark Perlman, editors, *Schumpeter in the History of Ideas* (Ann Arbor: University of Michigan Press, 1994).

Small, Helen, editor, *The Public Intellectual* (Oxford: Blackwell, 2002).

Smart, Barry, "An Economic Turn: Galbraith and Classical Sociology," *Journal of Classical Sociology* 3, no. 1, March, 2003, 47–66.

Speier, Hans, "Mannheim as a Sociologist of Knowledge," *International Journal of Politics, Culture, and Society* 2, no. 1, Fall, 1988, 81–94.

Sproule, J. Michael, "Progressive Propaganda Critics and the Magic Bullet Myth," *Critical Studies in Mass Communication* 6, no. 3, September, 1989, 225–46.

Sproule, J. Michael, "Propaganda Studies in American Social Science: The Rise and Fall of the Critical Paradigm," *Quarterly Journal of Speech* 73, 1987, 60–78.

Stabile, Donald, "Veblen's Analysis of Social Movements: Bellamyites, Workers, and Engineers," *Journal of Economic Issues* 22, no. 1, March, 1988, 211–26.

Stanfield, James, *John Kenneth Galbraith* (New York: St. Martin's, 1996).

Stones, Rob, editor, *Key Sociological Thinkers* (New York: New York University Press, 1998).

Swartz, David L., *Culture and Power: The Sociology of Pierre Bourdieu* (Chicago: University of Chicago Press, 1997).

Swartz, David L., "From Critical Sociology to Public Intellectual: Pierre Bourdieu and Politics," *Theory and Society* 32, nos. 5–6, December, 2003, 791–823.

Swedberg, Richard, *Joseph Schumpeter: His Life and Work* (Princeton, NJ: Princeton University Press; Oxford: Polity Press, 1991).

Swedberg, Richard, "Saint-Simon's Vision of a United Europe," *Archives Européennes de Sociologie* 35, no. 1, 1994, 145–69.

Thompson, E. P., "C. Wright Mills: The Responsible Craftsman," *Radical America* 13, no. 4, July–August, 1979, 61–73.

Tilman, Rick, *C. Wright Mills: A Native Radical and His American Intellectual Roots* (University Park: Pennsylvania State University Press, 1984).

Tilman, Rick, *The Intellectual Legacy of Thorstein Veblen* (Westport, CT; London: Greenwood, 1996).

Tilman, Rick, *Thorstein Veblen and His Critics, 1891–1963: Conservative, Liberal, and Radical Perspectives* (Princeton, NJ: Princeton University Press, 1992).

Tilman, Rick, "Veblen's Ideal Political Economy and Its Critics," *American Journal of Economics and Sociology* 31, 1972, 307–17.

Veblen, Thorstein (1923), *Absentee Ownership and Business Enterprise in Recent Times* (New York: Augustus Kelly, 1964).

Veblen, Thorstein (1921), *The Engineers and the Price System* (New York: Harcourt, Brace & World, 1963).

Veblen, Thorstein (1918), *The Higher Learning in America* (New Brunswick, NJ: Transaction, 1993).

Veblen, Thorstein, *Imperial Germany and the Industrial Revolution* (London: Macmillan, 1915).

Veblen, Thorstein (1914), *The Instinct of Workmanship and the State of the Industrial Arts* (New Brunswick, NJ: Transaction, 1990).

Veblen, Thorstein (1884), "Kant's Critique of Judgment," in *Essays in Our Changing Order*, edited by Leon Ardzrooni (New York: Augustus Kelly, 1964), 175–93.

Veblen, Thorstein (1906), *The Place of Science in Modern Civilization and Other Essays* (New Brunswick, NJ: Transaction, 1989).

Veblen, Thorstein (1904), *The Theory of Business Enterprise* (New York: Scribner, 1932).

Veblen, Thorstein, *A Veblen Treasury: From Leisure Class to War, Peace, and Capitalism*, edited by Rick Tilman (Armonk, NY: M. E. Sharpe, 1993).

Vidich, Arthur, "The Higher Learning in America in Veblen's Time and Our Own," *International Journal of Politics, Culture, and Society* 7, 1994, 639–68.

Vidich, Arthur, "Veblen and the Post Keynesian Political Economy," *International Review of Sociology* 3, 1992, 151–81.

Wacquant, Loïc, "For a Socio-Analysis of Intellectuals: On Homo Academicus," *Berkeley Journal of Sociology* 34, 1989, 1–29.

Wacquant, Loïc, "Pointers on Pierre Bourdieu and Democratic Politics," *Constellations* 11, no. 1, March, 2004, 3–15.

Wacquant, Loïc, "Reading Bourdieu's Capital," *International Journal of Contemporary Sociology* 33, no. 2, October, 1996, 151–70.

Weaver, Mark, "Weber's Critique of Advocacy in the Classroom: Critical Thinking and Civic Education," *Political Science and Politics* 31, 1998, 799–801.

Weber, Max, *Economy and Society: An Outline of Interpretive Sociology*, translated by Guenther Roth and Claus Wittich (Berkeley: University of California Press, 1978).

Weber, Max, *The Methodology of the Social Sciences*, translated and edited by Edward Shils and Henry Finch (New York: Free Press, 1949).

Weber, Max, *Political Writings*, edited and translated by Peter Lassman and Ronald Speirs (Cambridge; New York: Cambridge University Press, 1994).

Weber, Max (1919), "Politics as a Vocation," in *From Max Weber: Essays in Sociology*, translated by Hans Gerth and C. Wright Mills (New York: Oxford University Press, 1958), 77–128.

Weber, Max (1904), *The Protestant Ethic and the Spirit of Capitalism*, translated by Talcott Parsons (New York: Charles Scribner's Sons, 1958).

Weber, Max (1919), "Science as a Vocation," in *From Max Weber: Essays in Sociology*, translated by Hans Gerth and C. Wright Mills (New York: Oxford University Press, 1958), 129–56.

Wellen, Richard, "The Politics of Intellectual Integrity," *Max Weber Studies* 2, no. 1, November, 2001, 81–101.

Wilensky, Harold L., "Social Science and the Public Agenda: Reflections of the Relation of Knowledge to Policy in the United States and Abroad," *Journal of Health Politics, Policy and Law* 22, no. 5, October, 1997, 1241–65.

Wilson, William Julius, *Sociology and the Public Agenda* (Thousand Oaks, CA: Sage, 1993).

Zald, Mayer, and John McCarthy, "Organizational Intellectuals and the Criticism of Society," *Social Service Review* 49, no. 3, September, 1975, 344–62.

Znaniecki, Florian, *The Social Role of the Man of Knowledge* (New York: Harper & Row, 1968).

Index

absentee owners, Veblen on, 35
academia, 134–36; Bourdieu on, 106–7,
   115–16; Galbraith on, 83–84; Mills
   on, 86–87; Veblen on, 41–44; Weber
   on, 22, 27–28. *See also* education
Adorno, Theodor, 122n36
advisors, political, intellectuals as,
   138–39
Agger, Ben, 146n4
alienation, Mills on, 89
Alt, John, 95n1
alternative outlooks, intellectuals and,
   141–42
aristocracy, Comte and Saint-Simon on,
   3
arms race, Galbraith on, 85
authority: Comte and Saint-Simon on,
   9–10; intellectuals and, Schumpeter
   on, 61–62; Mills on, 92; Weber on, 22
authors, selection criteria for, xi
autonomy: Bourdieu on, 112–17; Weber
   on, 22

bankers, Veblen on, 35
Bell, Daniel, 45n6
Bellah, Robert, 149n28
Bender, Thomas, 147n11
Best, Joel, 149n25

bias: Bourdieu on, 107–8, 110; Comte
   and Saint-Simon on, 14; and
   education, 135; Schumpeter on, 59,
   62; social scientists and, 129; Veblen
   on, 40–41, 43; Weber on, 26–27
Bourdieu, Pierre, 101–24, 128, 133
Breiner, Peter, 33n16
Brubaker, Rogers, 121n34
Burawoy, Michael, 150n35
bureaucracy: Galbraith on, 81; Mills on,
   80; social scientists and, 128; Veblen
   on, 36; Weber on, 22, 30
business institutions: Bourdieu on, 117;
   Schumpeter on, 53; Veblen on, 35,
   37, 39–40, 42. *See also* corporations

Cannella, Gaile, 147n7
capitalism: Comte and Saint-Simon on,
   9; Mannheim on, 50; Schumpeter on,
   62–63; Veblen on, 35. *See also* state
   capitalism
careerism, 132
Chinese bureaucracy, Weber on, 30
civil liberties, Galbraith on, 83
class: Bourdieu on, 103; Mannheim on,
   60
classical liberalism, Comte and Saint-
   Simon and, 18n26

163

clergy, Comte and Saint-Simon on, 9–10
Coenen-Huther, Jacques, 120n18
Cold War: Galbraith on, 83, 85; Mills and, 98n33
collective unconscious, Bourdieu on, 103
collective work in science: Bourdieu on, 113–15, 118–19; Comte and Saint-Simon on, 14–15
Collins, Randall, 73n12
common good, Schumpeter on, 68
communication, technocracy of, Bourdieu on, 105
Communism, 50; Schumpeter on, 52–53, 67–68
complexity: Mills on, 89; of politics, ix–x; Veblen on, 39
compromise, Weber on, 29
Comte, Auguste, 1–19, 125; versus Saint-Simon, 15n2, 16n7, 18n32
Congi, Gaetano, 18n30
consensus, Mannheim on, 65
contemporary social research, dilemmas of, 132–34
corporations: Galbraith on, 81–84; transnational, 101; Veblen on, 35. *See also* business institutions
Coser, Lewis, 71n2, 76n55
creativity, Schumpeter on, 53, 67
critical stance: and alternative viewpoints, 141–42; education and, 135–36; on institutions, 145
critique: Comte and Saint-Simon on, 4; social science tradition of, 135–36
culture, Comte and Saint-Simon on, 7
curiosity: versus careerism, 132; Veblen on, 42–43

Dahms, Harry, 72n5
decision making, political: Bourdieu on, 102; Comte and Saint-Simon on, 6; intellectuals and, 136–41; Schumpeter on, 68–69; Weber on, 23–24, 26
deconstructionists, Bourdieu on, 109
democracy: Comte and Saint-Simon on, 11–13, 19n37; Galbraith on, 83;

Mannheim on, 65–66; Mills on, 78–79; Schumpeter on, 68; Weber on, 24, 26. *See also* masses
direct democracy, Weber on, 26
Discepolo, Thierry, 123n44
division of labor: Comte and Saint-Simon on, 9–11; Weber on, 30
double historicization, 115
Dreyfus affair, 113

education, 134–36; Bourdieu on, 102, 115–16; Comte and Saint-Simon on, 12; Galbraith on, 85, 93; Mannheim on, 66; Mills on, 92–93; Schumpeter on, 67–68; Veblen on, 43; Weber on, 27–28. *See also* academia
Emge, Richard, 16n12
empirical investigation, 130
ends, Weber on, 25, 28–29
engineers: Comte and Saint-Simon on, 9; Veblen on, 37, 45n6
entrepreneurial corporation, Galbraith on, 81
entrepreneurship: Mannheim on, 54; Schumpeter on, 53
ethics of intellectuals: Mills on, 88; Weber on, 28–31
existentialism, 102

Fascism, 49–50, 77
feudal system, Comte and Saint-Simon on, 2, 4, 9
first principles, 10
Fowler, Bridget, 121n33
France, Bourdieu on, 102, 104–5, 111–12
French Revolution, and social philosophy, 1
Frick, Jean-Paul, 19n37
functional rationality, Mannheim on, 54
funding for research, 134; Bourdieu on, 103–4, 117; Galbraith on, 85; Mills on, 88
future: advisors and, 140; Bourdieu on, 111–12, 118; Comte and Saint-Simon on, 7; Galbraith on, 83; Veblen on, 44; Weber on, 23

Galbraith, John Kenneth, 77–99, 127–28, 139; background of, 78
Germany, 49–50; Mannheim on, 69; Veblen on, 45n1, 47n27; Weber on, 22, 30
Giddens, Anthony, 148n19
globalization, Mannheim and, 51–52
goals of social science: Bourdieu on, 110–12; Comte and Saint-Simon on, 6; Mills on, 89; Weber on, 24, 28
Goldfarb, Jeffrey, 150n34
Gordon, Scott, 96n17
Gouhier, H., 18n30
Grange, Juliette, 19n42

habits of thought: Bourdieu on, 110; Veblen on, 38–39
Hegel, G. W. F., 39
Hession, Charles, 96n17
Hewa, Soma, 146n1
Hodder, H. J., 45n6
Horowitz, Irving, 95n1

idle curiosity, Veblen on, 42–43
idlers, Saint-Simon on, 17n24
individualism: Comte and Saint-Simon on, 14–15; Weber on, 22
inductive reasoning, Veblen on, 38–39
industry: Comte and Saint-Simon on, 2–3, 8, 18n32; Mannheim on, 51; Veblen on, 35–37; Weber on, 22
innovation: Galbraith on, 84; Mannheim on, 64; Schumpeter on, 53, 67; social science and, 131; Veblen on, 43–44
institutions: critical stance on, 145; domination by, 128; Mills on, 77–78; Weber on, 22
intellectual(s): Bourdieu on, 103, 105, 112–17; ethics of, 28–31, 88; Mannheim on, 59–61, 64, 74n37; mediatic, 105; Mills on, 86–87; power of, Bourdieu on, 113; responsibilities of, 9, 23, 44, 138; Schumpeter on, 61–64; social scientists as, 125–50; versus observer role, x. *See also* engineers; public role of intellectuals; savants

intellectual administrators, Mills on, 89
intellectual life, conditions of, Bourdieu on, 117–19
intelligence agencies, Galbraith on, 83
interconnectedness: Bourdieu on, 104–5; Comte and Saint-Simon on, 7; Mannheim on, 51–52; Mills on, 79
interdisciplinary teams, 133–34
international exchange of ideas, Bourdieu on, 115–17
invention, Schumpeter on, 53
Iraq war, media and, 149n29

Jacoby, Russell, 147n5

Kant, Immanuel, Veblen on, 38–39
Karakayali, Nedim, 122n36
Kenway, Jane, 122n40
Kettler, David, 72n10, 73n27, 74n38
knowledge: Bourdieu on, 106–7; Comte and Saint-Simon on, 10–11, 13–15; Mannheim on, 54–57, 60; Schumpeter on, 57–59; Veblen on, 38–39; Weber on, 27

Lasch, Christopher, 98n33, 99n44
Lazarsfeld, Paul, 99n36
leadership: Comte and Saint-Simon on, 6, 8, 12; Galbraith on, 82; Mills on, 78–80, 90; Schumpeter on, 63, 67–69; Veblen on, 35; Weber on, 22–23, 26, 30–31
Lemert, Charles, 121n25
Lévi-Strauss, Claude, 101
liberalism: classical, Comte and Saint-Simon and, 18n26; Mannheim and Schumpeter on, 49–50; Mills on, 78
liberal practicality, Mills on, 87
Lincoln, Yvonna, 147n7
Loader, Colin, 72n2, 74n37, 75n46

management of public opinion. *See* propaganda
managerial perspective in social sciences, Mills on, 87–88
Mannheim, Karl, 49–76, 126–27; background of, 49–50

market ideology: Galbraith on, 82; Schumpeter on, 50, 54, 62; Veblen on, 39–40

März, Eduard, 73n14, 75n41

masses: Comte and Saint-Simon on, 11–13; intellectuals and, 139–41; Mannheim on, 64; Mills on, 79–80; Weber on, 26. *See also* democracy

mature corporation, Galbraith on, 81–82

mature society, Schumpeter on, 58

McCarthy, John, 74n41

McDaniel, Susan, 147n10

McLeod, Julie, 122n40

mechanistic accounts, Veblen on, 39

Medearis, John, 76n61

media: Bourdieu on, 102, 104–5, 115–17; and Iraq war, 149n29; Mills on, 91–92; social scientists and, 143–44. *See also* propaganda

mediatic intellectuals, Bourdieu on, 105

Meja, Volker, 72n10, 73n27

metaphysical system of knowledge: Comte and Saint-Simon on, 3–5, 11–12; Veblen on, 39

Michael, John, 147n5

militarism, Comte and Saint-Simon on, 2–3, 6

Miller, Andrew, 124n61

Miller, Jim, 98n33

Mills, C. Wright, 77–99, 127–28, 139; background of, 77–78

monopoly of the universal, Bourdieu on, 102

morality: Comte and Saint-Simon on, 10–11; Mannheim on, 64–65; social scientists and, 142–43

Napoleon Bonaparte, 1, 3

nationalism, Comte and Saint-Simon on, 3

Nazism, 49

New Deal, Schumpeter on, 50

nuclear weapons, scientists and, 85

Oakes, Guy, 97n32

objectivism, Bourdieu on, 107–10

objectivity: Comte and Saint-Simon on, 13–14; Galbraith on, 85; Schumpeter on, 59, 62; Veblen on, 40–41; Weber on, 23, 26–27

observer role, x; Mannheim on, 56–57

Oestereicher, Emil, 75n46

options, political, understanding of, intellectuals and, 139–40

Parker, Richard, 95n2, 96n20

particular: Comte and Saint-Simon on, 7; Mannheim on, 55, 65; Schumpeter on, 59

Patton, Cindy, 119n5

peer review, 130–31

Pels, Dick, 123n48

Pelton, Leroy, 147n9

Pileggi, Mary S., 119n5

Pinto, Louis, 122n37

planning: Mannheim on, 51–52, 59–61, 64–67; Schumpeter on, 52–54

planning system: definition of, 82; Galbraith on, 80–86

policy consequences, social scientists and, Weber on, 25

political knowledge: Bourdieu on, 106–7; Mannheim on, 56

political role of social scientists, 136–41; Bourdieu on, 112–17; Mills on, 90; Schumpeter on, 63; Veblen on, 38–41; viewpoints on, x; Weber on, 23–31

politics: Bourdieu on, 102; complexity of, ix–x; Comte and Saint-Simon on, 2, 8; Mannheim on, 54–57, 64–67; as positive science, 5–7

positive philosophy: Comte and Saint-Simon on, 1–19; Mannheim on, 54–55; nature of, 3–5; and politics, 5–7

Posner, Richard, 150n33

postmodernism, Bourdieu on, 108–9

Poupeau, Franck, 123n44

poverty, Schumpeter on, 53–54

power elite, Mills on, 78–80, 86–87

practical knowledge, Veblen on, 43

prestige, Bourdieu on, 106

producers, Saint-Simon on, 17n24
propaganda, 141–42, 149n29; and
    education, 135; Mannheim on, 51,
    66; Mills and Galbraith on, 90–93;
    Schumpeter on, 67–68. *See also*
    media
public intellectuals. *See* intellectual(s)
public opinion: Mannheim on, 51,
    65–66; Mills and Galbraith on, 90–93;
    social scientists and, 141–44
public role of intellectuals, 125–50;
    Bourdieu on, 101–24; Comte and
    Saint-Simon on, 1–19; Mannheim and
    Schumpeter on, 49–76; Mills and
    Galbraith on, 77–99; Veblen on,
    35–47; Weber on, 21–34
public sociology, 145, 150n35

rational inquiry: Comte and Saint-Simon
    on, 2, 14; intellectuals and, 140;
    Mannheim on, 54; Schumpeter on,
    59, 68; Veblen on, 37–39
rationalization: of civilization, Weber on,
    22–23; Schumpeter on, 58, 69; in
    social sciences, Mills on, 87–88
reflexivity, Bourdieu on, 110–12
Reisman, David, 97n28
relativism: Bourdieu on, 109; Weber on,
    27
religion: Comte and Saint-Simon on, 4,
    9, 19n33; Mannheim on, 65–66
representative democracy, Weber on, 26
research: contemporary social,
    dilemmas of, 132–34; funding for, 85,
    88, 103–4, 117, 134; quality of,
    careerism and, 132
researchers: social scientists as, 129–31;
    teams of, 133–34
responsibilities of public intellectuals,
    138; Comte and Saint-Simon on, 9;
    Veblen on, 44; Weber on, 23
responsibility, ethic of, Weber on, 28–29
Riesman, David, 45n6
Robbins, Derek, 122n40
Roman bureaucracy, Weber on, 30
romanticization: Veblen on, 36; Weber
    on, 25

Rosenberg, Bernard, 45n6
Roth, Guenther, 34n37
Rutherford, Malcolm, 46n6

Sadri, Ahmad, 34n36
Saint-Simon, Henri de Rouvroy, 1–19,
    125; versus Comte, 15n2, 16n7,
    18n32
Sartre, Jean-Paul, 102
savants: characteristics of, 8; Comte and
    Saint-Simon on, 7–10; and morality,
    10
Schlesinger, Arthur, Jr., 97n20
Schluchter, Wolfgang, 34n37
Schumpeter, Joseph, 49–76, 126–27,
    142; background of, 50
science: Comte and Saint-Simon on, 2,
    8, 11; Galbraith on, 83–86; and
    morality, 10; Schumpeter on, 57–59;
    Tolstoy on, 28; Veblen on, 38–41
Scott, Alan, 34n38, 73n18
Sharpe, Myron, 97n23
skepticism: Mills on, 92; Veblen on, 42
Smart, Barry, 97n26
socialism, Schumpeter on, 52–53, 58
social science: contemporary, dilemmas
    of, 132–34; goals of, 6, 24, 28, 89,
    110–12; Mills on, 87–88; strengths of,
    130–31
social scientists, role of: as educators,
    134–36; Mills on, 88; as opinion
    leaders, 141–44; as political actors,
    136–41; as public intellectuals,
    125–50; as researchers, 129–31
societal management, 7–10; Comte and
    Saint-Simon on, 12–13
Soviet Union, Schumpeter on, 67–68
specialization, 132–33
Stabile, Donald, 46n6
state: Bourdieu on, 102, 104–5, 111–12;
    Comte and Saint-Simon on, 3; Veblen
    on, 36
state capitalism, 101; Veblen on, 36;
    Weber on, 21–34
Stehr, Nico, 72n10, 73n27
stockholders, Galbraith on, 81–82
stock market crash, 49–50

structuralism, 101–2
subjectivism, Bourdieu on, 107–10
substantial rationality, Mannheim on, 54
Swartz, David, 121n33, 123n46

teams, of researchers, 133–34
technical approach, Weber on, 24
technocracy: Bourdieu on, 105; Mills on, 88; Veblen on, 45n6
technology. *See* science
technostructure, Galbraith on, 81
theologians, Comte and Saint-Simon on, 9, 16n7
think tanks, 137
third way, Mannheim on, 50
Thompson, E. P., 98n33
Tilman, Rick, 46n6, 95n1
Tolstoy, Leo, 28
transformation, social, Schumpeter on, 58
transnational corporations, 101
trend analysis: Mannheim on, 57; Schumpeter on, 57–58; Weber on, 25

ultimate ends, ethic of, 28–29
understanding: of contemporary society, efforts at, ix–x; intellectuals and, Mannheim on, 60; of political options, intellectuals and, 139–40

unifying orientation: Comte and Saint-Simon on, 10–11; Mills and Galbraith on, 93; social scientists and, 143
United States, 49; Bourdieu on, 107; Mills on, 78–80; Veblen on, 35–38
universal, monopoly of, Bourdieu on, 102
university. *See* academia
urbanization, Mannheim on, 51
utilitarianism: Comte and Saint-Simon and, 17n25; Mannheim on, 55; Veblen on, 42

values: Comte and Saint-Simon on, 7; Galbraith on, 85; Mannheim on, 66; Mills on, 87; Schumpeter on, 68; social scientists and, 129; Weber on, 25
Veblen, Thorstein, 35–47, 125–26
Vidlich, Arthur, 47n19, 97n32

Wacquant, Loïc, 123n49
Weaver, Mark, 33n23
Weber, Max, 21–34, 125–26, 134–36
Wellen, Richard, 33n21
Wilensky, Harold L., 148n21
Wilson, William Julius, 149n22

Zald, Mayer, 74n41

About the Author

Charles F. Gattone received his Ph.D. from The New School for Social Research in 2000. He taught as a visiting professor in the Department of Sociology at Oberlin College, and joined the faculty at the University of Florida in the fall of 2001. His work addresses a host of questions on the place of social science in public affairs, and examines some of the underlying challenges social scientists have had to confront in today's highly competitive and bureaucratically organized academic environment. Dr. Gattone's research has also focused on the areas of media studies, the sociology of knowledge, and the sociology of culture. His earlier publications include *Image and Persuasion: The Machiavellian World of Advertising and Public Relations*, *The Role of the Intellectual in Public Affairs*, and *Media and Politics in the Information Age*.